Bloom's Modern Critical Interpretations

The Adventures of
  Huckleberry Finn
The Age of Innocence
Alice's Adventures in
  Wonderland
All Quiet on the
  Western Front
Animal Farm
The Ballad of the Sad
  Café
Beloved
Beowulf
Black Boy
The Bluest Eye
The Canterbury Tales
Cat on a Hot Tin
  Roof
Catch-22
The Catcher in the Rye
The Chronicles of
  Narnia
The Color Purple
Crime and
  Punishment
The Crucible
Darkness at Noon
Death of a Salesman
The Death of Artemio
  Cruz
Don Quixote
Emerson's Essays
Emma
Fahrenheit 451
A Farewell to Arms
Frankenstein
The Glass Menagerie
The Grapes of Wrath

Great Expectations
The Great Gatsby
Gulliver's Travels
Hamlet
Heart of Darkness
The House on Mango
  Street
I Know Why the
  Caged Bird Sings
The Iliad
Invisible Man
Jane Eyre
The Joy Luck Club
Julius Caesar
The Jungle
Long Day's Journey
  into Night
Lord of the Flies
The Lord of the Rings
Love in the Time of
  Cholera
The Man Without
  Qualities
The Metamorphosis
Miss Lonelyhearts
Moby-Dick
My Ántonia
Native Son
Night
1984
The Odyssey
Oedipus Rex
The Old Man and the
  Sea
On the Road
One Flew over the
  Cuckoo's Nest

One Hundred Years of
  Solitude
Persuasion
Portnoy's Complaint
Pride and Prejudice
Ragtime
The Red Badge of
  Courage
Romeo and Juliet
The Rubáiyát of Omar
  Khayyám
The Scarlet Letter
A Separate Peace
Silas Marner
Slaughterhouse-Five
Song of Solomon
The Sound and the
  Fury
The Stranger
A Streetcar Named
  Desire
Sula
The Tale of Genji
A Tale of Two Cities
"The Tell-Tale Heart"
  and Other Stories
Their Eyes Were
  Watching God
Things Fall Apart
To Kill a Mockingbird
Ulysses
Waiting for Godot
The Waste Land
Wuthering Heights
Young Goodman
  Brown

Bloom's Modern Critical Interpretations

Sandra Cisneros's
The House on Mango Street

Edited and with an introduction by
Harold Bloom
Sterling Professor of the Humanities
Yale University

BLOOM'S
LITERARY CRITICISM
An imprint of Infobase Publishing

Bloom's Modern Critical Interpretations: The House on Mango Street

Copyright © 2010 by Infobase Publishing

Introduction © 2010 by Harold Bloom

Bloom's Literary Criticism
An imprint of Infobase Publishing
132 West 31st Street
New York NY 10001

Library of Congress Cataloging-in-Publication Data

Sandra Cisneros's The house on Mango Street / edited and with an introduction by Harold Bloom.

    p. cm.—(Bloom's modern critical interpretations)

    Includes bibliographical references and index.

    ISBN 978-1-60413-586-2

    1. Cisneros, Sandra. House on Mango Street.   I. Bloom, Harold.

    PS3553.I78H633 2010

    813'.54—dc22

                         2009022142

Contributing editor: Pamela Loos

Cover designed by Alicia Post

Printed in the United States of America

IBT IBT 10 9 8 7 6 5 4 3 2

Contents

Editor's Note

My introduction contextualizes *The House on Mango Street* by invoking a classic analysis of male and female identity in Mexico by the greatest of Mexican writers, the poet-critic and Nobel Prize laureate Octavio Paz. In his *The Labyrinth of Solitude*, Paz analyzed the Mexican male myth that divides their women into incarnations either of Guadalupe the Virgin Mother or the *Chingada*, the violated mother who has sold herself to the Spanish conquerors. Historically she is identified with the mistress of Cortez, La Malinche. This is still the Mexican-American world of Sandra Cisneros.

All of the essays in this volume concern this background of male resentment and emergent, courageous female resistance to a malign and pervasive myth. Though there are nine fairly diverse approaches to the ways in which Cisneros handles this dilemma, it would be gratuitous and redundant to particularize these critical variations on a common theme.

HAROLD BLOOM

Introduction

Rereading *The House on Mango Street*, some years after first encountering this book by Sandra Cisneros, is not for me a literary experience. What matters about this series of linked narratives is social testimony or the anguish of a young woman confronting the dilemmas of Mexican-American identity. To an outsider, these in turn seem founded on the vexed issue of Mexican national identity. As background (one among many) to *The House on Mango Street*, I suggest that we turn to the greatest of Mexican writers, the poet-critic and Nobel Prize–winner Octavio Paz (1914–1998). His *The Labyrinth of Solitude* (1950) remains a disturbing guide to what could be called the Mexican myth of Mexico.

Doubtless there are and will be rival attempts to define what might be called the genius of Mexico, and some Mexican feminists already denounce *The Labyrinth of Solitude* for implicitly taking the side of what it exposes and criticizes, the Mexican male myth that their women first betrayed them to, and with, the invading Spaniards. And yet I cannot see how Paz could have been any clearer:

> In contrast to Guadalupe, who is the Virgin Mother, the *Chingada* is the violated Mother. Neither in her not in the Virgin do we find traces of the darker attributes of the great goddesses: the lasciviousness of Amaterasu and Aphrodite, the cruelty of Artemis and Astarte, the sinister magic of Circe and the bloodlust of Kali. Both of them are passive figures. Guadalupe is pure receptivity and the benefits she bestows are of the same order: she consoles,

1

quiets, dries tears, calms passions. The *Chingada* is even more passive. Her passivity is abject: she does not resist violence, but is an inert heap of bones, blood and dust. Her taint is constitutional and resides, as we have said earlier, in her sex. This passivity, open to the outside world, causes her to lose her identity: she is the *Chingada*. She loses her name; she is no one; she disappears into nothingness; she is Nothingness. And yet she is the cruel incarnation of the feminine condition.

If the *Chingada* is the representation of the violated Mother, it is appropriate to associate her with the Conquest, which was also a violation, not only in the historical sense but also in the very flesh of Indian women. The symbol of this violation is Doña Malinche, the mistress of Cortés. It is true that she gave herself voluntarily to the conquistador, but he forgot her as soon as her usefulness was over. Doña Marina [the name given to La Malinche by the Spaniards] becomes a figure representing the Indian women who were fascinated, violated or seduced by the Spaniards. As a small boy will not forgive his mother if she abandons him to search for his father, the Mexican people have not forgiven La Malinche for her betrayal. She embodies the open, the *chingado*, to our closed, stoic, impassive Indians. Cuauhtémoc and Doña Marina are thus two antagonistic and complementary figures. There is nothing surprising about our cult of the young emperor—"the only hero at the summit of art," an image of the sacrificed son—and there is also nothing surprising about the curse that weighs against La Malinche. This explains the success of the contemptuous adjective *malinchista* recently put into circulation by the newspapers to denounce all those who have been corrupted by foreign influences. The *malinchistas* are those who want Mexico to open itself to the outside world: the true sons of Malinche, who is the *Chingada* in person. Once again we see the opposition of the closed and the open.

Since Paz was writing as a poet, he received all the misunderstandings that he risked: "an elegant insult against Mexican mothers." More accurately, as Paz remarked, "*The Labyrinth of Solitude* was an attempt to describe and understand certain myths; at the same time, insofar as it is a literary work, it has in turn become a myth."

Whether or not Cisneros agrees with Paz, I cannot know, but his melancholy observations help me to contextualize *The House on Mango Street*.

MARIA ELENA DE VALDÉS

In Search of Identity in Cisneros's
The House on Mango Street

Sandra Cisneros (1954–), a Chicago-born poet of Mexican parentage, published her first novel in 1984.[1] *The House on Mango Street* is written in the manner of a young girl's memoirs.[2] The forty-four pieces are, however, not the day-to-day record of a preadolescent girl, but rather a loose-knit series of lyrical reflections, her struggle with self-identity and the search for self-respect amidst an alienating and often hostile world. The pieces range from two paragraph narratives, like "Hairs," to the four-page "The Monkey Garden."

There are a number of significant issues to be discussed concerning *The House on Mango Street*[3] but I believe that the most pressing issue is the ideological question of a poetics of identity in the double marginalization of a Chicana.[4] I am opposed to any critical strategy which ignores the qualitative perspective of the lyric narrative voice, the referential situation from which she is writing, and the issues she is writing about. In this study, I shall present the highly lyrical narrative voice in all its richness of a "persona" to which my commentary will seek to respond.

Cisneros's literary persona, Esperanza, is the lyric narrative voice to whom the reader responds and who the reader eventually knows. My theoretical position is closely allied and, to a large extent, indebted to Naomi Black's social feminism, which she defines as "the argumentation and process

From *Canadian Review of American Studies* 23, no. 1 (Fall 1992): 55–72. © 1992 by University of Toronto Press.

in which feminism is able to use the doctrine of difference not to obliterate differences of kind, but to change a society that uses difference as a basis for exclusion" (322). The feminist social criticism that I have developed over the last four years builds on the infrastructure of Black's work and the orientation of Julia Kristeva's writing, but also draws from Paul Ricoeur's hermeneutic mode of inquiry.

The plan of this paper is to move rapidly from a semiotic level to a semantic level of the text before attempting an intertextual interpretation of my reading. The final stage of my exposition is to present the significance of the reading experience in that dialogic relation between the text and the reader and the reader's community. The sensibility and feeling that the narrator captures from her experiences governs her relations with her world and its people, and is part of the long tradition of literature of the coming of age. As an aesthetic process, the apprehension of the world of Mango Street becomes a metaphor for identity. The consequence of this aesthetic process is that the reader is directed less toward the singularity of the places, events and persons of Mango Street than toward the eye/I that writes them. The protagonist, Esperanza, probes into her world, discovers herself and comes to embody the primal needs of all human beings: freedom and belonging.

I am aware that some feminists, especially in English-speaking North America, do not share my philosophical premises, but it is my conviction that they will listen and respond to this voice from the North American third world. The following passage from an article by Ricoeur will serve as an intellectual paradigm for my commentary on Chicana identity as a part of the reading experience. Ricoeur writes: "What we want to understand is not something hidden behind the text, but something disclosed in front of it. What has to be understood is not the initial situation of discourse, but what points toward a possible world. . . . To understand a text is to follow its movement from sense to reference, from what it says, to what it talks about" ("What is Text" 218). The organization of the study is, therefore, a strategy of communication. The main semantic focus of the text is the presentation of the narrating self.

My commentary is aimed at establishing a historically based, critical model of reading for the presentation of self. The narrating presence is a composite of a poetic enunciating voice and a narrative voice, and this presence can best be described as a formal function within the literary structure who, as a speaker, is only knowable as a storyteller in her response to the extratextual, societal, and historical, determinate referents. Notions of self or voice are implicitly controlled by the spectrum of the world of action as known to the reader, and notions of character are explicitly linked to the notions of person in the world. The union of the self and person is the hallmark of the lyrical text. If voice or self is an impulse toward the world, person or character is a social structure of dispositions and traits. In brief, the text in *The House on Mango Street* presents the exterior and the interior of living in the world.

The narrative situation is a familiar one: a sensitive young girl's reflections of her struggle between what she is and what she would like to be. The sense of alienation is compounded because ethnically she is a Mexican, although culturally a Mexican American; she is a young girl surrounded by examples of abused, defeated, worn-out women, but the woman she wants to be must be free. The reflections of one crucial year in her life are narrated in the present from a first person point of view. This was the year of the passage from preadolescence to adolescence when she discovered the meaning of being female and Mexican living in Chicago, but, most of all, this was the year she discovered herself through writing. The girl who did not want to belong to her social reality learns that she belongs to herself, to others, and not to a place.

The frame for the short narratives is simple but highly effective. The family has been wandering from place to place, always dreaming of the promised land of a house of their own. When they finally arrive at the house on Mango Street, which is at last their own house, it is not the promised land of their dreams. The parents overcome their dejection by saying that this is not the end of their moving, that it is only a temporary stop before going on to the promised house. The narrator knows better. The conflict between the promised land and the harsh reality, which she always recognizes in its full force of rejection, violence, fear, and waste, is presented without compromise and without dramatization. This is just the way things are on Mango Street, but the narrator will not give up her dream of the promised house and will pursue it. The lesson she must learn is that the house she seeks is, in reality, her own person. She must overcome her rejection of who she is and find her self-esteem. She must be true to herself and thereby gain control of her identity. The search for self-esteem and her true identity is the subtle, yet powerful, narrative thread that unites the text and achieves the breakthrough of self-understanding in the last pieces.

We can trace this search through some of its many moments. The narrative development begins in the first entry, "The House": "I knew then I had to have a house. A real house. One I could point to. But this isn't it. The house on Mango Street isn't it. For the time being, Mama says. Temporary, says Papa. But I know how those things go" (9). The narrator goes on to establish the family circle where she has warmth and love but is lonely and, most of all, estranged from the world outside. Her name, Esperanza, in English means hope: "At school they say my name funny as if the syllables were made out of tin and hurt the roof of your mouth. But in Spanish my name is made out of a softer something, like silver" (13). Fear and hostility are the alienating forces she tries to understand. Why do people of other colour fear her? And why should she fear others? That's the way it is. "All brown all around, we are safe" (29). Changes are coming over her, she is awakening to sexuality and to an adult world. It is in "Four Skinny Trees," that the identity question is explored: "They are the only ones who understand me. I am the only one who understands them" (71).

"A Smart Cookie" touches one of the most sensitive areas of the text: the mother–daughter relationship. Her mother remains nostalgic not for what was, but for what could have been: "I could've been somebody, you know?" (83) Being somebody is full of unarticulated significance, but in its impact on Esperanza, it means primarily to be herself and not what others wanted her to be. Her mother tells her she had brains, but she was also self-conscious and ashamed not to look as well as other more affluent girls. She quit school because she could not live looking at herself in the mirror of the other girls's presence. She states forthrightly: "Shame is a bad thing, you know. It keeps you down" (83). The syndrome is there; it is a closed circle. You are poor because you are an outsider without education; you try to get an education, but you can't take the contrastive evidence of poverty and "[i]t keeps you down." The constant movement of the narrative takes up one aspect after another of the circumstances of the emerging subject that is Esperanza Cordero.

There is a subtle sequential order to the short sections. The text opens with the description of the house and its significance to the narrator, moves on to a delicate image of the family group, and with the third piece, "Boys and Girls," begins the highly lyrical exposition of the narrator's world, punctuated with entries of introspection in the narrator's struggle with her identity. "My Name," "Chanclas, "Elenita, Cards, Palm Water," "Four Skinny Trees," "Bums in the Attic," "Beautiful and Cruel," "The Monkey Garden," "The Three Sisters," and "A House of My Own," are the most significant pieces because they mark the narrative development of identity. The text ends with the anticipated departure from the house and the literary return to it through writing. Although each piece can be seen as a self-contained prose poem, there is the subtle narrative unity of the enunciating voice's search for herself as she observes and questions her world and its social, economic, and moral conventions.

Esperanza Cordero observes, questions, and slowly finds herself determined through her relationship to the others who inhabit her world. She is drawn to the women and girls as would-be role models; within her family, her mother and her younger sister Magdalena (Nenny) are characterized, but the most searching descriptions are of girls her own age or, as she says, a few years older. Marin from Puerto Rico is featured in "Louie, His Cousin and

His Other Cousin" and "Marin," Alicia in "Alicia Who Sees Mice," Rafaela in "Rafaela Who Drinks Coconut and Papaya Juice on Tuesdays," and, most important of all, Sally in "Sally," "What Sally Said," "Red Clowns," and "Linoleum Roses." The older women are treated with a soft-spoken sympathy through imagery: Rosa Vargas in "There Was an Old Woman She Had So Many Children She Didn't Know What to Do," Ruthie in "Edna's Ruthie," the neighbour Mamacita in "No Speak English," and her own mother in "A Smart Cookie."

The enunciating voice never breaks her verisimilar perspective. She speaks about what she sees and what she thinks. Her style is one of subtlety, understatement, and generosity. When she reflects on social hostility or the brutality of wife-beating, it is not with violence or rancour, but with a firm determination to describe and to escape the vicious circle of abused women: Rosa Vargas is the mother "who is tired all the time from buttoning and bottling and babying, and who cries every day for the man who left without even leaving a dollar for bologna or a note explaining how come" (30); Marin who is not allowed out and hopes to get a job downtown so that she "can meet someone in the subway who might marry and take you to live in a big house far away" (27); "Alicia, who inherited her mama's rolling pin and sleepiness" and whose father says that "a woman's place is sleeping so she can wake up early with the tortilla star" (32); "Rafaela, who is still young but getting old from leaning out the window so much, gets locked indoors because her husband is afraid Rafaela will run away since she is too beautiful to look at" (76); "Minerva is only a little bit older than me but already she has two kids and a husband who left . . . she writes poems on little pieces of paper that she folds over and over and holds in her hands a long time" (80). And, there is Sally whose father hits her and "her mama rubs lard on all the places where it hurts. Then at school she'd say she fell. That's where all the blue places come from. That's why her skin is always scarred" (85).

The first person moves effortlessly from observer to lyrical introspection about her place in the world. The language is basic, idiomatic English with a touch of colloquial speech and a few Spanish words. The deceptively simple structure of sentences and paragraphs has a conceptual juxtaposition of action and reaction where the movement itself is the central topic. For example, "Those Who Don't," which consists of three short paragraphs, is about alienation and fear in a hostile society, but it is only fourteen lines in total. It begins with a direct statement about life as she sees it: "Those who don't know any better come into our neighborhood scared. They think we're dangerous. They think we will attack them with shiny knives. They are stupid people who are lost and got here by mistake" (29). The second paragraph, five lines long, begins with the "we" that is the implicit opposite of the "they" of

the preceding paragraph. "But we aren't afraid. We know the guy. . . ." With
the economy of a well-written sonnet the third five-line paragraph brings the
"they" and the "we" into an inverted encounter: "All brown all around, we are
safe. But watch us drive into a neighborhood of another color and our knees
go shakity-shake and our car windows get rolled up tight and our eyes look
straight. Yeah. That is how it goes and goes" (29). The description has been
that of a keen observer, the composition is that of a poet.

This structure operates through a conceptual back and forth movement
of images, like the action of the shuttle in the loom.[5] An image appears which
moves the reader forward, following the woof of the first-person through the
warp of referential world, but as soon as the image takes shape it is thrust
back toward the enunciator. The process is repeated again and again slowly
weaving the tapestry of Esperanza's Mango Street. For example, in "Those
Who Don't," the initial image is about the others, "Those who don't know
any better," but it reaches culmination with the observation that "they think
we're dangerous." The countermove is that "They are stupid people." The new
thrust forward is the reassurance of familiarity with the ostensible menacing
scene that greeted the outsiders and led them to fear they would be attacked.
But, when the shuttle brings back the narrative thread, it presents the inversion. The "we" are the "they" in another neighbourhood. The movement back
and forth will go on, the narrator says, "That is how it goes and goes." The
colour of the warp is different in each community, the woof keeps them next
to each other, but their ignorance and fear keeps them separate. The tapestry
that is being woven by this constant imagistic back and forth movement of
the narrator's perceptions and thoughts is not a plotted narrative, but rather
a narrative of self-invention by the writer-speaker. The speaker and her language are mutually implicated in a single interdependent process of poetic
self-invention.

The poetic text cannot operate if we separate the speaker from her language; they are the inseparable unity of personal identity. There is no utterance before enunciation. There is a fictional persona, Esperanza Cordero,
who will speak, and there is the implicit continued use of idiomatic American English. But the enunciation that we read is at once the speaker and
the spoken which discloses the subject, her subjectivity, and ours. An inescapable part of this subject is what she is expected to be: "Mexicans, don't
like their women strong" (12). "I wonder if she [my great-grandmother]
made the best with what she got or was she sorry because she couldn't be
all the things she wanted to be. Esperanza. I have inherited her name, but
I don't want to inherit her place by the window" (12). This close reading
of the text with attention to how it operates, suggests a movement and a
counter-movement which I have described metaphorically as the move-

ment of a loom weaving the presence of subjectivity. Subjectivity is always seen against the background of her community that is Chicago's changing neighbourhoods. This determinate background gives narrative continuation, or narrativity, to the narrator's thoughts. The narrative development of this text can be described as the elaboration of the speaker's subjectivity. The symbolic space she creates should not be abstracted from the writing, because the writing itself is the creation of her own space.[6] The structure of this text, therefore, begins as a frame for self-invention and as the writing progresses so does the subject. She is, in the most direct sense of the word, making herself and in a space of her own.

There are numerous empirical and verisimilar truth-claims about the way of life in the neighbourhood.[7] All of these references form a well-knit web of specific truth-claims about social reality. Simultaneous to these truth-claims is another kind of reference. The reference to the narrator's own sense of the world, her wonderment and search for answers of why things are the way they are for her and for those who are her family, friends, and neighbours: Minerva "comes over black and blue and asks what can she do? Minerva. I don't know which way she'll go. There is nothing I can do (80);" "Sally. What do you think about when you close your eyes like that? . . . Do you wish your feet would one day keep walking and take you far away from Mango Street, far away and maybe your feet would stop in front of a house, a nice one with flowers and big windows" (78). Esperanza meditates after her Aunt Lupe's death: "Maybe she was ashamed. Maybe she was embarrassed it took so many years. The kids who wanted to be kids instead of washing dishes and ironing their papa's shirts, and the husband who wanted a wife again. And then she died, my aunt who listened to my poems. And then we began to dream the dreams" (57). This quest for answers takes on an explicit tension because of the depth of the themes the narrator treats, but the manner in which she develops her search for answers is the fundamental dialectic of self-world. She describes what is around her, she responds to people and places, but, most importantly, she reflects on a world she did not make, and cannot change, but must control or she will be destroyed. She is a young, dark-skinned girl of Mexican parentage, born in Chicago, speaking English, and feeling alienated.

The use of these determinate features is of primary importance, for it is through the interplay between the lyrical introspection and the truth-claims that the fusion of self (enunciating voice) and person (character) takes place. The power of the text lies precisely in the creation of this presence. It is this human presence that transcends the time, place, and condition of the composition to create a literary metaphor for a woman coming of age. Readers halfway around the world, who have never seen Chicago and have never experienced what it is to live with the fear expressed in "All brown all around, we are safe," can, nevertheless, understand what it is to be lonely and alienated and how difficult it is to come out free from an environment that enslaves.

The images evoked by the text all signal a subject: Esperanza Cordero, an adolescent Mexican American girl who wants to be a writer. As critical readers, we read in a manner that creates ourselves as recipients, our own self-invention as the sympathetic listeners of the tale, attentive to actualize the words into images clothed in the colors of our own experience. The subject that emerges from our reading is neither the author's nor ours; she is a unique construct of intersecting designs and paradigms, those of the author's structure of the text, and those of the larger cultural context we share, in part, with the author. But this construct can only be reconstructed from its effects on us, its readers. Thus, the subject I am dealing with in these pages is a deliberate reconstruction from the effects of reading.

In order to draw out the subject of this text I will comment on three of the numerous images which are part of this work. The imagery in this text functions on three levels, in the manner of prose poems. Images in this text are effective because they function at the level of form, of plot, and of symbolic significance. Each of these images serves, first, to establish the identity of the enunciating voice; this is primarily a poetic function of creating the lyric presence who experiences and speaks. But, the images also have a narrative function as a part of the plot line which is the search for the promised house. And, finally, each image takes on symbolic proportions because it participates in the rich intertextuality of literature.

"Four Skinny Trees" presents the most iconic image in the entire text. The trees are personified in the image of the narrator: "Four skinny trees with skinny necks and pointy elbows like mine" (71), but the description is also markedly referential to the specific urban setting of the text: "Four who grew despite concrete" (71). At the primary level of the enunciating voice's identity, the image evokes a powerful statement about belonging and not belonging to the place where they happen to have grown: "Four who do not belong here but are here" (71). The narrative is composed of four short paragraphs. The first, with lyrical rhythm, establishes reciprocity between "I" and "they," "four skinny trees." The second completes the personification: "they" completely supplants "trees." The third paragraph introduces their function: "they teach"; and the fourth gives the lesson: to reach and not forget to reach and to "be and be."

At the level of plot, the trees serve as a talisman of survival in a hostile environment:

Let one forget his reason for being, they'd all droop like tulips in a glass, each with their arms around the other. Keep, keep, keep, trees say when I sleep. They teach.

When I am too sad and too skinny to keep keeping, when I am a tiny thing against so many bricks, then it is I look at trees. When there is nothing left to look at on this street. Four who grew despite concrete. Four who reach and do not forget to reach. Four whose only reason is to be and be. (71)

Esperanza's survival amidst surroundings that are negative and a rejection of her sensibility is not a denial of where she is and who she is, but rather a continuous fight to survive in spite of Mango Street as Esperanza from Mango Street. It is, however, at the symbolic level that the image of the trees attains its fullest significance. There is a secret to survival that the trees make manifest—an unconquerable will to fight without respite in order to survive in an urban setting:

Their strength is secret. They send ferocious roots beneath the ground. They grow up and they grow down and grab the earth between their hairy toes and bite the sky with violent teeth and never quit their anger. This is how they keep. (71)

I want to emphasize that the visual aspects of the textual imagery engage the reader in the visual figuration of vertical movement in trees. Is this a form of intertextuality? I think it would be more appropriate to say that this visual imagery is a woman's prose painting.

The highly lyrical presentation of "The Three Sisters" evokes the fairy godmothers of fairy-tale lore, each with a unique image and gift for the heroine. Their gift is the gift of self: "When you leave you must remember to come back for the others. A circle, understand? You will always be Esperanza. You will always be Mango Street. You can't erase what you know. You can't forget who you are" (98). This poem-piece is unlike any of the others in form because it combines the prose-poem quality of the rest of the book with the most extended dialogue sequence. The three sisters speak to Esperanza. The speaking voices are of crucial importance for through their enunciation they become full participants in the story-telling evocation with Esperanza.

At the level of plot the sisters serve as revelation. They are the narrative mediators that enter the story, at the crucial junctures, to assist the heroine in the trial that lies ahead. It is significant that they are from Mexico and appear to be related only to the moon. In pre-Hispanic Mexico, the lunar goddesses, such as Tlazolteotl and Xochiquetzal, were the intermediaries for all women (Westheim 105). They are sisters to each other and, as women, sisters to Esperanza. One has laughter like tin, another has the eyes of a cat, and the third hands like porcelain. This image is, above all, a lyrical disclosure of revelation. Their entrance into the story is almost magical: "They came with the wind that blows in August, thin as a spider web and barely noticed" (96), for they came only to make the gift to Esperanza of her selfhood. At the symbolic level, the three sisters are linked with Clotho, Lachesis, and Atropos, the three fates. Catullus depicts them weaving their fine web of destiny: "These sisters pealed their high prophetic song, / Song which no length of days shall prove untrue" (173).[8] The tradition of the sisters of fate runs deep in Western literature from the most elevated lyric to the popular tale of marriage, birth, and the fate awaiting the hero or heroine. In Cisneros's text, the prophecy of the fates turns to the evocation of self-knowledge.

The last image I shall discuss is based on the number two, the full force of opposition between two houses, the one on Mango Street and the promised house which is now the projection of the narrator. Although this image runs throughout the text, "The House on Mango Street," "Alicia," "A House of My Own" and "Mango Says Goodbye Sometimes," are the principal descriptions. The imagery of the house is in constant flux between a negative and a positive, between the house the narrator has and the one she would like to have: "I knew then I had to have a house. A real house. One I could point to. But this isn't it. The house on Mango Street isn't it" (9). On the level of the narrative voice's sense of belonging and identity, it is clear from the first piece that the house is much more than a place to live. It is a reflection, an extension, a personified world that is indistinguishable from the occupant. The oppositional pull and push continues throughout and reaches its climax in the last three pieces. In "Alicia and I Talking on Edna's Steps," it is in the form of reported dialogue: "No, this isn't my house I say and shake my head as if shaking could undo the year I've lived here. I don't belong. I don't ever want to come from here . . . I never had a house, not even a photograph . . . only one I dream of" (99). Because the house has become an extension of the person the rejection is vehement. She knows the person she is does not belong to the hostile ugly world she lives in.

"A House of My Own" expands on the promised house of her dreams in subtle, yet evocative, intertextuality to Virginia Woolf's *A Room of One's Own*:[9] "Only a house quiet as snow, a space for myself to go, clean as paper before the poem" (100). The house is now a metaphor for the subject and, therefore, the personal space of her identity. The last piece resolves the oppositional tension by transforming it into writing, into the metaphor of going away from Mango Street in order to return.

At the level of plot, the opposition of the house on Mango Street and a house of her own provides the narrative thread for the text. It is the movement implicit in the description of hostility and poverty and the belief in a better life that gives the story its inner cohesion and builds the consistency of the narrator's reflections. The fact that this conflict between alienation and the need to belong is common to persons of all cultures and across history gives the text its thematic link to world literature. There is a perfect circularity in the plot insofar as the text ends when the writing begins. The opening lines of the text are the closing. Esperanza has made her tension a tension creative of her subjectivity.

The idea of creative tension is well known to us through the work of Gaston Bachelard's *The Poetics of Space* and *The Poetics of Reverie* as well as Paul Ricoeur's *The Rule of Metaphor*, however, we must be reminded that this idea was already implicit in Aristotle's discussion of representation as the tension between the object known to be represented and the means used to represent it. In my work, I follow the theory that the image is not the residue of an impression, it is not an imprint that fades with time; on the contrary, the image that is produced through speech gives us the speaking subject and the subject spoken of, entwined in a unity of expression. If we move from speech to the written text, the situation becomes richer with possibilities. The text makes the image possible, the reader makes it actual and the image is something new in our language, an entity of reflection that was not there before, it is the poetic subjectivity in which we participate.

My commentary on these pages is reflective, aimed at participation and not at imposing closure on the text for other readers. As readers, regarding the self-invention of writing, we must respect the specificity of the self-invention, that is, a Chicana coming of age. In all patriarchal societies, but especially in this one, there is the imposition of the sign of gender which serves to silence women, to force them to particularize themselves through the indirect means of the way and style in which they serve others. This is the ideological meaning of "a daddy's house." By writing, this young woman has created herself as a total subject and not a gender role or a disembodied voice.

The symbolic level of the image of the house is the most basic expression of existence. Everything about the house on Mango Street repels the lyric narrator. This house is not hers and does not reflect her presence. The house of her dreams is first described in negative terms, by what it cannot be: "Not a flat. Not an apartment in back. Not a man's house. Not a daddy's" (100). This is followed by its attributes: "A house all my own. With my porch and my pillow, my pretty purple petunias. My books and my stories. My two shoes waiting beside the bed" (100). And it also excludes: "Nobody to shake a stick at. Nobody's garbage to pick up after" (100). The problem is that she belongs to the house on Mango Street and to deny it would be at the expense of herself, of her identity. She belongs to a world that is not hers; it is an opposition that will not be resolved in a synthesis or a compromise. The metaphor of a place of her own draws upon the continuing tensional opposition. She learns not only to survive but to win her freedom, and the text itself with its title and its search for the promised house is the creative tension of poetry. The semantic impertinence of belonging and not belonging creates the metaphorical meaning of identity as one who does not forget to reach and to reach and whose only reason is to "be and be."

The conclusion, "Mango Says Goodbye Sometimes," is lyrical and meditative:

> Friends and neighbors will say, What happened to that Esperanza? Where did she go with all those books and paper? Why did she march so far away?
>
> They will not know that I have gone away to come back. For the ones I left behind. For the ones who cannot out. (101–02)

The liberation of Esperanza through her writing draws from a rich tradition of a writer's self-creation. Reflection, in this tradition, is the movement toward the very core of being. Not only does the past become the present through the act of writing, but, of more consequence, the projection into the self's future is predicated on the self-knowledge of this existentialized consciousness. To remember, therefore, is not just to go back in time, it is the recovery of the past that makes the future. Cisneros writes it in these words: "You must keep writing. It will keep you free, and I said yes, but at that time I didn't know what she meant" (56).

Sandra Cisneros's text is a fictional autobiography of Esperanza Cordero. This is a postmodern form of fiction stitching together a series of lyrical pieces, "lazy poems" Cisneros calls them ("Writer's Notebook" 79), into the narrativity of self-invention through writing. In her study on autobiography, Sidonie Smith establishes a theoretical position which is at once lucid and fully applicable to my endeavor in this essay. Esperanza's position as a woman gives a particularity to the writing itself in four instances: (1) the fiction of memory, (2) of self, (3) of the reader, and (4) of the narrativity itself. Her position of authority to interpret herself must be asserted by writing, but it must be done against the grain, for she lives in a patriarchal Mexican American culture where stories about women silence and subjugate them as in the case of her namesake, her great-grandmother. Finally, Esperanza's basis of authority—she knows what she has lived and felt better than anyone else—is vulnerable unless she asserts her presence in a specific everyday reality; in other words, it cannot slip into a daydream escape route which would be an evasion, not a liberation; she must make her presence, the presence of a woman writing.[10]

Cisneros begins the end of her text with the affirmation of self-invention that displaces men's stories about women: "I like to tell stories. I am going to tell you a story about a girl who didn't want to belong" (101). By writing, Esperanza has not only gained control of her past, she has created a present in which she can be free and belong at the same time. Her freedom is the fundamental freedom to be herself and she cannot be herself if she is entrapped in patriarchal narrativity. Mango Street will always be part of this woman, but she has taken the strength of trees unto herself and has found the courage to be the house of her dreams, her own self-invention.

NOTES

1. Cisneros was National Endowment for the Arts Fellow in 1982 for Poetry and in 1988 for Narrative, graduated from the Iowa Writers Workshop, taught creative writing at one of Chicago's alternative high schools, and in 1988 held the Roberta Halloway writer-in-residence lectureship at the University of California, Berkeley. She has lectured extensively in North America and during the last three years has dedicated most of her time to writing another book of fiction, *Woman Hollering Creek and Other Stories*, published by Random House in 1991. *The House on Mango Street* was published in 1984 with a publication grant from the National Endowment for the Arts. The book was written from 1977 to 1982 and is now in its fourth printing which is the second revised edition (1988). In an interview I had with Cisneros on 30 December 1988 in New Orleans, she informed me that the first edition of *The House on Mango Street* had some overcorrections the publishers had made; she was not able to revise the edition until the fourth printing in 1988. It was reissued in 1991 by Vintage.

2. Dorrit Cohn has given us an analysis on the kinds of narrating voices we find in *The House on Mango Street* in what she terms "Diary and Continuity": "There are many reasons why the fictional diary is a close relative—and an important ancestor—of the autonomous monologue. For one thing, the two forms share the fiction of privacy; diarists ostensibly write, as monologists speak, only for themselves. Neither has any use for over exposition; the fiction of privacy collapses the moment either one of them explains his existential circumstances to himself in the manner of an autobiographer addressing future readers (or an oral narrator a listener)" (208).

3. In one of the first articles written about *The House on Mango Street*, Julián Olivares gives a sensitive reading of the text and also provides a balanced review of some of the debate provoked by this text. The two issues debated are genre and Chicano ideology. Olivares cites Cisneros's remarks on the question of genre: "I wanted to write a collection which could be read at any random point without hav-

ing any knowledge of what came before or after. Or that could be read in a series to tell one big story" ("Do You Know Me?" 78). She has done what she set out to do. The ideological debate is much more serious. I am in agreement with Olivares's assessment. He cites the review of Mango Street by Juan Rodríguez and comments on his ideological critique: "That Esperanza chooses to leave Mango St., chooses to move away from the social/cultural base to become more 'Anglicized,' more individualistic; that she chooses to move from the real to the fantasy plane of the world as the only means of accepting and surviving the limited and limiting social conditions of her barrio becomes problematic to the more serious reader." Olivares disagrees, he writes: "Esperanza transcends her condition, finding another house which is the space of literature. Yet what she writes about—third-floor flats, and fear of rats, and drunk husbands sending rocks through windows, anything as far from the poetic as possible—reinforces her solidarity with the people, the women, of Mango Street" (169).

4. My feminist criticism has developed out of my study of Kristeva's writings. Although I now have moved toward my own position of literary criticism as social critique, it would be less than forthright not to acknowledge my debt to Kristeva. It is primarily Kristeva's concept of language as social being and her insight into the *sujet en procès* which has given me the theoretical basis to examine all literary texts in a social critique that is neither coopted by the patriarchal system of historicist literary criticism nor by the reductionist tendencies of the feminist essentialists. I am primarily concerned in my criticism with the question of identity and gender in the third world of Latin America and its extension into the United States with the Chicana writing. In addition to her book *Desire in Language*, I have made use throughout the present study of the article "The System and the Speaking Subject."

5. I use the metaphor of the loom, not only because of its usefulness in describing the movement of the discourse, but also quite consciously that this is a woman's writing and it privileges the gradual emergence of a woman's poetic space rather than a plot. If my study were to concentrate on the topic of women's discourse, the metaphor of the quilt would have been more appropriate. But whether loom or quilt there is the unmistakable design of imagistic narrativity in place of employment. I am indebted to the work of Elaine Showalter and through her I have gained much greater insight into the recovery of women's art in the article by Lucy Lippard.

6. I find it essential to repeat that the critical strategy that effaces the female signature of a text is nothing less than the continuation of a patriarchal tradition of appropriation of the female's work through the destruction of her signature. Cisneros has created a female voice who writes with strength in a social context where doing so is an act of transgression, and she writes for "Alas mujeres/To the Women" as the dedication so poignantly states. I want to acknowledge the importance of Nancy K. Miller's article which has offered me the intellectual support for my recasting of text as texture.

7. I had occasion to have a second interview with Cisneros in Tijuana, Mexico, on 12 May 1989, at which time I asker her about the specific references to streets and establishments in Chicago. She said that Mango Street itself is a fictional composite of many streets and places. The references to other streets like Loomis, the church, businesses, etc. are referentially specific to Chicago in the sixties.

8. The Spanish Latin poet Catullus in his "The Marriage of Peleus and Thetes," describes the wedding gift of the three sisters, the Fates, all dressed in white, spinning their prophecy. The allusion of the spider web in Cisneros's text also gives the three sisters not only the gift of prophecy but an emblem of the weaver of tales of aunts as "the organizers and custodians of folklore and stories" (Showalter 233). The prophecy of Cisneros's three sisters is the gift of her identity.

9. An essential point to my argument is to emphasize the importance of an open text in writing by women. Virginia Woolf's characters after *Jacob's Room* are created for the reader to develop by inference and her essays, and especially *A Room of One's Own*, are for the reader to collaborate in a dialogical relationship with the writer. The metaphor of a room of one's own is, therefore, the highly charged space that comes to be through freedom to engage her other as equal in discussion, a right, not a privilege, traditionally denied to women.

10. In Sidonie Smith's discussion of Maxine Hong Kingston's *The Woman Warrior*, she touches the raw nerve of *The House on Mango Street*. Both texts, we have discovered through Smith, share in the complex act of writing about writing an autobiography, but in Cisneros's text, this is a fictional persona writing about writing her liberation. Cisneros's text, like that of Kingston, comes from the double marginalization of being female and an ethnic minority in the United States. Both force the issue of difference in terms of the community's narratives of selfhood.

Works Cited

Bachelard, Gaston. *The Poetics of Reverie.* Trans. Daniel Russell. New York: Orion, 1969.

———. *The Poetics of Space.* Trans. Maria Jolas. Boston: Beacon, 1969.

Black, Naomi. *Social Feminism.* Ithaca: Cornell UP, 1989.

Catullus. *The Poems of Catullus.* Ed. William A. Aiken. New York: 1960. 164–76.

Cisneros, Sandra. *The House on Mango Street.* Houston: Arte Publico P, 1988.

———. "From a Writer's Notebook: Do You Know Me? I Wrote *The House on Mango Street.*" *The Americas Review* 15:1 (1987): 77–79.

Cohn, Dorrit. "From Narration to Monologue." *Transparent Minds: Narrative Models for Presenting Consciousness in Fiction.* Princeton: Princeton UP, 1978. 173–216.

Kristeva, Julia. *Desire in Language: A Semiotic Approach to Literature and Art.* New York: Columbia UP, 1980.

———. "The System and the Speaking Subject." *The Tell-Tale Sign: A Survey of Semiotics.* Ed. Thomas A. Sebeok. Lisse, Netherlands: Ridder, 1975. 45–55.

Lippard, Lucy. "Up, Down and Across: A New Frame for New Quilts." *The Artist and the Quilt.* Ed. Charlotte Robinson. New York: Knopf, 1983.

Miller, Nancy K. "Arachnologies: The Woman, The Text and the Critic." *The Poetics of Gender.* Ed. Nancy K. Miller. New York: Columbia UP, 1986. 270–95.

Olivares, Julián. "Sandra Cisneros' *The House on Mango Street*, and the Poetics of Space." *The Americas Review* 15:3–4 (1987): 160–70.

Ricoeur, Paul. *The Rule of Metaphor.* Trans. Robert Czerny. Toronto: U Toronto P, 1977.

———. "What is a Text? Explanation and Understanding." "The Model of the Text: Meaningful Action Considered as a Text." *Hermeneutics and the Human Sciences.* Ed., trans. John B. Thomson. Cambridge: Cambridge UP, 1981. 145–64; 197–221.

Rodríguez, Juan. "*The House on Mango Street*, by Sandra Cisneros." *Austin Chronicle* (August 10, 1984). Cited in Pedro Gutierrez-Revuelta. "Genero e ideologia en el libro de Sandra Cisneros: *The House on Mango Street*." *Critica* 1:3 (1986): 48–59.

Showalter, Elaine. "Piecing and Writing." *The Poetics of Gender*. Ed. Nancy K. Miller. New York: Columbia UP, 1986. 222–47.

Smith, Sidonie. *A Poetics of Women's Autobiography*. Bloomington: Indiana UP, 1987.

Woolf, Virginia. *A Room of One's Own*. London: Harcourt Brace Jovanovich, 1929.

JACQUELINE DOYLE

More Room of Her Own:
Sandra Cisneros's The House on Mango Street

"Books continue each other," Virginia Woolf told an audience of young women some sixty years ago, "in spite of our habit of judging them separately" (*Room* 84). Books such as Ellen Moers's *Literary Women*, Elaine Showalter's *A Literature of Their Own*, Patricia Meyer Spacks's *The Female Imagination*, Tillie Olsen's *Silences*, and Alice Walker's *In Search of Our Mothers' Gardens* continue Virginia Woolf's own book, *A Room of One's Own*, extending her fertile meditations on the effects of economic deprivation on women's literature, and her pioneering efforts to reconstruct a female literary tradition. Tillie Olsen has uncovered a rich vein of writing by American working class women, and has offered poignant personal testimony to the obstacles to writing posed by gender and class. Alice Walker has explored the silences created by gender and race in America: "What did it mean for a black woman to be an artist in our grandmothers' time? In our great-grandmothers' day? It is a question with an answer cruel enough to stop the blood" (233).

While feminists following Woolf's advice to "think back through our mothers" have expanded the literary canon in the past two decades, too many have ignored the questions of race, ethnicity, and class in women's literature. Adrienne Rich laments the "white solipsism" of white feminists—"not the consciously held *belief* that one race is inherently superior to all others, but

From *MELUS* 19, no. 4 (Winter 1994): 5–35. © 1994 by *MELUS*.

a tunnel-vision which simply does not see nonwhite experience or existence as precious or significant" ("Disloyal" 306). Barbara Smith, Alice Walker, and Toni Morrison have angrily denounced the canon implicit in early studies of women's literature such as Moers's and Spacks's.[1] To Spacks's tepid defense that she preferred to dwell on authors depicting "familiar experience" and a "familiar cultural setting" (5), Walker counters: "Why only these? Because they are white, and middle class, and because to Spacks, female imagination is only that—a limitation that even white women must find restrictive" (372).

Confined by what Rich criticizes as the "faceless, raceless, classless category of 'all women'"[2] ("Notes" 13) women of color in the United States have all too often felt themselves compelled to choose between ethnicity and womanhood. Mitsuye Yamada speaks for many when she observes: "I have thought of myself as a feminist first, but my ethnicity cannot be separated from my feminism" (73). Sonia Saldívar-Hull writes of the damaging "color blindness" and "ideological erasure" of contemporary white feminist "sister-hood" (204). Yvonne Yarbro-Bejarano points out that while a Chicana femi-nist perspective shares "with the feminist perspective an analysis of questions of gender and sexuality, there are important differences between a Chicana perspective and the mainstream feminist one with regard to issues of race, culture and class" (140). Many women of color reject the monolithic notion of a "woman's voice." If Woolf in *A Room of One's Own* brought Shakespeare's silenced sister to life, María C. Lugones and Elizabeth V. Spelman point to new silences within contemporary feminist discourse itself: "Indeed, many Hispanas, Black women, Jewish women—to name a few groups—have felt it an invitation to silence rather than speech to be requested—if they are requested at all—to speak about being women (with the plain wrapper—as if there were one) in distinction from speaking about being Hispana, Black, Jewish, working-class, etc., women" (574). Sandra Cisneros recalls sitting in a University of Iowa seminar at the age of twenty-two and suddenly realizing that she was "different from everybody" there:

> It wasn't as if I didn't know who I was. I knew I was a Mexican woman. But, I didn't think it had anything to do with why I felt so much imbalance in my life, whereas it had everything to do with it! My race, my gender, and my class! And it didn't make sense until that moment, sitting in that seminar. That's when I decided I would write about something my classmates couldn't write about. (Aranda 65)

Cisneros's *The House on Mango Street*, dedicated in two languages "A las Mujeres/To the Women," both continues Woolf's meditations and alters the legacy of *A Room of One's Own* in important ways. Her series of vignettes is about the maturing of a young Chicana and the development of a writer; it is about the women she grows up with; it is also about a sense of community, culture, and place. Esperanza, the young protagonist, yearns for "a space for myself to go, clean as paper before the poem," and for a house of her own:

> Not a flat. Not an apartment in back. Not a man's house. Not a daddy's. A house all my own. With my porch and my pillow, my pretty purple petunias. My books and my stories. My two shoes waiting beside the bed. Nobody to shake a stick at. Nobody's garbage to pick up after. (*House* 108)

Instead she shares a bedroom with her sister Nenny, in a house marked by constriction and absence: "windows so small you'd think they were holding their breath," a front door "so swollen you have to push hard to get in," "no front yard," and a small garage out back "for the car we don't own yet" (4).

The dilapidated series of apartments and houses Esperanza inhabits with her mother, father, sister, and two brothers—particularly their dwelling on Mango Street—represents her poverty, but also the richness of her subject matter. "Like it or not you are Mango Street," her friend Alicia tells her, "and one day you'll come back too" (107). "You must remember to come back," the three aged sisters tell her, "for the ones who cannot leave as easily as you" (105). *A Room of One's Own* would seem to allow Esperanza this subject, even to encourage it. "All these infinitely obscure lives remain to be recorded," as Woolf told her young female audience. Pondering the shopgirl behind the counter, she commented, "I would as soon have her true history as the hundred and fiftieth life of Napoleon" (*Room* 93–94). But Woolf's class and ethnic biases might also deter Esperanza from achieving her own literary voice.

Cisneros's *The House on Mango Street* covertly transforms the terms of Woolf's vision, making room in the female literary tradition for a young working-class Chicana who "like[s] to tell stories": "I make a story for my life," Esperanza tells us, "for each step my brown shoe takes. I say, 'And so she trudged up the wooden stairs, her sad brown shoes taking her to the house she never liked'" (109). If Esperanza's name means "too many letters," means "sadness" in the life she knows in Spanish, it translates as "hope" in English (10). Thinking back through her mothers and their comadres and across through her sisters, she builds her house from the unfulfilled hopes and dreams around her. "I could've been somebody, you know?" sighs her mother (90). Edna's Ruthie next door "could have been [many things] if she wanted to," muses Esperanza, but instead she got married to a husband nobody ever sees (68). Esperanza inherited her name from her great-grandmother, a "wild horse of a [young] woman" who, tamed by marriage, spent her days confined in her husband's house. "She looked out the window all her life," says Esperanza: "I wonder if she made the best with what she got or was she sorry because she couldn't be all the things she wanted to be. Esperanza. I have inherited her name, but I don't want to inherit her place by the window" (11). As Esperanza revises and lays claim to her matrilineal inheritance, so Cisneros in *Mango Street* offers a rich reconsideration of the contemporary feminist inheritance as well.

1

No one has yet written *A Room of One's Own* for writers, other than women, still marginal in literature. Nor do any bibliographies exist for writers whose origins and circumstances are marginal. Class remains the greatest unexamined factor.

(Tillie Olsen Silences 146)

Woolf famously concluded *A Room of One's Own* with her hopes for the resurrection of Shakespeare's voiceless sister. "She lives in you and in me," Woolf told her young female listeners, "and in many other women who are not here tonight, for they are washing up the dishes and putting the children to bed" (117).[3] Woolf's all-inclusive vision of sisterhood, however, barely admits the possibility of actual artistic expression among those women "not here tonight"—particularly those marginalized by race, ethnicity, and class. The five hundred pounds a year that afford her first-person narrator the freedom and independence to write are a legacy from her aunt (37–38). While Woolf expresses the hope that young women of the future will actually be "capable of earning over five hundred a year," and suggests that they limit child-bearing to "twos and threes" rather than "tens and twelves" (117), she seems to overlook the obstacles to creative freedom that a job and motherhood might pose even for the woman privileged with an income and a room of her own. She sees little future for women without those privileges.

Arguing the necessity of economic security for artistic production, Woolf asserts that "genius like Shakespeare's is not born among laboring, uneducated, servile people. . . . It is not born today among the working classes" (50). When she numbers among the advantages of "being a woman" the fact that "one can pass even a very fine negress without wishing to make an Englishwoman of her," she excludes women of color both from her audience and from her implicit definition of "being a woman" (52).[4] Similarly, when she observes that "genius of a sort must have existed among women as it must have existed among the working classes" (50), she implicitly addresses a community of women in the middle and upper classes, and thereby excludes working-class women. Tillie Olsen's wry footnote to this passage some years later reads: "Half of the working classes are women" (*Silences* 11n). And Alice Walker invites us to recast Woolf's sentence to read: "Yet genius of a sort must have existed among slaves as it must have existed among the wives and daughters of sharecroppers" (239).

In *Silences*, Olsen supplements Woolf's well-known comments on the "Angel in the House" in "Professions for Women" with her working-class equivalent: "*another angel . . . the essential angel*, with whom Virginia Woolf (and most women writers, still in the privileged class) did not have to contend—the angel who must assume the physical responsibilities for daily living, for the maintenance of life" (34). So "lowly as to be invisible," the essential angel makes no appearance in *A Room of One's Own*. If Woolf nods to those women "not here tonight, for they are washing up the dishes and putting the children to bed" (117), Adrienne Rich draws our attention to "women whom she left out of the picture altogether—women who are washing other people's dishes and caring for other people's children, not to mention women who went on the streets last night in order to feed their children" ("When We Dead" 38).

In a tribute to the "essential angel" of her own childhood, Cisneros has acknowledged the importance of Woolf's belief that a room of one's own is a necessary precondition for writing. Allowing her room of her own, Cisneros's mother enabled her daughter to create: "I'm here," Cisneros explained to an audience of young writers, "because my mother let me stay in my room reading and studying, perhaps because she didn't want me to inherit her sadness and her rolling pin" ("Notes" 75). In "Living as a Writer," Cisneros again stresses that she has "always had a room of [her] own": "As Virginia Woolf has said, a woman writer needs money, leisure, and a room of her own" (71). Elsewhere Cisneros indirectly questions the class bias of Woolf's perspective, however, when she discusses her early "dream of becoming a writer" and the inspiration of Emily Dickinson as a female literary precedent for her poetry. "What I didn't realize about Emily Dickinson," Cisneros told a junior high audience, "was that she had a few essentials going for her":[5]

> 1) an education, 2) a room of her own in a house of her own that she shared with her sister Lavinia, and 3) money inherited along with the house after her father died. She even had a maid, an Irish housekeeper who did, I suspect, most of the household chores. . . . I wonder if Emily Dickinson's Irish housekeeper wrote poetry or if she ever had the secret desire to study and be anything besides a housekeeper. ("Notes" 75)

As Woolf speculated on Shakespeare's hypothetical, silenced sister, Cisneros speculates on Dickinson's housekeeper, comparing her to her own mother, "who could sing a Puccini opera, cook a dinner for nine with only five dollars, who could draw and tell stories and who probably would've enjoyed a college education" if she could have managed one ("Notes" 75). In *The House on Mango Street*, Esperanza's mother tells her that she herself should never have quit school (91). "Study hard," she tells her daughter, stirring the oatmeal, "Look at my comadres. She means Izaura whose husband left and Yolanda whose husband is dead. Got to take care all your own, she says shaking her head" (91).

Woolf stressed the importance of a female tradition for the woman writer: "we think back through our mothers if we are women" (*A Room* 79). For both Alice Walker and Sandra Cisneros, these mothers include women outside the "tradition" as it is conventionally understood, women who, perhaps anonymously, "handed on the creative spark, the seed of the flower they themselves never hoped to see; or . . . a sealed letter they could not plainly read" (Walker 240). Esperanza's mother—her encouragement, but also what she has not written, not expressed—is central to the community of female relationships informing her daughter's development as an artist. Esperanza's tribute to her mother, "A Smart Cookie," opens: "I could've been somebody, you know? my mother says and sighs." Her list of talents—"She can speak two languages. She can sing an opera. She knows how to fix a T.V."—is framed by her confinement in a city whose subway system she has never mastered, and extended in a list of unfulfilled desires: "Someday she would like to go to the ballet. Someday she would like to see a play" (*House* 90). *The House on Mango Street* strikingly enacts what Rachel Blau DuPlessis sees as a "specific biographical drama that has entered and shaped *Künstlerromane* by women": "Such a narrative is engaged with a maternal figure and . . . is often compensatory for her losses. . . . The daughter becomes an artist to extend, reveal, and elaborate her mother's often thwarted talents" (93). Esperanza's mother points to the girl's godmothers (her own *comadres*, or, literally translated, "comothers," powerful family figures in Chicano culture) as examples of the necessity "to take care all your own" (91). In the extended filiations of her ethnic community Esperanza finds a network of maternal figures. She writes to celebrate all of their unfulfilled talents and dreams and to compensate for their losses.

Cisneros loosely structures her series of prose pieces as a *Künstlerroman*, whereby the final piece circles back to the opening.[6] Esperanza's closing statement, "I like to tell stories. I am going to tell you a story about a girl who didn't want to belong," is followed by a repetition of the opening lines of the book that she is now able to write (109, 3). The paired sections opening and closing the book strongly evoke Esperanza's maternal muse. While the opening chapter describes their ramshackle series of third-floor flats and the unsatisfactory house on Mango Street where Esperanza has no room of her own, her mother's body in the second chapter provides all of the security and warmth and "room" that the small girl desires:

> But my mother's hair, my mother's hair, . . . sweet to put your nose into when she is holding you, holding you and you feel safe, is the warm smell of bread before you bake it, is the smell when she makes a little room for you on her side of the bed still warm with her skin, and you sleep near her, the rain outside falling and Papa snoring. The snoring, the rain, and Mama's hair that smells like bread. (6–7)

The two closing sketches, "A House of My Own" and "Mango Says Goodbye Sometimes," describe the grown Esperanza's ideal house of her own where she can create, "a space for myself to go, clean as paper before the poem" (100), and also her new relation to Mango Street and her origins. The house on Mango Street becomes an overtly maternal figure who collaborates in her freedom and creativity: "I write it down and Mango says goodbye sometimes. She does not hold me with both arms. She sets me free" (110).

DuPlessis sees the circular structure of the twentieth-century woman's *Künstlerroman* as a way of writing "beyond" the traditional endings available to women, what Woolf in *A Room of One's Own* called "breaking the sequence" of conventional plot (*A Room* 85, 95). "In these works," DuPlessis writes, "the female artist is given a way of looping back and reenacting childhood ties, to achieve not the culturally approved ending in heterosexual romance, but rather the reparenting necessary to her second birth as an artist" (94). The "maternal muse" and "reparenting motifs," DuPlessis suggests, are among the "strategies that erode, transpose, and reject narratives of heterosexual love and romantic thralldom" (94). Esperanza contrasts fairy tale romances with the lives of the women around her as she develops a new narrative form to tell their stories and give shape to her own vocation. "You must keep writing," her aunt tells her, "It will keep you free" (61).

2

There will be narratives of female lives only when women no longer
live their lives isolated in the houses and the stories of men.
(Carolyn G. Heilbrun *Writing a Woman's Life* 47)

In *A Room of One's Own*, Woolf looked ahead to the woman in the future who would write a different sort of "novel," "some new vehicle, not necessarily in verse, for the poetry in her" (80). She anticipated that women writers would need to break the sentence and to break the sequence, "the expected order," in order to develop forms "adapted to the [woman's] body" and expressive of women's lives (85, 95, 81). Women's books, she suggested, would possibly "be shorter, more concentrated, than those of men" (81), and would undoubtedly deal with new subjects (86–96). *The House on Mango Street* fulfills many of Woolf's prophecies, most obviously in its brevity and generic instability. Cisneros herself has called her stories "a cross between poetry and fiction,"[7] which she wanted her readers to be able to read both in and out of sequence: "I wanted to write a collection which could be read at any random point without having any knowledge of what came before or after. Or, that could be read in a series to tell one big story. I wanted stories like poems, compact and lyrical and ending with a reverberation" ("Do You Know Me?" 78).

Woolf specified gender and class as the two subject areas yet to be explored. The female writer of the future need no longer depict women exclusively in relation to men; she would be free to explore "relationships between women," particularly friendships, "those unrecorded gestures, those unsaid or half-said words, which form themselves, no more palpably than the shadows of moths on the ceiling, when women are alone, unlit by the capricious and coloured light of the other sex" (*A Room* 86, 88). Further, Woolf wrote, "she will not need to limit herself any longer to the respectable houses of the upper middle classes" (92). In lectures Cisneros has explained that her subject emerged in a "defensive and rebellious" reaction to her white middleclass fellow graduate students at the University of Iowa Writer's Workshop: "My intent was simply to chronicle, to write about something my classmates couldn't" ("Do You Know Me?" 78).

Poverty was the "ghost" she attempted to escape before she found her subject, Cisneros told an audience of young writers ("Ghosts" 72). "As a poor person growing up in a society where the class norm was superimposed on a t.v. screen, I couldn't understand why our home wasn't all green lawn and white wood like the ones in 'Leave It To Beaver' or 'Father Knows Best'" (72). The metaphor of the house emerged, Cisneros said, in a heated graduate seminar discussion of Gaston Bachelard's *Poetics of Space*: "What did I know except third-floor flats. Surely my classmates knew nothing about that. That's precisely what I chose to write: about third-floor flats, and fear of rats, and drunk husbands sending rocks through windows, anything as far from the poetic as possible" (73).

Julián Olivares argues that Bachelard's book delineates a "poetics of space" that is particularly the provenance of the privileged upper-class white male, "probably never having to do 'female' housework and probably never having been confined to the house for reason of his sex." Bachelard's reveries of "felicitous space," he contends, evoke "images of a house that a woman might not have, especially an impoverished woman raised in a ghetto" (160). Olivares overlooks a number of feminist writers, however, who have explored the special relation of women to houses and rooms, the traditional realm of their "separate sphere."[8] In *A Room of One's Own* Woolf described the creative power exerted by women in the drawing-room or nursery, "the centre of some different order and system of life" (90):

> One goes into a room—but the resources of the English language would be much put to the stretch, and whole flights of words would need to wing their way illegitimately into existence before a woman could say what happens when she goes into a room. . . . One has only to go into any room in any street for the whole of that extremely complex force of femininity to fly in one's face. How should it be otherwise? For women have sat indoors all these millions of years, so that by this time the very walls are permeated by their creative force, which has, indeed, so overcharged the capacity of bricks and mortar that it must needs harness itself to pens and brushes and business and politics. But this creative power differs greatly from the creative power of men. (91)

While it might be argued that Woolf's privileged experience of domestic space more closely approximates an upper-class white Englishman's than a contemporary woman of color's in the United States, Toni Morrison has also commented on the peculiar "intimacy" of a woman's sense of place, "a woman's strong sense of being in a room, a place, or in a house." "Sometimes my relationship to things in a house would be a little different from, say my brother's or my father's or my sons'," she told Robert Stepto in an interview, "I clean them and I move them and I do very intimate things 'in place': I am sort of rooted in it, so that writing about being in a room looking out, or being in a world looking out, or living in a small definite place, is probably very common among most women anyway" (Stepto 213).[9]

The domestic realm arouses a variety of responses in contemporary women writers. Tillie Olsen has most vividly described the difficulty of making space in a woman's daily life for writing: "habits of years—response to others, distractibility, responsibility for daily matters—stay with you, mark you, become you" (39). Esperanza boldly proclaims her intention to break these habits early: "I have begun my own quiet war. Simple. Sure. I am one who leaves the table like a man, without putting back the chair or picking up the plate" (*House* 89).[10] Gender roles, as well as class, condition Esperanza's response to women's confinement to the household. Olivares is largely correct in his central premise that "Cisneros . . . inverts Bachelard's pronouncement on the poetics of space; for Cisneros the inside, the here, can be confinement and a source of anguish and alienation" (161). In story after story of the women in her community, Esperanza recognizes that a room—if not of one's own—can be stifling.

Her own grandmother, unhappily married, "looked out the window all her life, the way so many women sit their sadness on an elbow" (11). Because Rafaela is beautiful, her husband locks her indoors on Tuesday nights while he plays dominoes; Rafaela is "still young," Esperanza explains, "but getting old from leaning out the window so much" (79). Louie's cousin Marin "can't come out—gotta baby-sit with Louie's sisters—but she stands in the doorway a lot" (23–24). "We never see Marin until her aunt comes home from work," Esperanza tells us, "and even then she can only stay out front" (27). Across the street on the third floor, Mamacita, who speaks no English, "sits all day by the window and plays the Spanish radio shows and sings all the homesick songs about her country" (77). Sally's father keeps her inside and beats her when he thinks of his sisters who ran away. Later Sally's husband won't let her talk on the phone or even look out the window:

> She sits at home because she is afraid to go outside without his permission. She looks at all the things they own: the towels and the toaster, the alarm clock and the drapes. She likes looking at the walls, at how neatly their corners meet, the linoleum roses on the floor, the ceiling smooth as wedding cake. (102)

"There Was an Old Woman She Had So Many Children She Didn't Know What to Do" suggests the Mother Goose character who lived in a shoe; "Rosa Vargas' kids are too many and too much" and even the neighborhood has given up trying to help (29). Throughout Esperanza's narrative shoes intersect with the theme of dwellings as images of constricting femininity.[11] The enormously fat Mamacita with her tiny feet arrives in the United States with "a dozen boxes of satin high heels" and then never leaves her room again, perhaps because she's fat, perhaps because she doesn't speak English, perhaps because she can't climb the three flights of stairs" (77). Sire ties his girlfriend Lois's shoes as Esperanza concludes that Lois doesn't know how. "Mama says those kind of girls, those girls are the ones that go into alleys. Lois who can't tie her shoes. Where does he take her?" (73). In "The Family of Little Feet," Esperanza and her girlfriends Lucy and Rachel spend a day teetering on high heels, sampling adult femininity. "It's Rachel who learns to walk the best all strutted in those magic high heels. She teaches us to cross and uncross our legs, and to run like a double-dutch rope, and how to walk down to the corner so that the shoes talk back to you with every step." The men on the corner "can't take their eyes off" them. The grocer tells them they're "too young to be wearing shoes like that," the shoes are "dangerous" and he's going to "call the cops." A bum accosts Rachel and offers her a dollar for a kiss. "Tired of being beautiful," the girls abandon the shoes and never wear them again (40–42).

Gender identity in "The Family of Little Feet" becomes an arbitrary cultural construct assumed like a pair of shoes.[12] "The boys and girls live in separate worlds," as Esperanza explains to us (11), yet it is possible to act like a male by refusing household chores, or to act like a female by wobbling helplessly on high heels. Even "scientific facts" marking gender difference, such as women's hips, become part of the cultural production of gender identity as the girls speculate on their functions:

> They're good for holding a baby when you're cooking, Rachel says turning the jump rope a little quicker. She has no imagination.
>
> You need them to dance, says Lucy.
>
> If you don't get them you may turn into a man. Nenny says this and she believes it. She is this way because of her age.
>
> That's right, I add before Lucy or Rachel can make fun of her. She is stupid alright, but she is my sister.
>
> But most important, hips are scientific, I say repeating what Alicia already told me. It's the bones that let you know which skeleton was a man's when it was a man and which a woman's. (47)

Like the high heels, hips require practice. "You gotta know how to walk with hips," Esperanza explains, "practice you know—like if half of you wanted to go one way and the other half the other" (50). As their jump rope game progresses, what separates Nenny from the three older girls is not the immaturity of her hips, but her inability to improvise new rhymes on hips as they swing the rope. "Not that old song, I say. You gotta use your own song. Make it up, you know? But she doesn't get it or won't. It's hard to say which. The rope turning, turning, turning" (50).

By improvising their own songs, Esperanza and her friends "write beyond the ending" of the cultural scripts confining the women around them,[13] rejecting "that old song" that Nenny repeats, or the "same story" that Minerva tells, every time she takes her husband back (50, 85). Esperanza observes that the "stories the boys tell in the coatroom" about her friend Sally are "not true," and also that Sally herself has perpetuated lies from the "storybooks and movies": "Sally, you lied. It wasn't what you said at all. . . . The way they said it, the way it's supposed to be, all the storybooks and movies, why did you lie to me?" (99). Just as the relationship between the two girls is more central to Cisneros's loosely structured plot than any heterosexual bonds, so Esperanza seems to feel Sally's betrayal more keenly than the rape she suffers while she waits for Sally at the carnival. "Sally Sally a hundred times," she says, hoping her friend will "make him stop" (100). And later she repeats over and over, "You're a liar. They all lied. All the books and magazines, everything that told it wrong. Only his dirty fingernails against my skin, only his sour smell again. The moon that watched" (100). When she cries, "I waited my whole life" (100), Esperanza bitterly evokes the "romance" of deflowering as well as the eternity she waited for Sally to rescue her.

Woolf suggested that twentieth-century women writers would be free to explore relationships between women, who in the past had "not only [been] seen by the other sex, but seen only in relation to the other sex" (*A Room* 86). The friendship between Esperanza and Sally in *Mango Street* recalls Clarissa's bond with another Sally in Woolf's experimental novel *Mrs. Dalloway*. Esperanza's Sally, like Clarissa's bohemian friend, represents danger and adventure: "Sally is the girl with eyes like Egypt and nylons the color of smoke" (*House* 81). While Clarissa's Sally is undone by the relatively benign institutions of bourgeois marriage and motherhood, Esperanza's Sally endures physical abuse from her father, the cruel gossip of the boys in the coatroom, and an unhappy marriage before she reaches eighth grade. When Sally ignores Esperanza's attempt to "save" her from Tito and his friends, who significantly will return her keys only if she kisses each of them, the grief-stricken Esperanza loses the Edenic innocence of her girlhood: "I looked at my feet in their white socks and ugly round shoes. They seemed far away. They didn't seem to be my feet anymore. And the garden that had been such a good place to play didn't seem mine either" (98).[14] Esperanza's "monkey garden," choked with weeds and abandoned cars, would seem "far away" from the flower-filled British terrace of Woolf's novel, where Clarissa and Sally's kiss was rudely interrupted by Clarissa's suitor Peter and the intrusive cultural expectations of adult heterosexuality (*Mrs. Dalloway* 52–53).[15] Yet within their disparate socioeconomic settings, both narratives self-consciously resist the closure of the conventional romance or marriage plot, which DuPlessis defines as "the use of conjugal love as a telos and of the developing heterosexual love relation as a major . . . element in organizing the narrative action" (200n22).

Tensions between Esperanza's new narratives and "all the books and magazines, everything that told it wrong" are most evident in her use of fairy tales as counterpoints to women's lives in the barrio. Locked in her room, Rafaela "dreams her hair is like Rapunzel's" and yearns to be rescued (79). Marin moons in the doorway under the streetlamp, hoping the boys will see her: "Is waiting for a car to stop, a star to fall, someone to change her life" (27). When they receive the gift of the discarded shoes, Esperanza and her friends shout, "Hurray! Today we are Cinderella because our feet fit exactly" (40). Their encounters with men as they strut in their glass slippers escalate in danger until they flee from the drunken "bum man," a leering Prince Charming whose kiss they refuse.[16]

Princes are conspicuously absent or threatening in almost all of Esperanza's stories. Rosa Vargas's husband "left without even leaving a dollar for bologna or a note explaining how come" (29). Minerva's "mother raised her kids alone and it looks like her daughters will go that way too" (84). Edna's daughter Ruthie sleeps on a couch in her living room and "says she's just visiting and next weekend her husband's gonna come back to take her home. But the weekends come and go and Ruthie stays" (69). Esperanza's godmothers' husbands left or died (91). Minerva's husband, who "left and keeps leaving," throws a rock through the window when she "finally" puts him out. "Then he is sorry and she opens the door again. Same story. Next week she comes over black and blue and asks what can she do? Minerva. I don't know which way she'll go. There is nothing *I* can do" (85). When Sally marries a marshmallow salesman out of state, she tells Esperanza she is in love, but Esperanza thinks "she did it to escape" her father's beatings. Trapped in her room with its linoleum roses and "ceiling smooth as wedding cake," Sally is imprisoned by the very prince who was to rescue her (102).

Most of the women yearn for different endings. Minerva secretly writes poems on "little pieces of paper that she folds over and over and holds in her hands a long time, little pieces of paper that smell like a dime" (84). On Tuesday nights Rafaela lowers a shopping bag on a clothesline from her locked room so that the children can send up coconut and papaya juice, "and wishes there were sweeter drinks, not bitter like an empty room, but sweet—sweet like the island, like the dance hall down the street where women much older than her throw green eyes easily like dice and open homes with keys" (80). Yet if Rafaela desires her own key, she continues to dream of what DuPlessis terms "romantic thralldom" (66–67), the same stories that locked her in her room: "And always there is someone offering sweeter drinks, someone promising to keep them on a silver string" (80). Marin also yearns for the silver string—a job downtown, where you "get to wear nice clothes and can meet someone in the subway who might marry you and take you to live in a big house far away" (26). Esperanza's little sister Nenny insists "she won't wait her whole life for a husband to come and get her," nor does she want to leave the house like Minerva's sister by having a baby: "She wants things all her own," Esperanza says, "to pick and choose. Nenny has pretty eyes and it's easy to talk that way if you are pretty" (88). Esperanza, whose hair "never obeys barrettes or bands" (6), tells us that she is the "ugly daughter," "the one nobody comes for" (82). She dreams of being a movie screen *femme fatale*, "beautiful and cruel": "Her power is her own. She will not give it away" (89). She has decided, she tells us, "not to grow up tame like the others" (88).

Indifferent to the prince's glass slipper, Esperanza seeks to develop an autonomous identity. She and Lucy and Rachel decisively abandon their high heels after a day of playing grownup princesses at the ball. In a related episode, Esperanza, dressed in new clothes for her cousin's baptism, is ashamed to dance because of her old and scuffed brown and white saddle shoes. Her feet "grow bigger and bigger" as she declines invitations to dance until her uncle pulls her onto the dance floor:

> My feet swell big and heavy like plungers, but I drag them across the linoleum floor straight center where Uncle wants to show off the new dance we learned. And Uncle spins me and my skinny arms bend the way he taught me and my mother watches and my little cousins watch and the boy who is my cousin by first communion watches and everyone says, wow, who are those two who dance like in the movies, until I forget that I am wearing only ordinary shoes, brown and white, the kind my mother buys each year for school. (47)

Esperanza reconciles herself to "ordinary shoes" as she will later reconcile herself to Mango Street. In both cases this reconciliation entails a new freedom, to dance, to imagine a house of her own with her "two shoes waiting beside the bed," a house "quiet as snow," "clean as paper before the poem" (108). The blank page allows her the freedom to imagine new scripts for women's lives. "You can never have too much sky," she tells us (33).

Woolf's Mary Beton in *A Room of One's Own* explained that her aunt's legacy of five hundred pounds a year "unveiled the sky" to her, "substituted for the large and imposing figure of a gentleman, which Milton recommended for my perpetual adoration, a view of the open sky" (39). Esperanza's first vision of a house with a room of one's own is inspired by her passionate sorrow for Sally, her wish that Sally could escape the life she leads on Mango Street:

> Sally, do you sometimes wish you didn't have to go home? Do you wish your feet would one day keep walking and take you far away from Mango Street, far away and maybe your feet would stop in front of a house, a nice one with flowers and big windows and steps for you to climb up two by two upstairs where a room is waiting

for you. And if you opened the little window latch and gave it a shove, the windows would swing open, all the sky would come in. (82–83)

In an environment where "there is too much sadness and not enough sky" (33), Esperanza's dream is collective and redemptive: to liberate the women around her from the tyrannies of male houses and male plots.

3

One day I will pack my bags of books and paper. One day I will say goodbye to Mango. I am too strong for her to keep me here forever. One day I will go away.

Friends and neighbors will say, What happened to that Esperanza? Where did she go with all those books and paper? Why did she march so far away?

They will not know I have gone away to come back. For the ones I left behind. For the ones who cannot out.

(Sandra Cisneros *The House on Mango Street* 110)

Pondering the doors shut by the male custodian of the library, Woolf in 1928 "thought how unpleasant it is to be locked out; and . . . how it is worse perhaps to be locked in" (*A Room* 24). To be confined within male structures might be as great a disadvantage to the female artist as to be outside them. To achieve the "freedom and fullness of expression" Woolf considered necessary to art, women must design new spaces appropriate to their dreams and needs. "A book is not made of sentences laid end to end," wrote Woolf, "but of sentences built . . . into arcades or domes. And this shape too has been made by men out of their own needs for their own uses" (80).

As Esperanza shapes her narrative, images of constricting, infelicitous space are balanced by powerful feminine images of what Bachelard terms "felicitous space." Their third-floor flat on Loomis above the boarded-up laundromat, which they had to leave "quick" when the water pipes broke, is an early source of shame to Esperanza, when the nun from her school says "'You live *there?*' . . . You live *there?* The way she said it made me feel like nothing" (5). The series of third-floor flats, on Loomis, and before that on Keeler, and before that on Paulina, more flats than Esperanza can remember, would not seem to exemplify Bachelard's intuition that "life begins well, it begins enclosed, protected, all warm in the bosom of the house" (7). What Esperanza "remember[s] most is moving a lot" (3). "I never had a house," she complains to Alicia on Mango Street, " . . . only one I dream of" (107). Yet the "maternal features of the house" that Bachelard describes are literally exemplified in the

felicitous peace of Esperanza's mother's body, "when she makes a little room
for you on her side of the bed still warm with her skin, and you sleep near
her," "when she is holding you, holding you and you feel safe" (6). Within this
shelter, the small girl can begin to dream.

The overcrowded house on Mango Street, with its "swollen" door,
"crumbling" bricks, and "windows so small you'd think they were holding
their breath," is "not the house we'd thought we'd get," Esperanza complains,
"not the way they told it at all" (3–4). Yet Mango Street becomes an integral
part of herself, the source of her art and her freedom. *Las comadres*, the three
magical sisters, tell Esperanza: "When you leave you must remember to come
back for the others. A circle, understand? You will always be Esperanza. You
will always be Mango Street. You can't erase what you know: You can't forget
who you are" (105). If Mango Street is "not the way they told it at all," then
Esperanza's developing resolve is to re-member herself through a new telling
that will not erase realities, and to begin by circling back to "what I remember
most . . . Mango Street, sad red house, the house I belong but do not belong to"
(110). Bachelard suggests that circular structures "help us to collect ourselves,
permit us to confer an initial constitution on ourselves," and advises that "by
remembering 'houses' and 'rooms,' we learn to 'abide' within ourselves" (234,
xxxiii). Esperanza's negotiation with her origins is more ambivalent and less
nostalgic than Bachelard's, but remembering Mango Street is nevertheless
intimately connected to the formation of her identity as a woman, an adult
member of her community, and a writer.

Through Mango Street, Esperanza is able to explore the tensions
between belonging and not belonging. Hers is a story, she tells us, "about a
girl who didn't want to belong" (109). In "My Name" she confides her rebellious desire to "baptize myself under a new name, a name more like the real
me, the one nobody sees. Esperanza as Lisandra or Maritza or Zeze the X.
Yes. Something like Zeze the X will do" (11). Her successive baptisms, like the
names for the shape-shifting clouds in "And Some More," keep Esperanza's
identity fluid. Yet she also acknowledges that the name Esperanza belongs to
her, a legacy from her great-grandmother, a "wild horse of a woman." "I have
inherited her name," Esperanza tells us, "but I don't want to inherit her place
by the window" (11). When Alicia tells her that "like it or not" she is Mango
Street and will come back, she replies:

> Not me. Not until somebody makes it better.
> Who's going to do it? The mayor?
> And the thought of the mayor coming to Mango Street makes
> me laugh out loud.
> Who's going to do it? Not the mayor. (107)

Through naming herself and her community, Esperanza returns both to accept and to alter her inheritance. Her most conspicuous alliances when she constitutes herself as speaking subject are ethnic and local. The "we" she speaks is Hispanic, herself and her barrio neighbors.[17] "Those who don't know any better come into our neighborhood scared," she says of outsiders:

> But we aren't afraid. We know the guy with the crooked eye is Davey the Baby's brother, and the tall one next to him in the straw brim, that's Rosa's Eddie V. and the big one that looks like a dumb grown man, he's Fat Boy, though he's not fat anymore nor a boy. (28)

Names and stories create an intimate realm of safety in Esperanza's early stories. "All brown all around we are safe" (29). In "And Some More," a litany of names punctuates the girls' conversation: Rachel's cousin who's "got three last names and, let me see, two first names. One in English and one in Spanish. . . . Phyllis, Ted, Alfredo and Julie. . . . Jose and Dagoberto, Alicia, Raul, Edna, Alma and Rickey . . ." (35–36). Musing on the Eskimos' thirty names for snow, Esperanza and her friends supply over fifty-two names of the people around them, drawing their magic circle to a close with the communal declaration of their own names: "Rachel, Lucy, Esperanza, and Nenny" (38).

Yet as Rachel, Lucy, Esperanza, and Nenny grow, this sense of community shifts. The dangers that threaten them come from without but also within their own neighborhood, even within their own households. Men's names appear far less frequently in the latter part of Esperanza's narrative, where women's names and the bonds between women predominate. Alicia is "young and smart and studies for the first time at the university," but her father defines her reality and her "place" when he insists that she is "just imagining" the mice in the kitchen and that "anyway, a woman's place is sleeping so she can wake up early with the tortilla star" (31). Rafaela's husband locks her in. Sally becomes a "different Sally" when she hurries "straight home after school," where her father beats her "just because [she's] a daughter" (82, 92). Minerva's husband leaves her "black and blue" (85), and though she "cries" and "prays" and "writes poems on little pieces of paper" she remains trapped in the "same story," the same cycle of violence. Esperanza and her girlfriends successfully flee the bum who wants to kiss them, but already Rachel, "young and dizzy," is tempted by the "sweet things" he says and the dollar in his pocket, and "who can blame her" (41). Later Esperanza endures the unwanted kiss of the "older Oriental man" at her first job, and the brutal sexual assault at the fair where she waits in vain by the grotesque red clowns for Sally.[18] "Why did you leave me all alone?" (100). Sally's escape from the violence of her father's household leads to a new form of confinement and a husband who sometimes "gets angry and once he broke the door where his foot went through, though most days he is okay" (101). Impatient with writers who "make our barrios look like Sesame Street," Cisneros told an interviewer that "poor neighborhoods lose their charm after dark. . . . I was writing about it in the most real sense that I know, as a person walking those neighborhoods with a vagina" (Aranda 69).

Esperanza's dream of a house of her own—"Not a man's house. Not a daddy's." (108)—is both solitary and communal, a refuge for herself and for others. In *Felicitous Space*, Judith Fryer dwells on the spaces women inhabit, as well as those they imagine:

> It is not only, then, as Virginia Woolf suggested, that women have had no space to themselves, not only that they have been forbidden spaces reserved for men. Trapped, as she has been at home, a home that in America has been "not her retreat, but her battleground . . . her arena, her boundary, her sphere . . . [with] no other for her activities," woman has been unable to move. She has been denied, in our culture, the possibility of dialectical movement between private spaces and open spaces. But let us not forget the room of one's own. . . . (50)

In Cisneros's reconstruction of Woolf's "room of one's own," Esperanza's "house of my own" simultaneously represents an escape from the barrio, a rejection of the domestic drudgery of "home" ("Nobody's garbage to pick up after" [108]), a solitary space for her creativity, and a communal expression of women's lives. Like her name, her dream of a house is a legacy from her family. "Our house would be white with trees around it," Esperanza explains in the opening chapter, "a great big yard and grass growing without a fence. This was the house Papa talked about when he held a lottery ticket and this was the house Mama dreamed up in the stories she told us before we went to bed" (4). The older Esperanza stops listening to her mother's stories of the house when she begins to develop her own (86). As she gazes longingly at the houses on the hill, "the ones with the gardens where Papa works," she vows that she'll allow space for bums in the attic when she owns her own house (86). The house becomes as well an imaginary dwelling—the "home in the heart," "house made of heart" prophesied by the witch woman Elenita (64)—as Esperanza's sympathy for Sally animates her vision of a house "with plenty of blue sky," providing shelter for laughter and imagination: "And you could laugh, Sally. You could go to sleep and wake up and never have to think who likes and doesn't like you. You could close your eyes and you wouldn't have to worry what people said because you never belonged here anyway and nobody could make you sad and nobody would think you're strange because you like to dream and dream" (83). Finally the house for Esperanza becomes a creative refuge, "quiet as snow, a space for myself to go, clean as paper before the poem" (108). Many women in the community help her to arrive there: Edna's Ruthie, who listens when she recites "The Walrus and the Carpenter"; Elenita, who tells her fortune; her Aunt Lupe, who listens to her read library books and her first poems; Minerva, who trades poems with her; the three sisters, who offer her prophecies; and her mother, who encourages her to study.

Esperanza dreams of release and of reunion. She will leave Mango Street, "the house I belong but do not belong to" (110), but, she tells us, "I won't forget who I am or where I came from" (87). Traditionally the *Künstlerroman* closes with a departure. Joyce's Stephen Dedalus in *Portrait of the Artist as a Young Man* leaves the poverty and numbing provinciality of Dublin behind him, ready to "fly" the "nets" of "nationality, language, religion" in order to devote himself to art (203). But Esperanza will go away "to come back": "For the ones I left behind. For the ones who cannot out" (102). Her book, dedicated "*A las Mujeres/*To the Women," will tell not only the story of her own artistic development but the stories of the many women around her. "You must remember to come back," Lucy and Rachel's mysterious aunt tells her, "for the ones who cannot leave as easily as you" (98).

4

First world feminist criticism is struggling to avoid repeating the same imperializing moves that we claim to protest. We must leave home, as it were, since our homes are often sites of racism, sexism, and other damaging social practices. Where we come to locate ourselves in terms of our specific histories and differences must be a place with room for what can be salvaged from the past and what can be made new.

(Caren Kaplan "Deterritorializations: The Rewriting of Home and Exile in Western Feminist Discourse" 194–95)

In *A Room of One's Own* Woolf suggested that the female writer is always "an inheritor as well as an originator" (113). Her own legacy has crossed color and class lines in the feminist community. Michèle Barrett, writing from a Marxist-feminist perspective, applauds Woolf's fruitful and still largely unexplored insight in *A Room of One's Own* that "the conditions under which men and women produce literature are materially different"

(103). Tillie Olsen uses *A Room* to meditate on the silences of women more marginal than Shakespeare's sister, exploring not only gender as one of the "traditional silencers of humanity," but also "class—economic circumstances—and color" (24).[19] *A Room of One's Own* serves explicitly as the foundation for Alice Walker's reconstruction of her African American mothers' and grandmothers' creative achievements in "In Search of Our Mothers' Gardens."[20] Elsewhere Walker numbers Tillie Olsen and Virginia Woolf among the artistic models indispensable to her development (14). Amy Ling stresses "how much we share as a community of women and how often our commonalities cross cultural and racial barriers": "Reading Barolini, like reading Alice Walker's 'In Search of our Mothers' Gardens' and *The Color Purple*, Audre Lorde's poems and essays, and Virginia Woolf's *A Room of One's Own* is like finding sisters I didn't know I had" (154).

While some women of color have expressed radical alienation from the privileged position of "our reputed foresister Virginia Woolf," others read Woolf through Olsen's class perspective.[21] "Ideally," the Chicana writer Helena María Viramontes comments, "it would be bliss to manipulate the economic conditions of our lives and thus free our minds, our hands, to write. But there is no denying that this is a privilege limited to a certain sex, race, and class. The only bad thing about privilege, Virginia Woolf wrote (I'm paraphrasing from Tillie Olsen) was that not every one could have it" (34). Viramontes and Cherríe Moraga have acknowledged the inspiration of contemporary African American women writers for their own writing.[22] Cisneros's "house of my own"—"Not a daddy's. A house all my own. With my porch and my pillow, my pretty purple petunias" (100)—may have been inspired not only by Woolf's "room of one's own" but also by a similarly complex crossing of Emily Dickinson's dwelling "in Possibility—/A fairer House than Prose—," Alice Walker's maternal gardens and "Revolutionary Petunias," and Audre Lorde's landmark statement "The Master's Tools Will Never Dismantle the Master's House.[23]

Jane Marcus has designated Virginia Woolf "the mother of us all" (Meese 91), who invited her feminist successors to become "co-conspirators against culture," and who envisioned "untying the mother tongue, freeing language from bondage to the fathers and returning it to women and the working classes" ("Thinking Back" 83, 73). Yet Woolf's relation to women of the working classes is frequently problematic. In 1930, when she was invited to write an introduction to a collection of papers by working women, Woolf found much of interest in "these voices ... beginning only now to emerge from silence into half-articulate speech." But she also asserted emphatically, "It is not from the ranks of working-class women that the next great poet or novelist will be drawn" ("Memories" 148, 147). Woolf and many of her contemporary defenders seem all too often to imagine speaking from a privileged position for the obscure, the silenced, and the oppressed. In "Still Practice, A/Wrested Alphabet," Marcus elaborates her well-known metaphor of Woolf as the swallow Procne voicing the tongueless Philomel's text:

> The voice of the nightingale, the voice of the shuttle weaving its story of oppression, is the voice which cries for freedom; an appropriate voice for women of color and lesbians, it speaks from the place of imprisonment as political resistance. The voice of the swallow, however, Procne's voice, is the voice of the reader, the translator, the middle-class feminist speaking for her sisters: in a sense, the voice which demands justice. The socialist feminist critic's voice is a voice of revenge, collaboration, defiance, and solidarity with her oppressed sister's struggle. She chooses to attend to her sister's story or even to explicate its absence, as Virginia Woolf told the story of Shakespeare's sister. (215–16)

While Procne may support and even empower her sister, Marcus neglects to address the possibility that Procne may fail to attend to her sister's story, may even herself silence Philomel in the process of explicating her story's "absence."

Certainly much of the anger and frustration voiced by the women of color in collections such as *This Bridge Called My Back* and *Making Face, Making Soul* derives from the easy assumption of power among white middle-class feminists, who seem either to ignore their presence or to usurp their voices. "What I mind is the pseudo-liberal ones who suffer from the white women's burden," Gloria Anzaldúa writes: "She attempts to talk for us—what a presumption! This act is a rape of our tongue and our acquiescence is a complicity to that rape. We women of color have to stop being modern medusas—throats cut, silenced into a mere hissing" ("La Prieta" 206). Chandra Mohanty firmly concludes her discussion of the position of "third world women" within Western feminist discourses with the directive: "It is time to move beyond the Marx who found it possible to say: They cannot represent themselves; they must be represented" (354). Countless Philomels have not lost their tongues. If she is truly to achieve "collaboration" and "solidarity" through her song, Procne needs to imagine more harmonious alternatives to her solo performance. Adrienne Rich and Audre Lorde are among the growing number of feminists voicing the urgent necessity for dialogue between groups divided by race, ethnicity, class, and sexual preference within the feminist movement.[24] While the editors of *This Bridge Called My Back* uncovered radical "separation" in their effort to forge a "connection" with white women, the aim of their anthology was nevertheless to "create a definition that expands what 'feminist' means to us" (*This Bridge* 61, xxiii).

By engaging *A Room of One's Own* in *The House on Mango Street*, Cisneros opens a dialogue. Preserving Woolf's feminist architecture, she enlarges and even reconstructs Woolf's room to make space for her own voice and concerns. "I like to tell stories," her protagonist announces simply. "I put it down on paper and then the ghost does not ache so much" (101). Woolf predicted that the female writer would remain conscious of "the experience of the mass . . . behind the single voice" and of "the common life which is the real life and not . . . the little separate lives which we live as individuals" (69, 117). The female writer would enjoy a greater anonymity than the male writer, who was unhappily prone to erect an "I" that overshadowed his subject (*A Room* 52, 115, 103–105). Esperanza, who often speaks as "we," and sometimes is not present at all in her stories, achieves a collective as well as an individual voice. In vignettes such as "What Sally Said" and "A Smart Cookie," she is primarily a listener, aware, as Woolf was, of the "accumulation of unrecorded life" on Mango Street (*A Room* 93). In "Geraldo No Last Name" we hear "what he told" Marin, the "story" that Marin told "again and again. Once to the hospital and twice to the police." And the story that no one told: "Only Marin can't explain why it mattered, the hours and hours, for somebody she didn't even know. The hospital emergency room" (65–66). Yvonne Yarbro-Bejarano has suggested that an impulse toward a "collective subject" is characteristic of the Chicana writer, who finds "the power, the permission, the authority to tell stories about herself and other Chicanas . . . from her cultural, racial/ethnic and linguistic community" (141).

Free to tell stories, Esperanza—hope—will speak for herself and her people, in her own voice, from a vividly imagined house of her own. "One day I'll own my own house," she assures us, "but I won't forget who I am or where I came from" (81). She will speak in two tongues, English and Spanish, from inside and outside the barrio. She will speak for the nameless: for "Geraldo No Last Name"—"just another wetback" who died in the emergency room before anyone could identify him.

> His name was Geraldo. And his home is in another country. The ones he left behind are far away. They will wonder. Shrug. Remember. Geraldo. He went north . . . we never heard from him again. (63)

She will speak for the speechless: for Mamacita, who "doesn't come out because she is afraid to speak English" (74), and whose son grows away from her in America.

And then to break her heart forever, the baby boy who has begun to talk, starts to sing the Pepsi commercial he heard on T.V.

No speak English, she says to the child who is singing in the language that sounds like tin. No speak English, no speak English, and bubbles into tears. No, no, no as if she can't believe her ears. (75)

She will speak for all the women shut in their rooms: for Rafaela, "who is still young but getting old from leaning out the window so much" (76), for Sally, who "sits at home because she is afraid to go outside without [her husband's] permission" (95), for her great-grandmother Esperanza, who "looked out the window all her life" (12). She will speak for the banished: for Louie's other cousin, who gave all the kids a ride in his yellow Cadillac before the cops took him off in handcuffs (25–26), for Marin, whose employers will send her back to Puerto Rico.

Marin, under the streetlight, dancing by herself, is singing the same song somewhere. I know. Is waiting for a car to stop, a star to fall, someone to change her life. (28)

She will speak for the dead: for her Aunt Lupe (54–57), for Geraldo, for her great-grandmother, for Lucy and Rachel's baby sister (96), for Angel Vargas, "who learned to fly and dropped from the sky like a sugar donut, just like a falling star, and exploded down to earth without even an 'Oh'" (31).

She will speak for herself: "I have decided not to grow up tame like the others who lay their necks on the threshold waiting for the ball and chain" (82). Instead, like the four trees "who grew despite concrete," "four who reach and do not forget to reach" (71), Esperanza survives to reach for her own freedom and to release the stories of those around her. "There are so few of us writing about the powerless," Cisneros said in a lecture, "and that world, the world of thousands of silent women, women like my mama and Emily Dickinson's housekeeper, needs to be, must be recorded so that their stories can finally be heard" ("Notes" 76).

NOTES

1. See Smith 160–62, Walker 371–79, and Tate interview with Morrison 121. Lillian Robinson also professes herself "disheartened" by the "increasingly hegemonic, essentialist tendencies in feminist scholarship and criticism," arguing force fully for the total reevaluation of women's literature that an open canon would entail: " . . . the difference of gender is not the only one that subsists among writers or the people they write about. It may not always be the major one. Women differ

from one another by race, by ethnicity, by sexual orientation, and by class. Each of these contributes its historic specificity to social conditions and to the destiny and consciousness of individual women. Moreover, these differences are not simply or even primarily individual attributes. They are social definitions, based on the existence and the interaction of groups of people and of historical forces. As scholarship—itself primarily or secondarily feminist—reveals the existence of a black female tradition or a working-class women's literature, it is insufficient simply to tack these works onto the existing canon, even the emerging women's canon. Once again, every generalization about women's writing that was derived from surveying only relatively privileged white writers is called into question by looking at writers who are not middle class and white" ("Feminist Criticism" 148, 146). See also Robinson, "Canon Fathers and Myth Universe"; Judith Kegan Gardiner, Elly Bulkin, Rena Grasso Patterson, and Annette Kolodny, "An Interchange on Feminist Criticism"; the writings by women of color collected in *This Bridge Called My Back*, edited by Cherríe Moraga and Gloria Anzaldúa, and *Making Face, Making Soul/Haciendo Caras*, edited by Gloria Anzaldúa; and Audre Lorde's collection of essays *Sister Outsider*, particularly "The Master's Tools Will Never Dismantle the Master's House" (also included in *This Bridge Called My Back*), "Age, Race, Class and Sex: Women Redefining Difference," "The Uses of Anger: Women Responding to Racism," and "Eye to Eye: Black Women, Hatred, and Anger."

2. See also essays by María C. Lugones and Elizabeth V. Spelman, Caren Kaplan, Cora Kaplan, and Chandra Mohanty. Mohanty writes: "What is problematical, then, about this kind of use of 'women' as a group, as a stable category of analysis, is that it assumes an ahistorical, universal unity between women based on a generalized notion of their subordination. Instead of analytically demonstrating the production of women as socioeconomic political groups within particular local contexts, this move limits the definition of the female subject to gender identity, completely bypassing social class and ethnic identities. What characterizes women as a group is their gender (sociologically not necessarily biologically defined) over and above everything else, indicating a monolithic notion of sexual difference. Because women are thus constituted as a coherent group, sexual difference becomes coterminous with female subordination, and power is automatically defined in binary terms: people who have it (read: men), and people who do not (read: women). Men exploit, women are exploited. As suggested above, such simplistic formulations are both reductive and ineffectual in designing strategies to combat oppressions. All they do is reinforce binary divisions between men and women" (344).

3. Jane Marcus leans heavily on this line in her defense of Woolf as a "socialist feminist"; see particularly "Still Practice, A/Wrested Alphabet" (235–36), and her discussion of the "romantic socialist vision of the charwoman" in "Daughters of Anger" (298–99). See also Lillian S. Robinson's "Who's Afraid of a Room of One's Own?" for a class-based critique of *A Room* and specifically of Woolf's stirring peroration (146).

4. I am indebted to Mary Lou Emery's discussion of this passage in her unpublished conference paper. "The sentence quoted above," Emery writes, "not only makes use of the no longer acceptable term 'negress,' but it constitutes its subject—'woman' and 'one'—as exclusively white. The subject of the sentence excludes black women from the category 'woman' and presumes to judge them as 'very fine' in the same breath that it criticizes masculine imperialist habits of

thought. My point here is not to smash the idol (feminism's 'great mother and sister') Virginia Woolf but, borrowing a term from Julia Kristeva, to demassify it in an exploration of the ways 'western feminist' writings constitute colonized and working-class women as outside of the subject 'woman.'" See also Mary Eagleton's discussion of this passage in "Women and Literary Production" (42) and Michèle Barrett's thoughtful deconstruction of a similar passage in her own earlier work "Ethnocentrism" (35).

5. Tillie Olsen makes similar observations on Emily Dickinson's privileges in her essay "Silences" (*Silences* 17).

6. This form evolved gradually. Cisneros describes piecing the book together like a patchwork quilt ("Do You Know Me?" 79). In an interview, she explained that originally she did not even conceive of Esperanza as a writer: "When I started the series she was not going to be a writer. The book started out as simply memories. Later on—it took me seven years—as I was gaining my class, gender and racial consciousness, the book changed, the direction changed. I didn't intend for her to be a writer, but I had gotten her into this dilemma, and I didn't know how to get her out. . . . So the only way that I could make her escape the trap of the barrio was to make her an artist" (Aranda 69).

7. Cisneros, who published two volumes of poetry before *The House on Mango Street*, in fact sees many of these sketches as unrealized poems: "If several of the stories read like poems it's because some of them originally had been poems. Either poems redone as a story ('The Three Sisters') or a story constructed from the debris of an unfinished or unsuccessful poem ('Beautiful and Cruel' and 'A House of My Own')" ("Do You Know Me?" 79). Elsewhere she has referred to these prose pieces as "vignettes" ("The softly insistent voice of a poet," *Austin American Statesman*, March 11, 1986, qtd. in Olivares 161).

8. See Judith Fryer's *Felicitous Space* for a particularly rich and imaginative meditation on women's interconnections with "the spaces they inhabit, break free from, transform" (xiii). In Nancy Mairs's memoir *Remembering the Bone House*—directly inspired by Catherine Clément, Hélène Cixous, and Bachelard's *Poetics of Space*—female embodiment unfolds in a series of domestic and erotic spaces (7).

9. Bachelard himself dwells on the phenomenology of "women's construction of the house through daily polishing," though he is perhaps more excited about the sacramental potential of housework than most housewives might be: "Through housewifely care a house recovers not so much its originality as its origin. And what a great life it would be if, every morning, every object in the house could be made anew by our hands, could "issue from our hands" (69).

10. In *My Wicked Wicked Ways*, Cisneros prefaces her title section with a line chosen from Maxine Hong Kingston's *The Woman Warrior*: "Isn't a bad girl almost like a boy?" The narrator in *The Woman Warrior* also flouts the female roles prescribed for her by deliberately spilling soup, breaking dishes, neglecting her grooming, and affecting an unattractive limp.

11. "Perhaps women were once so dangerous that they had to have their feet bound," Maxine Hong Kingston writes in *The Woman Warrior* (23). Cisneros uses a line from *The Woman Warrior* as an epigraph to a section in *My Wicked Wicked Ways*; in *The House on Mango Street* Esperanza explains that "the Chinese, like the Mexicans, don't like their women strong" (12).

12. See Sandra Gilbert ("Costumes of the Mind") for an illuminating discussion of costumes and the creation of sexual identity in female modernist texts such as Woolf's *Orlando*.

13. The term "writing beyond the ending" is from Rachel Blau DuPlessis, who writes: "When women as a social group question, and have the economic, political and legal power to sustain and return to questions of marriage law, divorce, the 'couverte' status, and their access to vocation, then the relation of narrative middles to resolutions will destabilize culturally, and novelists will begin to 'write beyond' the romantic ending" (4). DuPlessis explores a variety of strategies that undermine the romance plot, itself "a trope for the sex gender system as a whole": "Writing beyond the ending means the transgressive invention of narrative strategies, strategies that express critical dissent from dominant narrative. These tactics, among them reparenting, woman-to-woman and brother-to-sister bonds, and forms of the communal protagonist, take issue with the mainstays of the social and ideological organization of gender, as these appear in fiction" (5).

14. The Biblical resonance of Esperanza's loss of innocence in the monkey garden is underlined when the children spread the rumor "that the monkey garden had been there before anything" (96). Though Esperanza is the one who wants to "save" Sally from kissing the older boys, she is left feeling "ashamed" and displaced from her former Edenic child's play. The substitution of two young women—Esperanza and Sally—for Adam and Eve parallels the shift in narrative focus from the heterosexual romance plot to a female-centered *Künstlerroman*. Elizabeth Ordóñez has suggested three modes of discourse common to recent works by ethnic women writers that all seem clearly relevant to *Mango Street*: 1. "disruption of genre"; 2. "the power to displace 'the central patriarchal text,' that is, the Bible"; and 3. "the invention—either through inversion or compensation—of alternate mythical and even historical accounts of women" ("Narrative Texts" 19).

15. Possibly Cisneros also acknowledges Woolf's feminist agenda in *Mrs. Dalloway* when she adds solitude to a "room of one's own" as necessary for the creation of art: "And I'm here because I didn't marry my first boyfriend, that pest who never gave me any time alone, something crucial to every writer—'aloneness' breeds art" ("Notes" 75). Clarissa Dalloway rejects Peter's marriage suit on similar premises.

16. Erlinda González-Berry and Tey Diana Rebolledo also see echoes of "Little Red Riding Hood" in this scene, as the bum, like the wolf, asks the girls to come closer and closer (116). González-Berry and Rebolledo argue persuasively that Cisneros plays these fairy tales against a new model of the female *Bildungsroman* whereby the heroine is allowed the mythic quest and achievement of the traditional male hero.

17. María C. Lugones and Elizabeth V. Spelman explore "the differences among women and how these differences are silenced" through a dialogue. The Hispana in the dialogue reflects on the different contexts in which she uses the word "we." In the paper, "when I say 'we,' I am referring to Hispanas," she writes; "'you' refers to "the white/Anglo women that I address." However, she adds, "'we' and 'you' do not capture my relation to other non-white women," and in a footnote she meditates on her general use of "we" outside of the paper: "I must note that when I think this 'we,' I think it in Spanish—and in Spanish this 'we' is gendered, 'nosotras.' I also use 'nosotros' lovingly and with ease and in it I include all members of 'La raza

cosmica' (Spanish-speaking people of the Americas, la gente de colores: people of many colors). In the US, I use 'we' contextually with varying degrees of discomfort: 'we' in the house, 'we' in the department, 'we' in the classroom, 'we' in the meeting. The discomfort springs from the sense of community in the 'we' and the varying degrees of lack of community in the context in which the 'we' is used" ("Have We Got a Theory" 575). Although *The House on Mango Street* is clearly a feminist text, Esperanza does not use "we" to refer to women; instead "we" refers to herself and her family, herself and her childhood girlfriends, and herself and her neighborhood ethnic community ("brown all around").

18. Esperanza's "first job" is at the Peter Pan Photofinishers, where she para-doxically must appear grown up by pretending to be older than she is, and where the older man's kiss "on the mouth" damages her innocence. Both her violations come from men outside of her culture. For useful discussions of the rape in "Red Clowns" and violence against women in *Mango Street*, see María Herrera Sobek, Ellen McCracken, and Ramón Saldívar.

19. See Elizabeth Meese's discussion of Olsen's reshaping of Woolf's vision. Meese documents "almost forty appearances by Virginia Woolf" in Olsen's *Silences* (110).

20. Walker quotes repeatedly from *A Room of One's Own* in this landmark essay. Her bracketed substitutions in Woolf's prose revise Woolf's perspective to incorporate black women's experiences in often startling ways; however, she is clearly inspired by Woolf's essay. Elsewhere she mentions that she has taught Woolf and Kate Chopin in her course on black women writers, "because they were women and wrote, as the black women did, on the condition of humankind from the perspective of women" ("From an Interview" 260).

21. The phrase is from Trinh T. Minh-ha (246). See also Gloria Anzaldúa ("Speaking in Tongues" 170), and Nellie Wong, who writes: "You are angered by the arrogance of some articles that would tell you that Virginia Woolf is your spiri-tual mother, your possible role model, for the work you have to do: to write. And why are you angered except for the fact that she was white and privileged, yet so ill that she walked into the sea" (178). Toril Moi offers a somewhat useful discussion of Woolf's controversial position in contemporary white feminist theory in "Who's Afraid of Virginia Woolf?," though she is conspicuously uninterested in women writers of color.

22. "Once I discovered the Black women writers—Walker, Morrison, Brooks, Shange, again to name a few," Viramontes writes, "womanism as a subject matter seemed sanctioned, illuminating, innovative, honest, the best in recent fiction that I've seen in a long time" ("'Nopalitos'" 37). In an interview, Moraga remarked, "I feel that I am a part of a movement of women of color writers. I feel that I have gotten a lot of inspiration from Black women writers in this country" (Umpierre 66).

23. See Walker's discussion of the title poem in *Revolutionary Petunias* in "From an Interview" (266–69). Lorde's influential essay appears in both *Sister Outsider* and *This Bridge Called My Back*. Cisneros credits Emily Dickinson, her "favorite American poet," with giving her "inspiration and hope all the years in high school and the first two in college when I was too busy being in love to write" ("Notes" 74, 75). She prefaces the four sections of *My Wicked Wicked Ways* with epigraphs from Emily Dickinson, Gwendolyn Brooks, Maxine Hong Kingston, and the Portuguese feminist text *The Three Marias*. These choices seem

deliberately to suggest the national, international, class, and ethnic range of her feminist alliances.

24. See particularly Rich's "Disloyal to Civilization," the essays in Lorde's *Sister Outsider*, which also includes an "interview" dialogue between Lorde and Rich, and the essays in *Making Face, Making Soul/Haciendo Caras*, ed. Gloria Anzaldúa. Richard Ohmann has recently written of the challenges involved in all "alliance politics." Reflecting on his role as a white male who "work[s] in women's studies," he points out, "What we do there ['in feminism'] with our experience, our competence, and our gender and class confidence, is a matter to be negotiated through caution, flexibility, improvisation, listening, and often doubtless through a strategic fade into the wallpaper. But I don't see drawing back from the knowledge that feminism is our fight, too. So is racial equality, so is gay liberation, so is antiimperialism. I see the difficulties of our participation in these struggles as parallel to those of our joining in women's liberation, and in consequence I see alliance politics as our challenge and aim" ("In, With" 187).

Works Cited

Anzaldúa, Gloria. "La Prieta." In Cherríe Moraga and Gloria Anzaldúa. 198–209. ed. *Making Face, Making Soul/Haciendo Caras: Creative and Critical Perspectives by Feminists of Color*. San Francisco: Aunt Lute, 1990.

———. "Speaking in Tongues: A Letter to Third World Feminists." Cherríe Moraga and Gloria Anzaldúa, 165–74.

Aranda, Pilar E. Rodríguez. "On the Solitary Fate of Being Mexican, Female, Wicked and Thirty-three: An Interview with Writer Sandra Cisneros." *The Americas Review* 18 (Spring 1990): 64–80.

Bachelard, Gaston. *The Poetics of Space*. 1958. Trans. María Jolas. Boston: Beacon P, 1969.

Barrett, Michèle, and Mary McIntosh. "Ethnocentrism and Socialist-Feminist Theory." *Feminist Review* 20 (June 1985): 23–47.

Barrett, Michèle. "Ideology and the Cultural Production of Gender." *Women's Oppression Today: Problems in Marxist Feminist Analysis*. London: New Left, 1980.

Cisneros, Sandra. "Do You Know Me?: I Wrote *The House on Mango Street*." *The Americas Review* 15 (Spring 1987): 77–79.

———. "Ghosts and Voices: Writing from Obsession." *The Americas Review* 15 (Spring 1987): 69–73.

———. *The House on Mango Street*. 1984. New York: Vintage, 1988.

———. "Living as a Writer: Choice and Circumstance." *Revista Mujeres* 3 (June 1986): 68–72.

———. *My Wicked Wicked Ways*. Bloomington: Third Woman P, 1987.

———. "Notes to a Young(er) Writer." *The Americas Review* 15 (Spring 1987): 74–76.

DuPlessis, Rachel Blau. *Writing Beyond the Ending: Narrative Strategies of Twentieth-Century Women Writers*. Bloomington: Indiana U P, 1985.

Eagleton, Mary. "Women and Literary Production." *Feminist Literary Theory: A Reader*. Ed. Mary Eagleton. New York: Basil Blackwell, 1986.

Emery, Mary Lou. "The Voice of Witlessness: Displacing the Other/Demassifying an Idol." Women's Studies Conference, "Women's Bodies/Women's Voice: The Power of Difference." University of Iowa, April 14–16, 1988.

Fryer, Judith. *Felicitous Space: The Imaginative Structures of Edith Wharton and Willa Cather*. Chapel Hill: U of North Carolina P, 1986.

Gardiner, Judith Kegan, Elly Bulkin, Rena Grasso Patterson, and Annette Kolodny. "An Interchange on Feminist Criticism: On 'Dancing Through the Minefield.'" *Feminist Studies* 8 (Fall 1982): 629–75.

Gilbert, Sandra M. "Costumes of the Mind: Transvestism as Metaphor in Modern Literature." *Writing and Sexual Difference.* Ed. Elizabeth Abel. Chicago: U of Chicago P, 1982. 193–219.

González-Berry, Erlinda, and Tey Diana Rebolledo. "Growing Up Chicano: Tomás Rivera and Sandra Cisneros." *Revista Chicano-Rigiteña* 13 (Fall–Winter 1985): 109–19.

Heilbrun, Carolyn G. *Writing a Woman's Life.* New York: Ballantine, 1988.

Herrera-Sobek, María. "The Politics of Rape: Sexual Transgression in Chicana Fiction." *The Americas Review* 15 (Fall–Winter 1987): 171–81.

Joyce, James. *A Portrait of the Artist as a Young Man.* 1916. New York: Penguin, 1976.

Kaplan, Caren. "Deterritorializations: The Rewriting of Home and Exile in Western Feminist Discourse." *Cultural Critique* 6 (Spring 1987): 187–98.

Kaplan, Cora. "Pandora's Box: Subjectivity, Class and Sexuality in Socialist Feminist Criticism." *Sea Changes: Essays on Culture and Feminism.* London: Verso, 1980. 147–76.

Kingston, Maxine Hong. *The Woman Warrior: Memoirs of a Girlhood Among Ghosts.* New York: Vintage, 1977.

Ling, Amy. "I'm Here: An Asian American Woman's Response." *New Literary History* 19 (Autumn 1987): 151–60.

Lorde, Audre. *Sister Outsider.* Freedom: Crossing P, 1984.

Lugones, María C., and Elizabeth V. Spelman. "Have We Got a Theory For You! Feminist Theory, Cultural Imperialism and the Demand for 'The Woman's Voice.'" *Women's Studies International Forum* 6 (1983): 573–81.

Mairs, Nancy. *Remembering the Bone House: An Erotics of Place and Space.* New York: Harper and Row, 1989.

Marcus, Jane. "Daughters of Anger/Material Girls: Con/Textualizing Feminist Criticism." *Women's Studies* 15 (1988): 281–308.

———. *Art and Anger: Reading Like a Woman.* Columbus: Miami U and Ohio State U P, 1988.

McCracken, Ellen. "Sandra Cisneros' *The House on Mango Street*: Community-Oriented Introspection and the Demystification of Patriarchal Violence." *Breaking Boundaries: Latina Writing and Critical Readings.* Ed. Asunción Horno-Delgado, Eliana Ortega, Nina M. Scott, and Nancy Saporta Sternbach. Amherst: U of Massachusetts P, 1989. 62–71.

Meese, Elizabeth A. "Deconstructing the Sexual Politic: Virginia Woolf and Tillie Olsen." *Crossing the Double-Cross: The Practice of Feminist Criticism.* Chapel Hill: U of North Carolina P, 1986. 89–113.

Minh-ha, Trinh T. "Commitment from the Mirror-Writing Box." *Making Face, Making Soul/Haciendo Caras: Creative and Critical Perspectives by Feminists of Color.* Ed. Gloria Anzaldúa. San Francisco: Aunt Lute, 1990. 245–55.

Moers, Ellen. *Literary Women.* New York: Doubleday, 1976.

Mohanty, Chandra Talpade. "Under Western Eyes: Feminist Scholarship and Colonial Discourses." *boundary* 2.12–13 (Spring–Fall 1984): 333–58.

Moi, Toril. "Who's Afraid of Virginia Woolf?" *Sexual/Textual Politics: Feminist Literary Theory.* New York: Methuen, 1985. 1–18.

Moraga, Cherríe, and Gloria Anzaldúa, eds. *This Bridge Called My Back: Writings by Radical Women of Color.* Watertown: Persephone P, 1981.

Ohmann, Richard. "In, With." *Men in Feminism*. Ed. Alice Jardine and Paul Smith. New York: Methuen, 1987. 182–88.

Olivares, Julián. "Sandra Cisneros' *The House on Mango Street*, and the Poetics of Space." *The Americas Review* 15 (Fall–Winter 1987): 160–70.

Olsen, Tillie. *Silences*. New York: Delacorte/Seymour Lawrence, 1978.

Ordóñez, Elizabeth. "Narrative Texts by Ethnic Women: Rereading the Past, Reshaping the Future." *MELUS* 9 (Winter 1982): 19–28.

Rich, Adrienne. "Disloyal to Civilization: Feminism, Racism, Gynephobia." *On Lies, Secrets, and Silence: Selected Prose 1966–1978*. New York: W.W. Norton, 1979. 275–310.

———. "Notes Towards a Politics of Location." *Women, Feminist Identity, and Society in the 1980s*. Ed. Myriam Diaz-Diocaretz and Iris M. Zavala. Philadelphia: John Benjamins, 1985. 7–22.

———. "When We Dead Awaken: Writing as Re-Vision." *On Lies, Secrets, and Silence: Selected Prose 1966–1978*. New York: W.W. Norton, 1979. 33–49.

Robinson, Lillian S. "Canon Fathers and Myth Universe." *New Literary History* 19 (Autumn 1987): 23–35.

———. "Feminist Criticism: How Do We Know When We've Won?" *Feminist Issues in Literary Scholarship*. Ed. Shari Benstock. Bloomington: Indiana U P, 1987. 141–49.

———. "Who's Afraid of a Room of One's Own?" *Sex, Class, and Culture*. Bloomington: Indiana U P, 1978. 97–149.

Saldívar, Ramón. *Chicano Narrative: The Dialectics of Difference*. Madison: U of Wisconsin P, 1990.

Saldívar-Hull, Sonia. "Feminism on the Border: From Gender Politics to Geopolitics." *Criticism in the Borderlands: Studies in Chicano Literature, Culture, and Ideology*. Eds. Héctor Calderón and José David Saldívar. Durham: Duke U P, 1991. 203–20.

Showalter, Elaine. *A Literature of Their Own*. Princeton, NJ: Princeton U P, 1977.

Smith, Barbara. "Toward a Black Feminist Criticism." *But Some of Us Are Brave*. Ed. Gloria T. Hull, Patricia Bell Scott, and Barbara Smith. Old Westbury: Feminist P, 1982. 157–75.

Spacks, Patricia Meyer. *The Female Imagination*. New York: Avon, 1975.

Stepto, Robert. "'Intimate Things in Place': A Conversation with Toni Morrison." *Chant of Saints: A Gathering of Afro-American Literature, Art, and Scholarship*. Urbana: U of Illinois P, 1979. 213–29.

Tate, Claudia. "Interview with Toni Morrison." *Black Women Writers at Work*. Ed. Claudia Tate. New York: Continuum, 1983. 117–31.

Umpierre, Luz María. "With Cherríe Moraga." *The Americas Review* 14 (Summer 1986): 54–67.

Viramontes, Helena María. "'Nopalitos': The Making of Fiction." *Breaking Boundaries: Latina Writing and Critical Readings*. Ed. Asunción Horno Delgado, Eliana Ortega, Nina M. Scott, and Nancy Saporta Sternbach. Amherst: U of Massachusetts P, 1989. 33–38.

Walker, Alice. *In Search of Our Mothers' Gardens*. New York: Harcourt Brace Jovanovich, 1983.

Wong, Nellie. "In Search of the Self as Hero: Confetti of Voices on New Year's Night—A Letter to Myself." *This Bridge Called My Back: Writings by Radical Women of Color*. Ed. Cherríe Moraga and Gloria Anzaldúa. Watertown: Persephone P, 1981. 177–81.

Woolf, Virginia. "Memories of a Working Women's Guild." *Collected Essays*. Vol. 4. New York: Harcourt Brace, 1967.

———. *Mrs. Dalloway*. 1925. New York: Harvest, Harcourt Brace Jovanovich, 1953.

———. "Professions for Women." *Collected Essays*. Vol. 2. New York: Harcourt Brace, 1967. 284–89.

———. *A Room of One's Own*. 1929. New York: Harcourt Brace Jovanovich, 1957.

Yamada, Mitsuye. "Asian Pacific American Women and Feminism." Cherríe Moraga and Gloria Anzaldúa. 71–75.

Yarbro-Bejarano, Yvonne. "Chicana Literature from a Chicana Feminist Perspective." *The Americas Review* 15 (Fall–Winter 1987): 139–45.

THOMAS MATCHIE

Literary Continuity in Sandra Cisneros's
The House on Mango Street

In 1963 in a collection of articles entitled *Salinger*, Edgar Branch has a piece in which he explores the "literary continuity" between Mark Twain's *The Adventures of Huckleberry Finn* and J. D. Salinger's *Catcher in the Rye*. Branch claims that, though these two books represent different times in American history, the characters, the narrative patterns and styles, and the language are strikingly similar, so that what Salinger picks up, according to Branch, is an archetypal continuity which is cultural as well as literary (239). I would like to suggest a third link in this chain that belongs to our own time, and that is Sandra Cisneros's *The House on Mango Street*. Published in 1989, this novella is about an adolescent, though this time a girl who uses, not the Mississippi or Manhattan Island, but a house in Chicago, to examine her society and the cultural shibboleths that weigh on her as a young Chicana woman.

Though not commonly accepted by critics as "canonical" (McCracken, 62), *The House on Mango Street* belongs to the entire tradition of the bildungsroman (novel of growth) or the *Künstlerroman* (novel inimical to growth), especially as these patterns apply to women. One can go back to 19th-century novels like Harriet Wilson's *Our Nig* (1859), where a black woman working in the house of a white family in Boston is treated as though she were a slave. Later, Charlotte Gilman's *The Yellow Wallpaper* (1889) depicts a woman who

From *The Midwest Quarterly* 37, no. 1 (Autumn 1995): 67–79. © 1995 by Pittsburgh State University.

goes crazy when she is confined to a room in a country house by her husband, a doctor who knows little about feminine psychology. Finally, in Kate Chopin's *The Awakening* (1899), the protagonist literally moves out of the house to escape her Creole husband, but cannot find a male with whom to relate in this patriarchal culture.

In *Mango Street*, a hundred years later, Esperanza is actually part of a six-member family of her own race, but that does not prevent an enslavement parallel to Nig's. Though not limited to a single room as in *Yellow Wallpaper*, Esperanza's house is a symbol of sexual as well as cultural harassment, and she, like the narrator in Gilman's story, is a writer whose colorful images help her create a path to freedom. And as in *The Awakening*, Esperanza dreams of leaving her house, an action that like Edna's is related to all kinds of men who make up the power structure in her Chicana world.

So in a general way Cisneros's novel belongs to a female tradition in which culture and literary quality are important. But for her, far more significant as literary models are Huck Finn and Holden Caulfield, primarily because they are adolescents growing up in culturally oppressive worlds. Cisneros's protagonist, like them, is innocent, sensitive, considerate of others, but extremely vulnerable. Like them, Esperanza speaks a child's language, though hers is peculiar to a girl and young budding poet. And like her predecessors, she grows mentally as time goes on; she knows how she feels, and learns from the inside out what in Holden's terms is "phony," and what with Huck she is willing to "go to hell" for. There are, of course, other Chicano novels that are bildungsromans, such as Tomás Rivera's *. . . y no se lo Tragó la Tierra*, but none presents a better parallel to Huck and Holden than Cisneros's Esperanza.

It may seem that the two boy's books are really journeys, while *Mango Street* is limited to a house, and therefore set—the opposite of a geographical quest. But when one looks at the patterns of the novels, what the boys go out to see simply comes past Esperanza, so that the effect is the same. She is simply a girl, and does not have the cultural opportunity to leave as they do. What is more important is that *Mango Street* continues a paradigm of growth where a young person encounters an outside world, evaluates it in relationship to herself, and then forges an identity, something that includes her sexuality and the prominence of writing in her life. McCracken says that this character breaks new boundaries with her outward movement into "sociopolitical reality" (63–64).

Huckleberry Finn begins with young Huck leaving a father who has abused him, the Widow Douglas who has tried unsuccessfully to educate him, and nigger Jim's owner, Miss Watson, who perpetuates the system of slavery which Huck will undercut on his journey down the river. *Catcher in the Rye*, as we learn in the end, is really a story Holden Caulfield tells.

Recovering from a mental breakdown, he begins by saying he's leaving school, Pency Prep, where in his view the teachers, alumni, and students are all phony. Mr. Spencer, his history teacher, talks to him just before leaving, but is more interested in justifying his test, which Holden failed, than understanding what is actually happening to the boy. Holden then goes to New York City to visit, not his parents, but his little sister. His father is a wealthy corporate lawyer and investor who is apparently too busy for Holden. Neither Huck nor Holden, however, is an arrogant individual, or sees himself as a rebel. They simply move out because, bored and lonesome, they object to the conditions they live under, and instinctively seek more comfortable worlds. The reader, however, cannot help but evaluate what is askew in the systems that fail these boys.

Esperanza actually loves her father, though as with Holden's he is virtually absent from the narrative. As Marcienne Rocard points out, Chicanas concentrate intensely on "human relationships between generations" (57)—something not stressed in Twain and Salinger. Esperanza thinks her father is brave; he cries after the death of a grandmother, and his daughter wants to "hold and hold and hold him" (57). But this same father perpetuates a structure that traps women. The girl's mother, for instance, has talent and brains, but lacks practical knowledge about society because, says Esperanza, Mexican men "don't like their women strong" (10). Her insight into an abusive father comes through her best friend Sally, whose father "just forgot he was her father between the buckle and the belt" (93). So Sally leaves home for an early unhappy marriage. Another friend, Alicia, goes to the university to break the pattern of her dead mother's "rolling pin and sleepiness" (31), but in studying all night and cooking, too, she begins to imagine that she sees mice, whereupon her father belittles her. Esperanza says Alicia is afraid of nothing, "except four-legged fur. And fathers" (32). Gradually, Esperanza comes to see that the pressure on women in Chicana families comes from a system she simply, though painfully, has to leave. This act reflects the life of Cisneros herself, who says she had to leave home in order to "write about those ghosts inside that haunt me" ("Notebook," 72–73).

Truly, all three books are wrought with violence, which the protagonists seem to forgive. Huck is abused by his father. On the river he watches whole families kill each other off, including his friend Buck, whose senseless death he mourns. Ultimately he witnesses the tar and feathering of the King and Duke, conmen for whom he feels "sorry" (216). Holden is also beaten several times—once by his roommate Stradlater, whom he thinks is handsome and sexy, but who knocks Holden bloody for calling him on the way he treated Jane Gallagher (Holden's old girlfriend) in the back of his car. Holden feels "sorry" for most girls, including the prostitute, Sunny, with whom he would rather talk than have sex, whereupon her pimp Maurice socks him in the stomach to get his five bucks. Holden is also concerned about the suicide of a Pency student, James Castle, who after being humiliated by other boys for not taking something back, jumped out a window. Holden was touched when Mr. Antonelli, his English teacher, went down and picked him up, blood and all. This violent death is crucial for Holden, probably because he sees himself in Castle, and needs someone older to understand.

Esperanza also feels for the victims of violence. What is interesting is that she sometimes interprets violence in a broad sense as injustice, or something in society that keeps people homeless, or in shabby housing. In the attic of her new house she'll have, not "Rats," but "Bums" (87) because they need shelter. She has visions of the violence done to Geraldo, "another wetback," who rented "two-room flats and sleeping rooms" (66) while he sent money back to Mexico; killed one night by a hit-and-run driver, he (in the minds of his people) simply disappeared. That violence becomes worse when individuals are confined to their homes. Mamacita, the big woman across the street, is beautiful but cannot get out because she "No speak English" (78)—a phenomenon doubly tragic because her baby sings Pepsi commercials. But mostly Esperanza identifies with wives mistreated by men who confine them to their homes. Raphaela is locked in because she is too beautiful for her jealous husband. Earl, a jukebox repairman, and Sire, who drinks beer, hold their wives tight lest they relate to anybody else. Things like this make Esperanza's "blood freeze" (73). She dreams of being held too hard. Once, after letting a man kiss her because he was "so old," she says he "grabs me by the face with both hands and kisses me on the mouth and doesn't let go" (55). So, like Holden and Huck, this girl cares for others because of the violence done to them (and herself) in all kinds of contexts.

All three protagonists have a favorite place to escape oppression. For Huck, it's the raft, where he gets to know Jim—who becomes both friend and "father." Twain catches the harmony of their relationship in a natural setting through the poetic (melodic and imagistic) voice of Huck:

> We had the sky up there, all speckled with stars, and we used to lay on our backs and look up at them, and discuss about whether they was made or only just happened; I judged it would have took too long to *make* so many. Jim said the moon could 'a' *laid* them. (111)

Holden finds his main refuge in Central Park where he watches the ducks in the lagoon, once naively asking a cab driver where they go in winter. At another time walking through the park he sees a boy with his family singing and humming "If a body catch a body, comin' through the rye." Here

Holden, like Huck, voices in a poetic way his unconscious longing for community—and the setting is again in nature. Later, he tells us that he would like to be that "catcher" (173), as though one could save the innocent ones lost in the world of adults.

Ironically, Esperanza already has a family whom she loves, but that does not free her, for her father is gone and her mother stuck. She too longs for friends, talking first about a temporary friend Cathy who then moves away. Later, she takes some of her sister's money to buy a share in a bike with her neighbors Rachel and Lucy so she can play with them, but that is fleeting. As she matures and sees what is happening to people, she picks four trees, which like her have "skinny necks and pointy elbows" (74). Others, like Nenny, do not appreciate those trees, but for Esperanza, they "teach" (75), helping her to realize that like them she is here and yet does not belong. And like the trees Esperanza, who thinks in images, must continue to reach. Her goal, like that of Huck and Holden, is not to forget her "reason for being" and to grow "despite concrete" (75) so as to achieve a freedom that's not separate from togetherness.

All three protagonists have friends who fail them, usually in some kind of romantic context. Huck rejects his friend Tom Sawyer because of Tom's "A-rabs" and "elephants" (13), and in the end Huck gets impatient with Tom's excessive charades to free Jim. "What I want is my nigger" (230), says Huck. Holden's critique of romanticism has to do with girls. He gets disgusted with the abusive way his friends treat them. Ackley, for instance, is a "terrible personality," always raving about "giving it" (37) to some girl, but Ackley is just a talker. It is Stradlater who actually takes out Holden's friend Jane Gallagher and abuses her in the back of his car and then brags about it. Later, Holden recalls some beautiful moments with Jane, with whom he always felt "happy" (79), and of whom he never took advantage.

Esperanza's best friend Sally is also a kind of romantic. She paints her eyes like Cleopatra and likes to dream. In an autobiographical note, Cisneros says she "glamorized living" in shabby neighborhoods where "the best friend I was always waiting for never materialized" ("Notebook," 70). Tragically, it is Sally who betrays her friend and admirer in the monkey garden (an animal pen turned old car lot) where she trades the boys' kisses for her lost keys, while all concerned laugh at Esperanza for trying to defend her friend with a brick. Later, Sally leaves Esperanza alone at the fair next to the "red clowns" (at once comical and tragic figures) where she is molested because her romantic friend "lied" (100). Actually, the whole experience is a lie, given what she had been led to expect.

Still, all three have a moral center, a person they can count on, or should be able to. Huck, of course, comes to appreciate Jim, who has "an uncommon level head for a nigger" (71). Ultimately he will literally "go to hell" (200) for this man he has come to trust and love. Holden puts his trust in his English teacher, Mr. Antonelli, who invites the boy to his house overnight, listens and gives him sound advice. He tells Holden his father is really concerned, and that he's heading for a special kind of fall (187). In the end, however, Antonelli makes sexual advances toward Holden, so the boy leaves and consequently does have a breakdown. The one person Holden loves and trusts, of course, is his sister Phoebe, and his memories of the innocent fun they had together are touching. But she is too little to be a source of emotional help, and when she follows him out of the house, he puts her on a carousel at the zoo where she can play. It's that wonderful image of childhood that Holden cannot get beyond because of his acute sensitivity toward a world he sees as phony, but in which he feels he is going "down, down, down" (197).

Esperanza also has a little sister, Nenny, for whom she feels responsible. Nenny, however, is again too little. Esperanza often refers to her as "stupid" and in the chapter on "Hips," where Esperanza is becoming more aware of the sexual role of a woman's body, she says Nenny just "doesn't get it" (52). Her real hope comes in Aunt Lupe who is dying—"diseases have no eyes," says the young poet. In a game the girls invent, they make fun of Lupe, and for this Esperanza, like Huck, feels she will "go to hell" (59). Actually, it is Lupe who listens to the girl's poems and tells her to "keep writing" (61). That counsel becomes the basis of Esperanza's future apart from Mango Street.

It is important to recognize that the three novels contain religious language that at once seems to undercut traditional religion, and in the mouths of the young seems to say more than they realize. Huck, for instance, is supposedly an uneducated soul, and when Miss Watson talks about going to "the good place," he replies that if she's going there he "doesn't think he'll try for it" (2). This is not only humorous, but unknown to Huck juxtaposes for the reader the fact that Miss Watson does not seem to connect her practice of religion with ownership of slaves. Christianity has to do with compassion, and that Huck will put into practice in his friendship with Jim. Likewise, Holden might see religions and ministers as phony, and himself as an atheist, but in arguing with one of his school mates, he says that he has an attraction to Jesus, and does not like the Disciples because they let Jesus down. And he can't imagine Jesus sending even Judas to hell. For the reader, Jesus' compassion only parallels Holden's own life, where he feels so deeply for others, though so many fail him.

For Esperanza, religion is a cultural thing; in her Catholic world, God the father and Virgin Mother are household terms. But for this young poet, religion takes on mythic or poetic dimensions. She sees herself, for instance, as a red "balloon tied to an anchor" (9), as if to say she needs to transcend present conditions where mothers are trapped and fathers abusive. She even sees herself molested in a monkey garden (a modern Eden) among red clowns (bloodthirsty males). She appeals to Aunt Lupe (Guadalupe, after the Mexican Virgin Mother), who tells her to write, to create. In the end, when Esperanza meets three aunts, or sisters (her trinity), she in effect has a spiritual vision, one which she describes in concrete language. One is cat-eyed, another's hands are like marble, a third smells like Kleenex. The girl uses these sights, smells, and touches to envision poetically her future house. As with Huck and Holden, there is something she does not fully understand. What she knows is that through these *comadres* (co-mothers) she will give birth to something very new. Like the two male protagonists, she longs for a respect and compassion absent in her experiences on Mango Street, and these women are her spiritual inspiration.

The ending of *Mango Street* is also very significant in terms of literary continuity. Just prior to the end Esperanza meets the three aunts at the funeral of a sister of her friends Lucy and Rachel; they tell her she cannot forget who she is and that if she leaves she must come back. In the end the girl recognizes that she both belongs and does not belong to Mango street. Then she vows to return to the house because of the "ones who cannot" leave. One reason for this is her writing, which has made her strong. She plans to "put it down on paper and then the ghost does not ache so much" (110). What this means relative to other women's novels is that she reverses a trend. In *Our Nig*, Nig is dissipated in the end. The protagonist of *Yellow Wallpaper* goes crazy before literally crawling over her dominating husband's body. Edna in *The Awakening* swims to her death rather than face a culture that will not recognize her identity. Not so with Esperanza. She is strong (something Mexican women should not be), perfectly aware of the problems with a patriarchal culture, and because of her love for her people, albeit abused and dehumanized, vows to return, and it is the writing which gives her the strength.

Here is where Cisneros returns to Huck and Holden for her cue. Consciously or not, Huck has challenged the very basis of a pre–Civil War culture. In the last fifth of the novel, however, it's not clear whether he returns to the ways of Tom Sawyer in staging Jim's escape or whether he's come to a new level of consciousness where he confronts Tom in the name of Jim. In the end he lights out into the territory so, in his words, they won't "civilize me" (274). In this way he seems to reject the culture of slavery, even though in *Tom Sawyer among the Indians*, written afterwards, Huck returns to that culture by adopting with Tom old romantic ways. In any case, the notion of going back, even to join an abusive culture, or not going back, is a key issue in Twain's handling of Huck in *The Adventures of Huckleberry Finn*.

Holden is slightly different. In the end he is recovering from the shock he received from living in a post–World War II world. It has devastated him. But in telling his story he seems to come back to normal, so that the very telling has the effect of giving him strength. Indeed, he says,

> I sort of *miss* everybody I told about. Even old Stradlater and Ackley, for instance. I think I even miss that goddam Maurice. (214)

It's not clear how Holden will relate to his phony world again, any more than it is with Huck, except that he consciously chooses it, perhaps because he needs people, no matter what they are like. But the fact is he's going back. Esperanza's choice has a different twist. Thoroughly aware of the abusive nature of her culture, she comes to the decision that though she does not want to come from Mango Street, and does not want to go back till somebody "makes it better" (107), she nevertheless chooses to return for the sake of the others. She is "strong" (110) and, in contrast to Huck, feels drawn back, not just because she needs people, like Holden, but because they need her.

There is one other way in which Cisneros seems to look to her predecessors for literary and cultural continuity, and that is the way she as an author comes into the text. Mark Twain, of course, creates in Huck the authentic voice of an illiterate river boy. At times, however, it is not clear whether it is Huck speaking, or Twain the satirist. When Huck tears up his letter to Miss Watson, for instance, he may think he's going to hell, but we know he's acted morally, indeed courageously. And sometimes Twain uses a tone and style quite different from Huck's, as in Col. Sherburn's lecture to the mob on cowardice after the killing of Boggs. Here Twain seems to be talking directly to his reader, and if we can connect the two incidents, the author may be directly lecturing us all on how cowardly we are compared to the growing, thinking, choosing Huck. In *Catcher* Holden speaks in the language of an immature adolescent, often using words like "sonofabitch" and "goddam," while in his own mind he's becoming a "madman" (134). Still, we sympathize with him as sensitive, perceptive, and highly moral. At times, however, Salinger seems to break through the text, as in the person of Antonelli, who tells Holden "you're not the first person who was ever confused and frightened and even sickened by human behavior." Then he continues, "You'll learn from them—if you want to. Just as someday if you have something to offer, someone will learn something from you" (171–72). It is as if Salinger is telling his audience to read Holden's story if you really want to know what is wrong with this age.

In *Mango Street* Cisneros has created the voice of a child, who is also a poet, a writer. For the most part that voice is consistent, but sometimes not. Once when Esperanza is playing an outside voice puts her friends and herself in perspective:

Who's stupid?
Rachel, Lucy, Esperanza and Nenny. (38)

In this case it is the author who seems to be speaking. And when Lupe is dying, and Esperanza helps lift her head, suddenly we are inside Lupe: "The water was warm and tasted like metal" (61). Here the author's presence is unmistakable. Perhaps Cisneros's most significant intrusion comes when Esperanza says that Mexican men do not "like their women strong" (10)—a comment that belongs more to an adult than a child, and it seems to underpin the whole novel. Shannon Sikes claims that Esperanza as writer plays with the narratorial voice throughout the book, so that it's difficult to distinguish between the younger and a later, older person who is both character and author (12–13).

So Cisneros, like Twain and Salinger, seems to enter the narrative to help define its ultimate meaning. Unlike the boys' quests, however, this novel is a collection of genres—essays, short stories, poems—put together in one way to show Esperanza's growth, but in another to imitate the part-by-part building of an edifice. Indeed, the house on Mango Street does not just refer to the place Esperanza is trying to leave, but to the novel itself as "a house" which Esperanza as character and Cisneros as author have built together. Huck may go out to the territory, rejecting civilization, and Holden may tell his story to gain the strength to return, but Esperanza through her writing has in fact redesigned society itself through a mythical house of her own.

In this regard, Lupe once told Esperanza to "keep writing," it will "keep you free" (61). At that time the girl did not know what she meant, but in the end Esperanza says "she sets me free" (110), so in a sense the house is already built—a monument to her people and her sex. Andrea O'Reilly Herrera says that Esperanza's house is an imaginative version of Mango Street "resurrected, reconstructed, and rendered through language" (4). Indeed, Esperanza is very different from the other women in the text. She has learned from them and not made their mistakes. So she is not trapped like her mother, Alicia, or Sally, or the others. Like Huck and Holden, she is the example for other Chicana women whom Cisneros would have us take to heart. Indeed, as the witch woman Elenita predicted earlier, Esperanza elects to build a "new house, a house made of heart" (64). And in the tradition of, but distinct from, Huck and Holden, that is just what she has accomplished.

Bibliography

Branch, Edgar. "Mark Twain and J. D. Salinger: A Study in Literary Continuity." *Salinger: A Critical and Personal Portrait.* Ed. Henry Anatole Grunwald. New York: Harper and Row, 1962. 226–40.

Chopin, Kate. *The Awakening.* New York: W. W. Norton, 1976. Originally published in 1899.

Cisneros, Sandra. "From a Writer's Notebook." *America's Review* 15: 1 (1987), 69–73.

———. *The House on Mango Street.* New York: Vintage, 1989. Originally published by Arte Publico Press in a somewhat different form in 1984.

Gilman, Charlotte Perkins. *The Yellow Wallpaper.* New York: Feminist Press, 1973. Originally published in 1889.

González-Berry, Erlinda, and Tey Diana Rebolledo. "Growing up Chicano: Tomás Rivera and Sandra Cisneros." *Revista Chicano-Riqueña,* 13:3–4 (1985), 109–19.

Herrera, Andrea O'Reilly. "Sandra Cisneros & The Big House on Mango Street: The Development of Self." Unpublished essay.

McCracken, Ellen. "Sandra Cisneros' *The House on Mango Street*: Community-Oriented Introspection and the Demystification of Patriarchal Violence." *Breaking Borders.* Ed. Asunción Horno-Delgado, et al. Amherst: University of Massachusetts, 1989. 62–71.

Rivera, Tomás. *. . . y no se lo Tragó la Tierra.* Houston: Arte Público Press, 1987.

Rocard, Marcienne. "The Remembering Voice in Chicana Literature." *America's Review,* 14:3–4 (1986), 150–59.

Salinger, J. D. *Catcher in the Rye.* Boston: Little, Brown, 1945.

Sikes, Shannon. "Narratorial Slippages and Authorial Self-Construction in Sandra Cisneros' *The House on Mango Street.*" Unpublished essay.

Twain, Mark. *The Adventures of Huckleberry Finn.* New York: Holt, Rinehart and Winston, 1948. Originally published in 1885.

———. *Tom Sawyer among the Indians.* Berkeley: University of California, 1989.

Wilson, Harriet E. *Our Nig; or Sketches from the Life of a Free Black.* New York: Vintage, 1983. Originally published in 1859.

ANNIE O. EYSTUROY

The House on Mango Street:
A Space of Her Own

By writing I put order in the world, give it a handle so I can grasp it. I
write to record what others erase when I speak, to rewrite the stories others have miswritten about me, about you. To discover myself, to preserve
myself, to make myself, to achieve self-autonomy.

—Gloria Anzaldúa

The House on Mango Street (1985) by Sandra Cisneros is probably the
best-known Chicana novel to date. The winner of the American Book
Award in 1985, it has received more critical attention than any other Chicana novel. Set in a contemporary Latino neighborhood of a big American
city, *The House on Mango Street* is composed of forty-four interrelated
stories narrated by Esperanza, the female "I" and central consciousness
of the novel.[1] In each story Esperanza narrates her own perception of her
sociocultural context, that is, the barrio, its people, its conditions of life,
and how she is inextricably connected to that context, an engagement
with her immediate surroundings that brings about a gradual coming into
consciousness about her own identity as a woman and as a Chicana. Sandra Cisneros gives voice to the ordinary experiences of a young Chicana
by letting Esperanza tell her own coming-of-age story, thus articulat-
ing the subjective experiences of the female "I" who resists entrapment
within sociocultural norms and expectations. The narrating "I" stands in

From *Daughters of Self-Creation: The Contemporary Chicana Novel*, pp. 89–112, 143. © 1996
by the University of New Mexico Press.

a dialectic relationship to her sociocultural context, and it is through the very act of constructing and telling her own story that Esperanza resolves the contradictions that inform her life. Her *Bildungs* process is thus closely linked to her development as an artist in the process of discovering, synthesizing, and narrating her experiences within the community of Mango Street, a development that turns *The House on Mango Street* into what we may call "a portrait of the artist as a young woman," that is, a *Künstlerroman*. It is through the process of telling her stories that Esperanza discovers the power of her own creativity, that "language is a way of becoming" (Seator, 32), a way of imagining herself beyond the confinements of the status quo, a way of imagining a different ending to her own *Bildungs* story. Collectively these stories reveal a female *Bildungs* process that moves from rejection of prescribed roles to the recognition of creativity as a path toward a self-defined identity.

* * *

As the title indicates, both "the house" and "Mango Street" are central symbols throughout the novel. Mango Street and the house Esperanza lives in constitute her world, the world she has to come to grips with as she grows up. It is her response to this particular environment, the interplay between psychological and social forces, that determines the direction of her *Bildungs* process. It is through her dialectical relationship to the house—in other words, the private sphere, the family, the collective memory—as well as to Mango Street—that is, the social sphere, the larger Hispanic community— that the narrating "I" comes to an understanding of her own individual self. Esperanza's world on Mango Street is a world unto its own, an Hispanic barrio of a large American city, yet unspecified in respect to its exact geographical and historical setting, a symbolic "microcosm for the larger world" (Gonzáles-Berry and Rebolledo, 114) that lends a universal quality to this Chicana *Bildungsroman*.

It is significant that the initial word in this Chicana quest novel is "We": "We didn't always live on Mango Street" (7). Esperanza recalls her family history of moving from one dilapidated house to another until they finally move into their own house on Mango Street, yet the house is not what the family had hoped for: "The house on Mango Street is ours. . . . But even so, it's not the house we'd thought we'd get" (7). Esperanza's sense of self is here firmly lodged within the collective identity of her family. It is, however, in this initial story, homonymous with the novel itself, that the narrating "I" becomes aware of her own subjective perceptions as she begins to differentiate between family dreams and social realities and becomes conscious of her parents' inability to fulfill their promises of the perfect house. "They always told us that one day we would move into a house, a real house" (7). The "real house" Esperanza expected would be "like the houses on TV":

> Our house would be white with trees around it, a great big yard and grass growing without a fence. This was the house Papa talked about when he held a lottery ticket and this was the house Mama dreamed up in the stories she told us before we went to bed.
>
> But the house on Mango Street is not the way she told it at all. (8)

The house is just the opposite of what she had been told would be their house one day, a fact that stands in direct opposition to the words of her parents. This contrast between expectation and reality awakens her awareness of herself as a social being and provokes her own interpretations of the significance the house holds in her life.

Esperanza sees the house on Mango Street as a symbol of poverty that she associates with the humiliation she has felt in the past, living in similar places:

> Where do you live? she said.
> There, I said, pointing up to the third floor.
> You live *there*?
> *There.* I had to look to where she pointed—the third, the paint peeling, wooden bars Papa had nailed on the windows so we wouldn't fall out.
> You live *there*? The way she said it made me feel like nothing.
> *There.* I lived *there*. I nodded. (8–9)

In another situation a teacher prejudicially assumes that Esperanza, because she is Chicana, lives in a building that "even the raggedy men are ashamed to go into" (43), thus automatically identifying her with the poverty and degradation the house represents. Made to feel ashamed of living in houses other people show obvious contempt for, thus ashamed of "her entire social and subject position" (Saldívar, 1990, 182), Esperanza sees the house as a symbol of the shame that threatens her own self-perception. To Esperanza the house on Mango Street is an emblem of the oppressive socioeconomic situation that circumscribes her life and is the source of her feelings of alienation. It is this alienation that becomes a catalyst for her desire to distance herself from this "sad red house" (101) she does not want to belong to.

This psychological rejection of the house on Mango Street is further underscored by her own description of the house as narrow and confining, where even the windows appear to be "holding their breath" (8), a description that shows an almost claustrophobic reaction to her parents' house. According to Cirlot, breathing is a process whereby one assimilates spiritual power. Esperanza's perception of the house as not breathing is indicative of the spiritual suffocation the house represents. This depiction of the house is, as Julián Olivares points out, "a metonymical description and presentation of the self" (162), a self that feels constrained as well as ashamed when identified with a house that represents only confinement and therefore knows that she needs another house, one that would liberate her from the oppression of her present situation:

> I knew then I had to have a house. A real house. One I could point to. But this isn't it. The house on Mango Street isn't it. For the time being, Mama said. Temporary, said Papa. But I know how these things go. (9)

The last phrase, "But I know . . . ," indicates the emerging consciousness of the protagonist, that her passage from childhood innocence to knowledge has begun, a development that marks the beginning of her *Bildungs* process. Through her own interpretative agency she now knows that she cannot rely on what her parents tell her and that they will not be able to provide her with the house that she needs. Although at this point she imagines a "real house" to be something like the Dick and Jane reader's version of an American home, the importance of the house lies not so much in its physical features as in its symbolic value in a sociocultural context. Her desire for a house is, as Ellen McCracken points out, "not a sign of individualistic acquisitiveness" (64); she wants a house she can "point to," that is, one she can point to as hers without feeling "like nothing" (9), one that does not destroy her sense of self, clearly connecting the house with her own self-perception. By rejecting the house of her parents she rejects a structure that threatens her sense of self and takes the first step toward claiming her right to self-definition.

In this initial story, "The House on Mango Street," the image of the house serves a twofold symbolic function: it is a symbol of the socioeconomic condition in which Esperanza finds herself and its alienating effect on her, and more importantly in the context of the novel, as a symbol of human consciousness. Her search for a new house, that is, her search for a viable self, becomes a leitmotif throughout the novel. It is significant that in the course of the story the initial "we," Esperanza's sense of herself being part of the collective identity of her family, gives way to the subjective "I" who begins to analyze her neighborhood on Mango Street.

Like the house, Mango Street is the physical and psychological marker of an oppressive socioeconomic situation that makes Esperanza conscious of her own status in a socioeconomic hierarchy: "The neighborhood is getting bad," she says, and this is why people have to move "a little farther away every time people like us keep moving in" (15). Much as with the house, a negative analogy is established between Esperanza and her barrio; she lives there and therefore the neighborhood is "getting bad," the narrating "I" again being defined by her external, socioeconomic circumstances:

> Those who don't know any better come into our neighborhood scared. They think we're dangerous. They think we will attack them with shiny knives. They are stupid people who are lost and got here by mistake. (29)

The implications of being defined by a poor, deteriorating neighborhood and prejudicial stereotypes make Esperanza conscious of the particular socioeconomic conditions that circumscribe her life and trap her in a marginalized world of "too much sadness and not enough sky" (33).

Despite the cumulative threat the house and Mango Street present to her sense of self, however, she begins to imagine herself beyond Mango Street, determined to "make the best of it" (33). Estranged by the social implications of living in this environment, Esperanza disavows her relationship to Mango Street—"I don't ever want to come from here" (99)—identifying herself with the only piece of nature present in the barrio, four trees "who do not belong here but are here":

> Their strength is secret. . . . When I am a tiny thing against so many bricks, then it is I look at trees. When there is nothing left to look at on this street. Four who grew despite concrete. Four who reach and do not forget to reach. (71)

This identification with a small piece of nature in this urban environment exemplifies the primacy of nature in female development, when the adolescent feels "a sense of oneness with cosmos" (Pratt, 1981, 17) as an alternative to her alienation from an oppressive environment. In her longing to escape her present circumstances, Esperanza sees the trees as role models for her own liberation: they grow "despite concrete," thus symbolizing Esperanza's own struggle to grow in a hostile environment, her desire to reach beyond the concrete, beyond class and race boundaries, for self-definition.

Esperanza's process of individuation is thus initiated by her resolution to escape the confinements of her socioeconomic condition represented by the house and by Mango Street, and she does this by seeking refuge in her own imagination:

> I like to tell stories. I tell them inside my head. . . . I make a story
> for my life, for each step my brown shoe takes. I say, "And so she
> trudged up the wooden stairs, her sad brown shoes taking her to
> the house she never liked." I like to tell stories. I am going to tell
> you a story about a girl who didn't want to belong. (101)

It is through the process of making "a story for my life," that is, the imaginative re-creation of her own experiences and interactions with her environment, that the narrating "I" begins her search for meaning and a new way of being in the world. Through the act of participating, interpreting, and narrating her life, she gradually comes to an understanding of herself and her relationship to the community on Mango Street.

Esperanza makes a clear link between language and identity when she turns to the act of narrating her experiences on Mango Street from her own experiential perspective as a strategy to escape social oppression and the threat this oppression presents to her own budding sense of self. Naming her own experiences is a way of defining and validating these experiences as well as her own perspectives. It is, at the same time, an affirmation of her own being that is grounded in language, in a new naming of self and her sociocultural reality. In this process of constructing herself as a subject through language, she begins to analyze the significance of her name, Esperanza, as a marker of her own identity. Her attempt to decode the meaning of her name becomes an attempt to come to terms with her bicultural identity:

> In English my name means hope. In Spanish it means . . . sadness,
> it means waiting. . . . It is the Mexican records my father plays on
> Sunday mornings when he is shaving, songs like sobbing. . . . At
> school they say my name funny as if the syllables were made out
> of tin and hurt the roof of your mouth. But in Spanish my name is
> made out of a softer something like silver. (12, 13)

To Esperanza her name embodies contradictory meanings—hope or sadness and waiting—much as the very pronunciation of her name changes with language and cultural context. Her name is thus a sign of a complex bicultural context that requires her to negotiate among opposing cultural meanings to come to terms with her own self.

This multiplicity of meanings that intersect in her name is further underscored by the female legacy the name Esperanza carries in the family. Named after her Mexican great-grandmother, Esperanza is linked through her name to her cultural past and to her identity as a woman within a particular sociocultural context. The grandmother, a recurring character in Chicana literature, often figures as the embodiment of Chicano cultural heritage: "For the most part *abuelitas* form a complex of female figures who are nurturing, comforting, and stable. They are linked symbolically and spatially to the house and home, and are often associated with an idealized cultural space" (Rebolledo, 1987, 150). In the story Esperanza has inherited about her great-grandmother, however, her *bisabuelita* does not inhabit such an idealized cultural space:

> My great-grandmother. I would've liked to have known her, a wild horse of a woman, so wild she wouldn't marry until my great-grandfather threw a sack over her head and carried her off. Just like that, as if she were a fancy chandelier. That's the way he did it. And the story goes she never forgave him. She looked out the window all her life, the way so many women sit their sadness on an elbow. (12)

This story of her namesake, of a strong and rebellious woman who nevertheless had to succumb to patriarchal coercion and control, makes Esperanza conscious of the position women in general hold within her own cultural framework, that the fact that "Mexicans don't like their women strong" (12) kept her great-grandmother from being "all the things she wanted to be" (12). Esperanza links her great-grandmother's fate, her confinement, her sadness and lost hope, with her own name, that is, her self, making her name tantamount to her culture's definitions of gender roles, definitions she can only reject: "Esperanza. I have inherited her name, but I don't want to inherit her place by the window" (12). She thus makes a clear distinction between the wild great-grandmother she would have liked to have known, her cultural foremother, and the sociocultural system that subdued her. By accepting her name, but refusing to accept a heritage of female confinement, Esperanza carries on a metonymic legacy of rebellion against patriarchal definitions of female selfhood.

In the process of analyzing the significance of the conflicting cultural connotations that intersect in her name—hope, sadness, rebellion, confinement—Esperanza becomes conscious of a complex, and, to her, confusing cultural framework that calls forth some ambivalence in respect to her own cultural heritage. This ambivalence is suggestive of a complicated relationship between ethnic heritage and female quest for a self-defined identity. If one's name is, as Mary Dearborn argues, "inextricable from identity" (93), then Esperanza's name carries some cultural implications that threaten her identity as a woman. She does not, as Renato Rosaldo points out, "stand in one place, looking straight ahead, and shout, 'Yo soy Esperanza'" (163), as that would mean, among other things, embracing patriarchal values and patriarchal definitions of herself. Rather, her ruminations on the cultural implications of her name lead her to wish for a new naming of herself. "I would like to baptize myself under a new name, a name more like the real me, the one nobody sees. . . . Something like Zeze the X will do" (13). Her choice of name, Zeze the X, indicates that what she wants is a name that carries no contradicting cultural connotations; it is, culturally speaking, a "hollow" name she would have to invest with meaning and identity, and unlike her name "Esperanza," it is not "culturally embedded in a dominating, male-centered ideology" (Olivares, 163). Much as she wants a new house, one she can point to, so she wants to give herself a new name that is more attuned to herself, "the one nobody sees." This desire is indicative of her refusal to be externally defined either by her house, by her socioeconomic circumstances, or by her name, that is, by traditional patriarchal values, in her quest for a self-defined identity.

In her exploration of the "real" Esperanza, the emerging female self "nobody sees" (13), the narrating "I" becomes increasingly aware of her own emerging sexuality. Her biological transformation marks a crucial point in Esperanza's self-development, as it is then that she begins to note not only her own sexual difference but also its implications for her as a woman.

The first notions of the changes her body is undergoing fill her with expectancy: "Everything is holding its breath inside me. Everything is waiting to explode like Christmas. I want to be all new and shiny" (71); she feels like "a new Buick with the keys in the ignition. Ready to take you where?" (47). This last question is crucial, indicating Esperanza's own awareness of the importance of sexuality in her own development and to her future self, as it is exactly through the control of female sexuality that women are socialized into accepting culturally prescribed roles of wives and mothers. The threat sexuality presents to the female self appears within the context of play when Esperanza and her friends, dressed in "magic high heels," are confronted with men who "can't take their eyes" off them and a "bum man" who says, "come closer. I can't see very well. Come closer. Please. . . . If I give you a dollar will you kiss me?" (39). This scene, with the shoes as symbols of female sexuality and the man's attempt to lure her closer, is a Chicana version of "Little Red Riding Hood," the fairy tale about "the curbing and regulation of sexual drives . . . that has always been used as a warning to children, particularly girls, a symbol and embodiment of what might happen if they are disobedient and careless. She epitomizes the good girl gone wrong" (Zipes, 1). Esperanza's confrontation with the "bum man" becomes an implicit demonstration of the danger sexuality, in a patriarchal context, presents to her own sense of self.

Through her interactions with Sally, Esperanza becomes increasingly aware that her friend already adheres to prescribed feminine behavior and has "her own game" (89), which, as it turns out, is not "her own game" but a male game into which she enters:

> One of the boys invented the rules. One of Tito's friends said you can't get the keys back unless you kiss us and Sally pretended to be mad at first but she said yes. It was that simple.... Something wanted to say no when I watched Sally going into the garden with Tito's buddies all grinning.... So what, she said. (89)

The socializing and conditioning effect of games is clearly evident in this episode where, pretending to be playing, the boys imitate patriarchal power by setting the rules of the game, and Sally, imitating what she thinks are female means of gaining male approval, passively acquiesces to sexual control. Whereas Esperanza intuits that "something wasn't right" (89), that the boys are violating Sally's natural right over her own body, Sally, having internalized male definitions of her sexuality, sees her own actions as a sign of being a grown-up woman.

In the role she has assumed as the streetwise, grown-up woman, Sally becomes Esperanza's guide to what to her are the secrets of womanhood—how to put on make-up, how to dress—with the implication that Sally also becomes the transmitter of cultural values in respect to how girls are supposed to relate to boys. The initial presentiment, however, that something is wrong in the way the adolescent boys interact with Sally is confirmed when Esperanza, left alone by Sally and her boyfriend in an amusement park, is confronted with male power and sexually attacked by a group of boys. To Esperanza the reality of this brutal sexual initiation stands in sharp contrast to what she has been told about sexual relationships: "Sally, you lied. It wasn't what you said at all. What he did. Where he touched me. I didn't want it, Sally. The way they said it, the way it's supposed to be, all the storybooks and movies, why did you lie to me?" (93).

This last question is central to Esperanza's sexual initiation, as it shows that she feels violated, not only physically by the boys, but also psychologically by a framework of omnipresent cultural myths that shroud the reality of patriarchal violence in idealistic romance. Her disillusionment with the reality of sexual encounters is thus aggravated by her bewilderment as to why

"they"—Sally, other women, mass media—have lied to her and left her vulnerable to male sexual advances and domination. As Herrera-Sobek points
out, Esperanza's diatribe is directed particularly against the community of
women who participate in a "conspiracy of silence": "The protagonist discovers a conspiracy of two forms of silence: silence in not denouncing the 'real'
facts of life about sex and its negative aspects in violent sexual encounters,
and complicity in embroidering a fairy-tale-like mist around sex" (1988, 178).
Thus Esperanza expresses her sense of alienation and betrayal:

> Why did you leave me all alone? I waited my whole life. You're a
> liar. They all lied. All the books and magazines, everything that told
> it wrong. Only his dirty fingernails against my skin, only his sour
> smell again. . . . He wouldn't let me go. He said, I love you, I love
> you, Spanish girl. (94)

Realizing that cultural stories do not tell the whole story, Esperanza con-
demns this cultural conspiracy around sexuality which—as the deprecia-
tory epithet "Spanish girl" indicates—makes her particularly vulnerable.
Esperanza's sexual initiation is thus an initiation into knowledge about
herself as a sexual subject who has been manipulated by a framework of
cultural myths. By telling her own version of her sexual initiation, however,
Esperanza creates a text that stands in direct opposition to the cultural texts,
the storybooks, magazines, and movies "that told it wrong," thus refusing to
participate in the conspiracy of silence which co-opts women into partaking
in their own oppression.

In her attempt to deconstruct sociocultural lies by telling the truth, Esperanza turns her narrative attention to the women on Mango Street. Realizing
that their fate can be hers, she begins to examine their lives in order to come
to an understanding of her own relationship to the sociocultural world of
the barrio. Perceived from Esperanza's female perspective, this environment
takes on distinct characteristics, in that she, in her evolving consciousness
about herself as a woman, becomes increasingly aware of the contradictions
between her emerging female self and the circumstances that inform women's
lives on Mango Street. It is through a continuous tension between herself and
her environment and through her interaction with the women in the barrio,
that she becomes aware of the true nature of patriarchal ideology and her own
position as a woman within her particular sociocultural context.

In her adolescent search for role models, Esperanza observes the lives
of the women in the neighborhood in order to get some clues to her own
future life as a woman. In narrating the stories about these women, Esperanza constructs an image of the women around her that is predominantly

one of entrapment and constraint. Women are behind windows, entrapped in their own houses, entrapped in the circumstances that determine their lives as women in a poor Latino barrio. There is Mamacita, who "doesn't come out because she is afraid to speak English" (74); and Rosa Vargas, "who is tired all the time from buttoning and bottling and babying, and who cries every day for the man who left without even leaving a dollar . . . or a note explaining how come" (30); and Minerva, who

> is only a little bit older than me but already she has two kids and a husband who left . . . and keeps leaving. . . . He comes back and sends a big rock through the window. Then he is sorry and she opens the door again. Next week she comes over black and blue and asks what can she do? . . . Her mother raised her kids alone and it looks like her daughters will go that way too. (80)

The women portrayed here exemplify the triple oppression poor Latino women on Mango Street have to face in their daily lives and how "women's marginality leads to economic and social dependence on the male" (Herrera-Sobek, 1988, 175); unable to break the cycle of poverty or their dependency on men, the daughters are often doomed to repeat the fate of their mothers.

A common denominator uniting almost all the different women Esperanza portrays is, not only their entrapment in oppressive sociocultural circumstances, but their internalization of a definition of self that is determined by phallocentric cultural values. They are thus not only confined within their own houses, but also confined by their own minds, by the conditioned limitations of their own self-perception. Their lives and actions, dominated by fathers and husbands, are physically and psychologically entrapped within oppressive patriarchal structures, and they can envision themselves only in the seemingly inescapable roles of future wives and mothers. Rafaela, for instance, who "gets locked indoors because her husband is afraid she will run away since she is too beautiful to look at . . . leans out the window . . . and dreams her hair is like Rapunzel's" (76), dreams of being liberated from her prison, but as in the fairy tale, by a man. And so Rafaela dreams of going dancing where "always there is someone offering sweeter drinks, someone promising to keep them on a silver string" (76); dreaming of being released of her present imprisonment, she can only dream of walking into another. This dependency on a man to liberate you from the oppressive circumstances of your present life also conditions Marin's dreams of the future, of

> a real job downtown because that's where the best jobs are, since you always get to look beautiful and get to wear nice clothes and

can meet someone on the subway who might marry and take you
to live in a big house far away. (27)

Like Esperanza, Marin wants to escape from Mango Street, but unlike
Esperanza she envisions marriage as the only possible way of getting away.

It is, however, in her attempt to understand her friend Sally that the narrating "I" begins to see why girls repeat the fate of their marginalized mothers
and become caught in a cycle of patriarchal violence and control. Esperanza
wants to be beautiful like Sally, dress like Sally, whose father thinks that "to
be this beautiful is trouble" (77) and whom the whole world expects "to make
a mistake" (79). Yet by narrating Sally's story, she begins to understand that to
be Sally also means to end up confined within patriarchal prisons like most of
the women on Mango Street.

Sally, who becomes different when she has to go home, cannot leave her
house because of her father: "He hits me . . . with his hands just like a dog . . .
like if I was an animal. He thinks I'm going to run away like his sisters who
made the family ashamed. Just because I'm a daughter" (85). Constant scars
on her skin are signs of her father's continuous violent attempts to control her
sexuality and force her into adhering to his patriarchal definition of womanhood. This violent drama culminates one day when "he just went crazy, he just
forgot he was her father between the buckle and the belt" (85). Making connections between female behavior and patriarchal violence, Esperanza begins
to understand why Sally, like Minerva and all the other women on Mango
Street, went "that way too" (80) and exchanged her father's prison for that of
a husband, believing, like Rafaela, in someone promising to give her "sweeter
drinks," to keep her on "a silver string" (76):

> Sally got married like we knew she would, young and not ready
> but married just the same. . . . She has her husband and her house
> now, her pillowcases and her plates. She says she is in love, but I
> think she did it to escape. Sally says she likes being married because
> now she gets to buy her own things when her husband gives her
> money. . . . Except he won't let her talk on the telephone. And he
> doesn't let her look out the window. . . . She sits at home because
> she is afraid to go out without his permission. (96)

Confined physically and psychologically to her house, Sally is trapped in an
existence that is completely circumscribed and controlled by her husband;
aware of no other alternatives, she leads a life that reflects a recurrent pattern in patriarchal cultural myths, one in which "women do not grow up.
They simply change masters—from a beastly father to a fatherly beast"

(Rose, 223). Narrating Sally's story, Esperanza comes to understand that, by marrying, Sally remains under the control of a man, and that the house she inhabits, rather than being a liberating space, is a stifling confinement in which Sally is trapped, "looking at walls, the linoleum roses on the floor, the ceiling smooth as a wedding cake" (95). She is, in effect, trapped between the myth and the reality of women's lives.

Sally's house stands as an antithesis to the house Esperanza dreams of inhabiting one day; it is also a far cry from Gaston Bachelard's image of a house as "felicitous space" (xxxv), or Tomás Rivera's definition of *la casa* as a "constant refuge" (1979, 22) from a hostile world. In Bachelard's reveries, a house is "the non-I that protects the I" (5), "a roomy home" where a family can live "in security and comfort" (30), where one shivers "merely from well-being" (31). He deems this experience of the house as a "material paradise" (7) to be so universal that it can be used as "a tool for analysis of the human soul" (xxxvii). It is obvious that this image of the house has its roots in Bachelard's own comfortable background and that his reveries on the house are circumscribed by a male-centered middle-class ideology. His "nostalgic and privileged utopia" (Olivares, 160) is based on experiences that differ dramatically from those of women like Sally and Esperanza.

There is a marked economic and cultural difference between Bachelard's concept of the house as "material paradise" and Tomás Rivera's concept of *la casa* as a "constant refuge" (1979, 22) from a hostile environment. In his article "Fiesta of the Living," Rivera presents *la casa*, *el barrio*, and *la lucha* as constant and essential elements in the struggle for cultural survival in a hostile environment. To Rivera, *la casa* is the center of cultural continuity, a safe haven where ethnic pride and family solidarity are perpetuated. Central to this concept of *la casa* is also the image of the much eulogized *madre abnegada*, who sacrifices herself for her family. This concept of the traditional family may perpetuate ethnic integrity and mitigate the blows of oppression, but for the Chicana it may also be the very concept that perpetuates her own oppression. Despite their differences, both Bachelard and Rivera see the house as a protective sphere, "the non-I that protects the I," a concept that does not always apply to women, as it is often within the very confines of the home that violence is visited upon her. To Sally, the house is neither a "material paradise" nor a "constant refuge"; in order to escape the physical violence in her father's house, she marries, only to realize that she has exchanged one prison for another.

Esperanza comes to realize, in examining the lives of the women on Mango Street, that a woman's house is often a confining patriarchal domain rather than the house of liberation she imagines for herself. Having arrived at this realization, Esperanza begins to resist the social conditioning that leads women on the path to marriage:

My mother says when I get older my dusty hair will settle and my blouse will learn to stay clean, but I have decided not to grow up tame like the others who lay their necks on the threshold waiting for the ball and chain. I have begun my own quiet war. Simple. Sure. I am one who leaves the table like a man, without putting back the chair or picking up the plate. (82)

Esperanza's refusal to adhere to social expectations of female behavior goes far beyond the mere action itself, as it is a symbolic refusal to "grow up tame," to accept a prescribed female destiny. Esperanza's action has been interpreted as a "somewhat adolescent gesture" that is likely "to increase the work for another woman in Esperanza's household" (McCracken, 72) and as an attempt "to increase her own power by starting out to be as rude as men" (Alarcón, 1989, 100), yet her refusal to do so-called female chores marks an important step toward breaking the cycle of female self-sacrifice. With her self-defining assertions, "I have decided not to grow up tame . . . , I am one who leaves the table," Esperanza claims control over her own *Bildungs* process by envisioning a role for herself that stands in direct opposition to the sociocultural roles and expectations imposed on women by a male-defined culture. In her own "quiet war," Esperanza begins to assert a self-defined destiny by "daring to be selfish" (Huf, 157), by daring to kill the "angel in the house" (Woolf, 1942, 236), so that she can inhabit her own liberating space, a house of her own making:

Not a flat. Not an apartment in the back. Not a man's house. Not a daddy's. A house all my own. With my porch and pillow, my pretty purple petunias. My books and my stories. My two shoes waiting besides the bed. Nobody to shake a stick at. Nobody's garbage to pick up after. Only a house as quiet as snow, a space for myself to go, clean as paper before the poem. (100)

Her initial wish for an illusive "real house," one she can point to, is thus in the course of her narrative transformed into a more defined desire for a place that transcends the mere physical living quarters to mean a life of her own creation. She wants not only a house but also a life that is unconfined by either a father or a husband or prescriptive social expectations, a nonpatriarchal space in which she can create herself and a self-defined destiny.

In the process of her exploration of her sociocultural context, of discovering, synthesizing, and narrating her own experiences within the community on Mango Street, Esperanza has come to understand that the "real house" she has been searching for is an unconfining creative space. Telling her own story, the narrating "I" participates in the process of her own self-formation, while she at the same time creates a poetic space that stands as an alternative to the confining conditions on Mango Street: "I like to tell stories. . . . I put it down on paper and then the ghost does not ache so much. I write it down and Mango Street says goodbye sometimes. She does not hold me with both arms. She sets me free" (101). This sense of liberation through the creative act of writing and narrating her own stories is predicted early on by a dying aunt who encourages Esperanza to write: "'That's nice. That's very good,' she said in her tired voice. 'You just remember to keep writing, Esperanza. You must keep writing. It will keep you free,' and I said, 'yes,' but at that time I didn't know what she meant" (56). Attention here turns to the narrating "I," who, through the creative reconstruction of this encounter, comes to understand that in writing about her experiences she has come to inhabit a liberating poetic space of her own.

Esperanza's vision of creativity as a form of liberation takes on social and cultural dimensions, as it becomes clear that *The House on Mango Street* is the narrator/author's textual return to Mango Street. The narrating "I," initially ashamed of her entire "social and subject position" (Saldívar, 1990, 182), is driven throughout the narrative process by the desire to escape not only her great-grandmother's "place by the window," but also the confinement of her socioeconomic circumstances on Mango Street. Yet in the course of telling her stories she comes to recognize the significance of Mango Street in her life, that it forms an inextricable part of her own self.

In the course of her *Bildung*, Esperanza encounters several guides, each of whom connects her with her cultural context in vital ways and provides important messages about the uniqueness of her own identity. There is her mother who "could've been somebody" (83) if it had not been for the shame of being poor: "Shame is a bad thing, you know. It keeps you down. You want to know why I quit school? Because I didn't have nice clothes. No clothes, but I had brains" (84). That the feeling of shame can entrap one in the very situation one wants to escape becomes a crucial lesson for Esperanza, who, throughout the narrative, has expressed being ashamed of her position on Mango Street. Her friend Alicia, furthermore, insists that Mango Street, the very place Esperanza wants to escape, forms an integral part of Esperanza's identity: "Like it or not you are Mango Street and one day you will come back" (99). This emphasis on her connection to Mango Street is reiterated by three *comadres*, three indigenous guides—reminiscent of the three Fates in Greek mythology who govern human destiny—who tell her that she is "special," that she will "go far" (97), but also that she must not forget that she comes from Mango Street:

> Esperanza . . . a good, good name.
>
> When you leave you must remember always to come back, she
> said. . . . When you leave you must remember to come back for
> the others. A circle, understand? You will always be Esperanza.
> You will always be Mango Street. You can't erase what you know:
> You can't forget who you are. You must remember to come back.
> For the ones who cannot leave as easily as you.
>
> Yes, yes, I said a little confused.
>
> I didn't understand everything they had told me. (98)

Once more the attention turns to the narrating "I" who, through the creative
reconstruction of her life on Mango Street, has come to understand that
she will always be Esperanza. She will always be a Chicana, and Mango
Street will always form a part of her identity. The *comadres* predict a different destiny for Esperanza, yet remind her at the same time that her origins,
her cultural and socioeconomic roots, form an important part of her future
self. When Esperanza in the end envisions her own departure from Mango
Street, it is with the intention of returning, of creating *esperanza* for those
she leaves behind:

> One day I will pack my bags of books and paper. One day I will say
> goodbye to Mango. I am too strong for her to keep me here forever.
> One day I will go away.
>
> Friends and neighbors will say, What happened to that Espe-
> ranza? Where did she go with all those books and paper? Why
> did she march so far away? They will not know that I have gone
> away to come back. For the ones I left behind. For the ones who
> cannot get out. (102)

By the end of her *Bildungs* experience, Esperanza has thus gained an awareness of herself as a potential writer who ventures into the larger world with
a firm sense of who she is, where she comes from, and where she is going.

* * *

The House on Mango Street is a narrative of self-discovery in which Esperanza narrates her own quest for a house, a life of her own making. Through
the act of narrating, the Chicana protagonist becomes the conscious subject
of her own *Bildungs* story. She is a female *Bildungsheld* who dismantles "the
cultural text as she grows up in resistance to it" (J. Frye, 109), resisting cultural norms that demand that women "grow down rather than up" (Pratt,

1981, 168). In the process she creates a text that subverts the traditional female quest story of the "thwarted or impossible journey" (Heller, 14) that inevitably leads to sociocultural entrapment of the female hero. Narrating her own *Bildungs* story, the narrating "I" engages in the subversive act of replacing the cultural text with her own. This aspect of the narrative lends a poetic dimension to this Chicana quest story: Esperanza's search for a "real" house is at the same time a quest for self-expression, for a liberating self-creation that dismantles traditional male-defined myths and texts that have locked the Chicana into confining stereotypes.

When Esperanza at the end of her self-discovering narrative envisions the "real" house she has been searching for, she defines it as "not a man's house. Not a daddy's. A house all my own.... A house quiet as snow, a space for myself to go, clean as paper before the poem" (100). This connection between the house and the text—her house is a poem yet to be written—turns her rejection of a "man's house" into a rejection of what Gilbert and Gubar have termed "patriarchal poetics" (72); her escape from the house of the fathers is an escape from male texts. Her own quest for a "real" house is thus a quest for a new Chicana text, one that names her own experiences and represents her as a Chicana in all her subjective complexity, one that does not make her "feel like nothing."

This use of the house as a metaphor for a new Chicana poetic space is further underscored by Esperanza's image of her own house as a place of ethnic consciousness and with room for outsiders: "One day I'll own my own house, but I won't forget who I am or where I came from. Passing bums will ask, Can I come in? I'll offer them the attic, ask them to stay, because I know how it is to be without a house" (81). Esperanza's house/text, the poem that is yet to be written, is thus going to include the traditional outsiders, the sociocultural "others," who have been excluded from inhabiting houses/texts of their own. And in fact, many of these "others" inhabit the finished text, *The House on Mango Street*, as for example Geraldo, who did not have a last name, who was "just another *brazer* who didn't speak English. Just another wetback. You know the kind. The ones who always look ashamed" (63). By making room for the story of a *mojado* in her text, Esperanza gives poetic space to one of the many outsiders who otherwise sink into oblivion, name-less and forgotten.

The House on Mango Street is a text that houses outsiders, where those who look ashamed because they do not have houses/texts of their own can feel at home. It is a concern that may stem from Cisneros's own feelings of textual exclusion. In a biographical essay, Sandra Cisneros recalls her encoun-ter with Gaston Bachelard's *The Poetry of Space* in college. She did not under-stand Bachelard's reveries on the house of the imagination, yet everyone else was quite comfortable with this book, and that made her feel "foreign from the others, out of place, different" (63):

> They seemed to have some communal knowledge which I did not have, did not understand—and then I realized that the metaphor of the *house* was totally wrong for me, that it did not draw from any archetype in my imagination, in my past culture. Suddenly I was homeless. There were no attics, and cellars, and crannies. I had no such house in my memories. (63)

Cisneros's feelings of homelessness in Bachelard's text stem from her inability to relate to a concept of the house that is based on a male-centered, middle-class ideology that is foreign to her. Bachelard's "felicitous space" finds no echo in Cisneros's imagination, and the house of her childhood was not the "material paradise" (7) that Bachelard seems to presume is a universal given. *The House on Mango Street* is thus a countertext to Bachelard's *The Poetics of Space*, a Chicana poetics of space that houses images which reverberate in the Chicana imagination. With *The House on Mango Street*, Cisneros has created a text that, unlike Bachelard's text, can house the imagination of the textual outsider.

Much in keeping with Esperanza's promise to return for the women she leaves behind, "the ones who cannot get out" (102), *The House on Mango Street* stands as a symbolic return to the women in a Latino barrio. Not only is this Chicana *Bildungsroman* dedicated "A las Mujeres/To the Women," but the narrative itself centers on the community of women on Mango Street who form part of Esperanza's *Bildungs* process. Elsewhere Sandra Cisneros argues that "the world of thousands of silent women . . . needs to be, must be recorded so that their stories can finally be heard" (76). Through the narrator/protagonist, Esperanza, Sandra Cisneros gives voice to a Chicana *Bildungsheld* who tells her own story, who in the process of constructing herself as a subject "dares to confront lies and to deconstruct myths" (Gonzáles-Berry, 14) about la Chicana. Esperanza grows up, not down, and gains in the process a clear understanding of her social, cultural, and sexual identity as a Chicana. Through her role as a writer, as a teller of stories, however, her *Bildung* is not merely individual, but takes on communal significance, as she, with the text, is reaching back to the women on Mango Street so that her own liberating self-creation may in turn become a symbolic *Bildungs* experience for those "who cannot get out":

> Marin, under the streetlight, dancing by herself, is singing the same song somewhere. I know. Is waiting for a car to stop, a star to fall, someone to change her life. Anybody. (28)

The communal significance of Esperanza's *Bildung* is further underscored by the fact that, while her primary concern is for the women who cannot escape marginalization, the text goes beyond an exclusive portrayal of the oppression of Chicanas to name and give voice to other outsiders in the community. *The House on Mango Street* thus exemplifies how Esperanza's *Bildung* involves an understanding of her own relationship to the entire Chicano community and that such understanding is essential to a true Chicana *Bildungs* process.

NOTE

1. There is a wide discrepancy among critics about how to define the narrative structure, the genre, of *The House on Mango Street.* I have chosen to define its narrative structure as interrelated stories that in their entirety form a novel, a *Bildungsroman*. For a discussion on the question of genre in *The House on Mango Street* see "Género e ideología en el libro de Sandra Cisneros: *The House on Mango Street*" by Pedro Gutiérrez-Revuelta.

NICHOLAS SLOBODA

A Home in the Heart:
Sandra Cisneros's The House on Mango Street

In *The House on Mango Street,* Sandra Cisneros presents Esperanza Cordero and her remembered experiences after her family moves to their new "sad red house" on Mango Street. She assembles, in forty-five short chapters, a collage of recollections by the young female protagonist. Esperanza, in her introspective narrative, looks back and remembers (and, in a sense, re-creates) her childhood in a depressed Mexican-American neighborhood. While this character has become an important figure in the development and expression of female subjectivity in recent Mexican-American fiction, all too often she is read exclusively as a voice of opposition to dominant-culture practices of oppression and hegemony. Ellen McCracken announces that "Cisneros links both the process of artistic creation and the dream of a house" to "enable" or promote "social rather than individualistic issues" (1989, 66). McCracken proceeds to describe Esperanza as a "positive objectification" (65) that critiques "bourgeois individualism" (64). Barbara Harlow similarly asserts that Cisneros's text is "premised on the alienation between the young girl's emergent sense of a socially conditioned self and the new neighborhood" (1991, 160). Harlow also contends that "the Mango Street house has failed to actualize the child's aspirations of status and comfort raised by the promise of 'moving'" (160). While such interpretations correctly point to Esperanza's desire to "redress humiliation and establish a

From *Aztlán* 22, no. 2 (Fall 1997): 89–106. © 1997 by the UCLA Chicano Studies Research Center Press.

dignified sense of her own personhood" (McCracken 1989, 65), they tend to overlook the value of Esperanza's distinctly playful nature and its effect on both her individual character and communal consciousness. I intend to show that Esperanza develops a self-resilience and acceptance that retains no "aspirations of status." Cultivating these attributes in conjunction with her playfulness, the young protagonist gains a self-understanding that extends well beyond any desire for mere "comfort." Her character, accordingly, is not merely confined to and contained by her often oppressive environment.

Beyond Oppositional Readings

Oppositional readings often typify the novel's protagonist. Terry DeHay uses such an approach to interpret Esperanza's experiences predominantly in the context of her growing awareness of her cultural, economic, and social objectification. DeHay restricts Esperanza's insights to "understanding . . . what it means to be both a member of a minority and a woman in a white patriarchal culture" (1994, 40). By claiming that Esperanza's memories and stories "*all* focus on the social, cultural, and sexual alienation she experiences as a child" (40, italics mine), DeHay, like McCracken, neglects Esperanza's positive experiences. DeHay, in fact, perceives Esperanza's conscience as focused exclusively on surviving, as exercising a "commitment to saving herself" (40). Cisneros, however, does not limit her central character to a static agent of counterdiscourse. Depicting Esperanza's active negotiation of her identity in light of both constricting social conditions and, significantly, liberating personal aspirations, she presents the young protagonist as a vital and dynamic individual. In the process, Cisneros demonstrates how a subject can be defined but, at the same time, not totally restricted by its material (representative) and psychological (cognitive) space. Not focusing on the superficial, exotic qualities of her young protagonist's otherness, Cisneros, instead, shows how Esperanza "waits" to gain her appropriate voice in light of the prevalent hegemonic forces, patriarchal oppression, and ethnic marginalization in urban America. In particular, she juxtaposes Esperanza's burgeoning awareness of the harsh socioeconomic realities around her with her personal dreams and playful spirit. The different aspects of the protagonist's character are hinted at in her name itself. Esperanza explains that, "In English my name means hope. In Spanish it . . . means sadness, it means waiting" (Cisneros 1984, 10). Through her minimalist narrative voice, Esperanza enters into a "dialogue" with her new home environment and learns to apply her hopefulness in the fashioning of her dream for a home of her own.

Cisneros opens *The House on Mango Street* by demonstrating how a home space plays a major role in shaping life and world experiences. She establishes the prominence of setting through a series of images that depict life in a predominantly Chicano urban American slum. Through these images, she exemplifies what Edward Soja, in his theoretical analysis of "postmodern geographies," terms a "social hieroglyphic" (Soja 1989, 7). The short novel begins with an all too typical scene for new or recent immigrants in America: a large family on the move. Esperanza, a member of such a family, is already accustomed to the migratory nature of lower-class life. Through Esperanza's differentiating between a "house" and "home," Cisneros specifically addresses the issue of transiency and shows how the local neighborhood can temper dreams and aspirations. In her "materialist interpretation of spatiality" (Soja 1989, 120), to draw from Soja's interpretive framework, Cisneros exposes a connection between spatiality and being. Soja contends that this type of "ontological spatiality situates the human subject in a formative geography" (8). Through her initial focus on the nature of Mango Street, Cisneros draws attention to the "formative," but not deterministic, role of the protagonist's new home space.

From the outset of the novel, Cisneros captures both the protagonist's individual plight and the general struggles of a lower-class family. Esperanza recalls her life as a young girl in a Mexican-American family: "But what I remember most is moving a lot" (3). Here, Cisneros implicitly distinguishes the perspective (and life) of her protagonist from the middle-class child (who would likely remember and describe other things). Esperanza then summarizes her life before Mango Street by listing the different streets where she has already lived: "We didn't always live on Mango Street. *Before* that we lived on Loomis on the third floor, and *before* that we lived on Keeler. *Before* Keeler it was Paulina, and *before* that I can't remember" (3, italics mine). The repetitive and cyclic quality of the moving experience reveals that the constant shifting to different locales does not lead to a dramatic improvement in living conditions. With Esperanza explaining that her family's relocations are out of economic necessity, Cisneros exposes the limitations of living as members of a minority and the lower class in America. She also points to the difficulty in breaking from a life of poverty.

In this opening section of the short novel, Cisneros establishes the house on Mango Street as a sign—at once real and symbolic—of the rift between the reality and dreams of Esperanza and others living in this ghetto. From this perspective, *The House on Mango Street*, as Harlow generalizes, "radically critiques the inherently political ideology of the 'American dream'" (1991, 160). Cisneros continues to unveil the harsh living conditions in Esperanza's new neighborhood by establishing a contrast between the ideal and the real. Although Esperanza recognizes the value of her family living in their own house and appreciates the lack of "a landlord banging on the ceiling with a broom" (3), she nonetheless realizes that "it's not the house we'd thought we'd get" (3). While listing what she perceives to be the general advantages of ownership—not paying rent or sharing the yard—Esperanza also reiterates that the house is "not the way *they* told it at all" (4, italics mine). Her use of the indefinite pronoun "they" refers to those in mass communication and the media that propagate the myth of the "better life." With this comment, the protagonist reveals that she is aware of her family's position outside of the comforts and serenities typically associated with the American dream. Later, in fact, she further acknowledges her neighborhood's separation from mainstream America by noting that "the thought of the mayor coming to Mango Street makes me laugh out loud" (107). Upon moving to Mango Street, Esperanza also alludes to her own already long-standing disappointment with her living conditions by sadly conceding that their new house is still not a "real" house that she could "point to" (5). Even though her mother describes their move as "for the time being," and her father calls it "temporary," Esperanza now understands, "But I know how those things go" (5). Although the young protagonist dreams of a "real house" and, implicitly, a better life, Cisneros shows that, even at this early stage of her life, Esperanza is already less idealistic and has learned to condition or temper her dreams.

Cisneros, however, also shows that, in spite of finding herself in another depressed neighborhood, her young protagonist does not abandon her hope and ideals. Almost immediately after moving to Mango Street, Esperanza contrasts her new house with her dream "home" environment. First she describes her ideal, "real house": "[O]ur house would have running water and pipes that worked. And inside it would have real stairs, not hallway stairs, but stairs inside like the houses on T.V." She also imagines the external features: "Our house would be white with trees around it, a great big yard and grass growing without a fence" (4). At this early point in the short novel, Cisneros reveals that her protagonist maintains her vitality and hopefulness. Through her awareness of the less than ideal nature of her new home and, at the same time, her determination not to abandon her dream, Esperanza begins to fashion her consciousness—at once socially informed and individually hopeful. Shortly thereafter, Cisneros again draws attention to Esperanza's playful and creative spirit by immediately contrasting the protagonist's bleak depiction of her new house on Mango Street with a scene in which she playfully describes the "different hair" (6) in her family. By consistently including the positive aspects of Esperanza's perspective, Cisneros reveals another significant dimension of her protagonist's character.

Cultural Tensions

In her new neighborhood, Esperanza learns that the issue of a respectable house and neighborhood is linked not only to people's economic plight, but also to their cultural identity. By drawing attention to the interconnection of these different facets of life on Mango Street, Cisneros addresses what Alberto Sandoval theorizes as the struggle of the "Latin American" woman to survive the "dialectics of a bi-cultural identity" (1989, 203). Esperanza gains an understanding of the nature of the cultural tensions in the neighborhood through her observations of Mamacita, a new immigrant who struggles with her sense of loneliness and isolation. She describes how a man worked two jobs to bring Mamacita, his "big mama," and her baby boy to the country. After arriving in their neighborhood, the new immigrant does not learn English; instead, she "sits all day by the window and plays the Spanish radio show and sings all the homesick songs about her country" (77). Mamacita not only longs for her homeland, but also faces an impoverished life in her new home. Cisneros actualizes Eliana Ortega and Nancy Saporta Sternbach's theories about cross-cultural contact by describing how Mamacita longs for "Home . . . a house in a photograph, a pink house, pink as hollyhocks with lots of startled light" (77). This poignant image illustrates that a home space, as a physical and psychological site of familiarity and comfort, plays a vital role in the (re)settling of the subject on both an individual and communal level.

Cisneros continues to highlight conflicts arising on Mango Street from differences between many of the residents' "home" culture and their new homes in America. Mamacita tries to preserve her sense of identity in her new country by speaking only in her mother tongue and not in English, the language "that sounds like tin" (78). She is aghast upon hearing her baby singing a Pepsi commercial in English. "No speak English, no speak English," she chants, "and bubbles into tears" (78). Presenting Mamacita's disquietude as a typical part of life on Mango Street, Cisneros exposes how the "Latina," according to Ortega and Sternbach, is "inscribed into two symbolic orders: English, the language of the hegemonic culture, and Spanish, the mother-tongue" (1989, 14). This "bicultural" subject, Ortega and Sternbach explain further, engages in a process of "constantly . . . negotiating her alliances with one or both of these orders" (14). The man, frustrated at Mamacita's sadness and constant longing for "home," exclaims: "We are home. This is home. Here I am and here I stay" (78). Refusing to even consider the possibility of this locale becoming her new home, Mamacita responds to her "man" and predicament by occasionally letting out a "cry, hysterical, high, as if he had torn the only skinny thread that kept her alive, the only road out to that country" (78). By watching how Mamacita struggles to adapt to her new homeland, Esperanza begins to appreciate the immigrant woman's feeling (and knowledge) that she does not "belong" (78).

Within this backdrop of transiency and strife on Mango Street, Cisneros shows how Esperanza must struggle to experience what other children in middle-class America take for granted. While looking for new friends, Esperanza confronts the negative stereotype of her otherness. She describes how Cathy, the "Queen of Cats," agrees to be her friend, "But only til next Tuesday" (12). Cathy then reveals, "That's when we move away" (13). Cathy's comment reminds Esperanza of the transient nature of life in her type of neighborhood. It also verifies for her that other families do not want to live near to or be associated with her class and people. In response to Cathy's remark, Esperanza states: "Then as *if* she forgot I just moved in, she says the neighborhood is getting bad" (13, italics mine). Her use of the conditional tense alludes to her melancholic awareness of the way in which she is perceived by those around her. Cathy proceeds to explain to Esperanza that her family will be inheriting the family house in France. Even though Esperanza most likely realizes that Cathy's story is a fantasy, she still becomes sad, as she seems to realize that she cannot even dream the same dreams as her friend. She gloomily concludes that Cathy's family will "just ... move a little farther north from Mango Street, a little farther away every time people like us keep moving in" (13). Through her experience of having to keep looking for new friends, Esperanza soon discovers that friendships can be tempered or even lost due to factors quite apart from personal compatibility and from her control. Cisneros also uses this exchange between the two young girls to expose the alienating effect of social stratification on a community, especially its children.

Cisneros further confirms how the difference in living conditions between the slum areas, with its run-down houses, and mainstream America, with its picket fences, leads to divisiveness. One day, Esperanza thinks about a neighborhood far away from Mango Street: "I want a house on a hill like the ones with the gardens where Papa works" (86). She, however, decides that she no longer wants to go with the rest of her family on Sundays to visit these gardens, as she now finds herself "ashamed" at "all of us staring out the window like the hungry" (86). Emphatic about her decision, Esperanza directly states: "I am tired of looking at what we can't have" (86). She then describes the attitudes of the rich over the poor: "People who live on the hills sleep so close to the stars they forget those of us who live too much on earth" (86). Cisneros uses Esperanza's reaction against her family's weekly drive to show how hope, when constantly set in the reality of impoverishment, wears thin.

Throughout her childhood, Esperanza faces people from the middle who, intentionally or not, differentiate and relegate her to a disempowered space. Once, at school, Esperanza had to stand at the window and point to where she lived. She remembers the Sister Superior's response: "That one? she said, pointing to a row of ugly three-flats, the ones even the raggedy men are ashamed to go into" (45). Even though these houses are worse than those in her neighborhood, Esperanza finds herself unable to do anything but nod her head and cry. Earlier, when Esperanza lived on Loomis, Esperanza experiences a similar scene of degrading objectification. One day, a nun from her school passes by. Spotting Esperanza, she stops and asks her whether she lived "there," pointing to the third floor of a decrepit house. Her feeling of embarrassment is still vivid in her memory: "*There*. I had to look where she pointed—the third floor, the paint peeling, wooden bars Papa had nailed on the windows so we wouldn't fall out" (5). Now understanding the nun's tone, Esperanza reflects on her experience and forced resignation: "The way she said it made me feel like nothing. *There*. I lived *there*. I nodded" (5). Through these seemingly innocent exchanges, Cisneros not only highlights the carelessness with which entire communities are negatively typified, but she exposes an irony, as Esperanza is repeatedly treated insensitively by someone who is supposed to be aware of the plight of the lower class and oppressed.

Alternative Voices

The House on Mango Street, however, is not merely a critical social commentary that articulates the anger and frustration of the victimized. In her narratives, Esperanza also establishes a hopeful voice that playfully "dialogues" with those in the local community. Notwithstanding the aforementioned hardships of life on Mango Street, Esperanza formulates a positive, personal vision. By accentuating the vibrancy of her protagonist, Cisneros develops, to apply Renato Rosaldo's terms, "a fresh vision of self and society" (1991, 85). While describing Cisneros's innovative narrative technique as exemplifying "the experimentation and achievement of recent Chicana narrative," Rosaldo explains that such Chicana writers in general have "opened" a "heterogeneous world within which their protagonists no longer act as 'unified subjects,' yet remain confident of their identities" (85). Esperanza, Rosaldo specifies, "acts assertive and playful . . . moving through a world laced with poverty, violence, and danger" and, in the process, "subverts oppressive patriarchal points of cultural coherence and fixity" (85). Scenes that expose Esperanza's playful and creative side include her experiences with Rachel, Nenny, and Lucy, such as their sharing a bicycle (14–16), naming clouds (33–38), trying on pairs of fancy shoes (38–42), playing jump rope (49–52), and spending time in what they call "the monkey garden" (94–98). Cisneros, accordingly, does not restrict Esperanza to a socially typified agent who merely exposes the disempowerment of ghettoized peoples in the United States. Instead, she shows how her protagonist uses her dynamic, individual attributes to maintain a positive perspective and, later, to begin to effect change in her life and in the community around her.

In formulating her own response to the neighborhood around her, Esperanza gains inspiration from the actions and the decisions made by her friend Minerva. Even though this young woman is about the same age as Esperanza, she already has two children whom she is raising herself, as her husband has left "and keeps leaving" (85). During the day, Minerva handles all her familial responsibilities. After her children are asleep, however, she writes poems "on little pieces of paper that she folds over and over and holds in her hands a long time" (84). Sharing creative interests, Esperanza and Minerva exchange poems. In the process, Esperanza realizes that her friend writes her hardships into her poetry; she describes Minerva's verses as "sad like a house on fire" (84). Through this striking image, Cisneros affirms the centrality of the house motif in the life of Esperanza and those around her. She also reiterates that local socioeconomic reality makes it difficult to break the cycle of poverty. Esperanza, in fact, soon discovers that Minerva is beaten regularly by her husband. In a tragic scene, Minerva arrives, "black and blue," at Esperanza's house and asks Esperanza what she can do. Through this scene, Cisneros illustrates that in neighborhoods like Mango Street oppression and even abuse often pervade the lives of the young women. Although Esperanza appreciates her friend and gains strength from her perseverance, she also sadly realizes that "There is nothing I can do" (85).

Esperanza learns to use her playful perspective and creative imagination to respond to the diverse forms of oppression around her on Mango Street. In particular, Cisneros develops Esperanza's alternative viewpoint through a highly poetic and stylistic writing. Along these lines, McCracken describes Cisneros's textual style as distinct from "the complex, hermetic language of many canonical works" (1989, 64). Esperanza employs a seemingly simple and direct language in expressing her creativity, as when she takes note of the differences in the hair of the members of her family. She describes Papa's hair as being "like a broom," her own as "lazy," Carlos's as "thick and straight," Nenny's as "slippery," and, Kiki's as being "like fir." Esperanza then concentrates on her mother's hair, focusing on its beauty:

> But my mother's hair, my mother's hair, like little rosettes, like little candy circles all curly and pretty because she pinned it in pincurls all day, sweet to put your nose into when she is holding you, holding you and you feel safe, is the warm smell of bread before you bake it, is the smell when she makes room for you on her side of the bed still warm with her skin, and you sleep near her, the rain outside falling and Papa snoring. The snoring, the rain, and Mama's hair that smells like bread. (6–7)

By switching to the second person point of view during the description, Cisneros brings readers closer to Esperanza s stream-of-consciousness and, in the process, enhances the scene's mood and tone. Her use of repetition, rhythmic language, and simple but effective figures of speech not only accurately portrays a child's point of view but also creates both striking and positive images.

Esperanza's playful and creative use of language extends beyond her personal moments of reflection to her social activities on Mango Street. One afternoon, Esperanza, her sister Nenny, and her friends Lucy and Rachel, talk about their "hips." Lucy then begins to dance, while Esperanza and Nenny twirl their skipping ropes. Esperanza describes the process: "It's gotta be just so, I say. Not too fast and not too slow. Not too fast and not too slow" (50). The repetitive and rhythmic language helps draw attention to both the motion of the skipping ropes and the girls' bodily movements, while the songs and choruses further establish the scene's playful atmosphere. Rachel is the first to introduce a refrain:

Skip, skip,
snake in your hips.
Wiggle around
and break your lip. (51)

By including other genres in this chapter, Cisneros not only playfully represents language but, in a sense, sets it in motion. This narrative strategy can be interpreted in light of Bakhtin's call for the deliberate incorporation of genres into moments of heteroglossia that "further intensify its speech diversity in fresh ways" (1981, 321). By refreshing the children's utterances, Cisneros creates a "dialogized heteroglossia" (272). In the process, she points to Esperanza's creative use of language and how this positively influences her character.

Cisneros's presentation of a variety of opposing and competing forces in Esperanza's world can be further understood in terms of Bakhtin's notions of "centrifuge" and "centripede." Bakhtin theorizes about this simultaneous inclusion of diverse, even competing socio-ideologic voices within the "environment," or "dialogized heteroglossia," of "every concrete utterance of a speaking subject." He explains that "processes of centralization and decentralization, of unification and disunification, intersect in the utterance" (272). "Centripetal" forces, accordingly, strive for a unified voice and a singular meaning, whereas "centrifugal" forces seek to fragment voices and enact a pluralistic discourse. Cisneros depicts Esperanza as a subject in the process of developing a voice of her own amidst these types of conflicting forces. She shows how Esperanza's creative means of "dialoguing" with her neighborhood helps her establish a space of her own. Watching four trees by her house, she notes that she is the "only one who understands them. Four skinny trees with skinny necks and pointy elbows like mine. Four who do not belong here but are here" (74). Aware that "[f]rom our room we can hear them [the trees]" (74), Esperanza formulates a link between the trees and her home, between her inner and outer worlds. Appreciative of the trees, Esperanza explains how they survive in the city: "Their strength is secret. They send ferocious roots beneath the ground. They grow up and they grow down and grab the earth between their hairy toes and bite the sky with violent teeth and never quit their anger. This is how they keep" (74). With these four trees now a noticeable part of her world, Esperanza learns from them and gains inspiration from their strength.

Transforming Spaces

Continuing to carve out a space for themselves in their neighborhood, Esperanza and her friends transform their living environment from a wasteland into a play-land. While describing some of Esperanza's experiences in this modified space, Cisneros also alludes to the dynamic interrelationship among individual consciousness, social expression, and spatiality. Soja, in his linking of "space" and "social ontology," theorizes about this type of spatial transformation in terms of a process of "incorporation": "Not only are the spaces of nature and cognition incorporated into the social production of spatiality, [but] they are [also] significantly transformed in the process" (1989, 120). Establishing their own particular "ideational space," to apply Soja's term, the neighborhood children on Mango Street take over a lot in which a man used to keep monkeys, but that now lies empty. The "garden" is filled with flowers, bees, spiders, thistles, weeds, rotting wood, and abandoned cars (95). The children play and find solace in their *recycled* space, this place where "things had a way of disappearing" (95). Esperanza remembers this lot as "[f]ar away from where our mothers could find us. We and a few old dogs who lived inside the empty cars" (95). She further recalls how, in no time at all, their play space acquired magical qualities: "Somebody started the lie that the monkey garden had been there before anything." Esperanza proceeds to describe the "garden" in almost mythical terms: "We liked to think the garden could hide things for a thousand years. There beneath the roots of soggy flowers were the bones of murdered pirates and dinosaurs, the eye of a unicorn turned to coal" (96). From what was essentially a dump, Esperanza and the neighborhood children transform the lot and create, for themselves, a sanctuary, a space very different from the depressed streets in their neighborhood. As part of the neighborhood's heteroglossic environment, the "monkey garden," however, is not totally separate from the reality of life on Mango Street. In this empty lot, Sally soon starts to spend time apart from Esperanza and, instead, with Tito and the local boys. At first, Esperanza tries to stop the boys from their game playing, but Sally tells her to go away. Esperanza wants to run away and hide "at the other end of the garden, in the jungle part, under a tree" (97). After watching Sally play with the boys, Esperanza feels angry. The lot that had been "such a good place to play" (98), now is beginning to lose its special attributes. In fact, after this event, Esperanza never returns to the "monkey garden."

In the midst of her varied experiences on Mango Street, Esperanza's long-standing dream for a house of her own begins to take shape. One day, Esperanza visits Elenita, the "witch woman" for a palm reading. Upon asking her specifically about the possibility of a house in her future, she is told, "Ah yes, a home in the heart. I see a home in the heart." Elenita then repeats this phrase, "I see a home in the heart" (64). Not satisfied with this answer, Esperanza asks, "Is that it?" (64). Recognizing Esperanza's sadness, the "witch woman" again rechecks the cards, Esperanza's palm, and her "special water" but, much to Esperanza's disappointment, reiterates: "A new house, a house made of heart" (64). Esperanza, at the time, does not understand that Elenita is offering an insight about the spiritual (and not material) nature of her character. Later, Esperanza comes to integrate Elenita's revelation into her dream of a house of her own. While affirming that "One day I'll own my own house," Esperanza does not ignore her social reality: "but I won't forget who I am or where I came from" (87). She then imagines how she'll offer "passing bums" a place to stay, in the attic, "because I know how it is to be without a house" (87). By detailing Esperanza's fantasy of "Bums in the Attic," Cisneros clarifies that Esperanza's aspiration for a home indeed includes "heart."

Cisneros contrasts Esperanza's burgeoning personal and social awareness with the changes in her friend, Sally. Esperanza wonders about Sally's decision to dress up like someone older and to change her lifestyle. She notices that her friend is now "different" and no longer laughs (82). Later, she discovers that Sally is beaten by her father (92). Esperanza then recounts how Sally met a marshmallow salesman at a school bazaar and quickly married in another state, where underage marriages are legal. By highlighting the results of Sally's actions, Cisneros unveils the consequences of a path followed by many young women in depressed neighborhoods. Upon seeing her friend in her new home and life, Esperanza observes that her friend is "young and not ready but married just the same" (101). Although Sally had hoped to "escape" (101), she now lives an even more confined life, as her husband does not let her talk on the phone or even look out the window. Her friends can visit only when he is at work. Esperanza summarizes the bittersweet quality of Sally's victory, by noting that her friend "sits at home because she is afraid to go outside without his permission. She looks at all the things they own" (102).

Esperanza recognizes that while Sally gains material wealth, she loses her autonomy, character, and, perhaps most important, her dignity.

In spite of her friends falling victim to various forces of economic and social oppression, Esperanza, nonetheless, does not abandon her idealism. Instead, she recognizes the need to broaden the scope of her dream to include the reality of her life on Mango Street. Esperanza, in fact, has a glimpse into her future, on visiting with her three aunts at the funeral of a baby cousin. One of the aunts takes Esperanza aside and, after looking at her for a long time, states: "When you leave you must remember always to come back" (105). The aunt then repeats that line and adds, "A circle, understand? You will always be Esperanza. You will always be Mango Street. You can't erase what you know. You can't forget who you are" (105). The repetition of this simple sentence draws attention to Esperanza's increasing awareness of a bond between her individual identity and her home space. The aunt, then, for the third time, reiterates her call for Esperanza to remember to come back; this time, however, she clarifies the reason for returning: "For the ones who cannot leave as easily as you" (105). Esperanza's meeting with her aunt further verifies for her the importance of developing her individual talents and accepting the social consequences of her actions.

While gaining insights about her own belonging, Esperanza benefits from her time with her friend Alicia. Realizing that her friend "doesn't want to spend her whole life in a factory or behind a rolling pin" (31–32), Esperanza understands and respects Alicia's commitment to studying hard at the university. Later, Esperanza recalls a conversation during which Alicia confirms the bond between Esperanza's sense of self and her life on Mango Street. Esperanza begins to tell Alicia about her "sadness" at not having a house: "You live right here, 4006 Mango, Alicia says and points to the house I am ashamed of" (106). At the time, Esperanza passionately rejects Alicia's declaration: "No, this isn't my house I say and shake my head as if shaking could undo the year I've lived here." Not wanting to associate herself with her neighborhood, she adds: "I don't belong. I don't ever want to come from here" (106). Alicia, however, verifies the intimate nature of the relation between Esperanza and the neighborhood: "Like it or not *you are* Mango Street" (107, italics mine). Through this exchange, Cisneros exposes the core of the young protagonist's conflict: on the one hand, Esperanza does not want to be associated with this type of neighborhood, with its oppression and poverty; on the other hand, however, she wants to accept her life, family, and friends, not in some fantasy or abstract space, but in the actual locale where she lives. Esperanza eventually resolves this seeming contradiction in her life by realizing that, first, she must affirm her presence in her own community and then try to improve it, to be a "somebody" who "makes it better" (107).

In light of her encounters and experiences with those around her on Mango Street, Esperanza begins to fashion her desire for a house of her own in a manner that includes both integrity and "heart." She realizes that in order for her own self to emerge to its fullest, her ideal house, in turn, must be her own and "Not a man's house. Not a daddy's" (108). Esperanza, accordingly, distinguishes herself from Sally by rejecting her friend's decision to attain material wealth and status at the expense of her personal character and integrity. Esperanza, instead, imagines that her dream house will be filled with "My books and my stories" (108). With Esperanza realizing that she cannot separate her living space from her creative perspective, Cisneros affirms the interconnection between an individual's physical and psychological reality. By adapting Virginia Woolf's famous novel title, *A Room of One's Own*, in describing Esperanza's dream for "A House of My Own" (108), Cisneros suggests a possible comparison between Woolf and Esperanza, particularly in terms of their shared strength of character, resolve, and rejection of imperial and patriarchal hegemony. Through this literary reference, Cisneros also echoes Woolf's promotion of communal (over colonial) dynamics, specifically, her recognition of the role and value of the individual in the context of a people.

The novel closes with Esperanza accepting the neighborhood as her own but, at the same time, refusing to become another of its victims. She announces her intention to tell stories about herself, "a girl who didn't want to belong" (109). Esperanza acknowledges that the "sad red house" is "the house I belong but do not belong to" (110). About her future, she remains hopeful. She talks about how, one day, she will leave "Mango" with her books and paper but, with a strong sense of purpose and direction in her life. She explains that her friends and neighbors "will not know I have gone away to come back. For the ones I left behind. For the ones who cannot out" (110). By ending the short novel with this deliberate stylized expression that omits a word of action, Cisneros uses Esperanza's personalized and minimalist language to accentuate the despair of those left behind and their inability to enact change. Overall, through her encounters with a variety of people—young and old—in the neighborhood, Esperanza gains the strength and perspective to challenge the prevalent socioeconomic oppression that, as she has seen, all too often entraps individuals in a life without hope. By realizing that her personal aspirations to be a writer and to have a home of her own carry a social duty, Esperanza also understands that she will become her real and true self only by fulfilling both her personal and communal responsibilities.

Self Re-vision

In *The House on Mango Street*, Cisneros brings to the surface the tensions between individual aspirations and societal restrictions (economic, social, racial, gender) inscribed in and, in part, regulating a local community. The short novel's young protagonist quickly learns about the limitations of life in an urban slum and the nature of the struggle she faces to realize her dream of a house of her own. By observing her friends Minerva and Sally, Esperanza also begins to understand the particular difficulties facing young women in the neighborhood. She, in fact, has an encounter of her own that involves inappropriate sexual behavior. While at work at her first job at Peter Pan Photo Finishers, she is confronted by an older Oriental man who, Esperanza recalls, "grabs my face with both hands and kisses me hard on the mouth and doesn't let go" (55). Such vignettes expose Cisneros's double focus, prevalent throughout the novel. On the one hand, she draws attention to the difficulties facing minority populations in ethnic ghettos arising from their economic, gender, and social stratification. On the other hand, she demonstrates that, nonetheless, it is possible to develop and maintain a positive, but not automatically naive, perspective. During these moments, Cisneros shows how Esperanza comes to recognize that only by accepting who she is—deep in her heart—and where she came from will she truly achieve her dream for a "home." Esperanza later realizes that, through her own talents as a writer, she can use her artistry to effect change in her self and her neighborhood. That is, she gains an awareness that she can use her voice as a poet to not only affirm her own sense of self but also to convey this positive energy and life-spirit to others. Esperanza thus begins to learn about the power of the written word and to understand what her aunt had once said to her: "You must keep writing. It will keep you free" (61). She recognizes that her poetry is a means of actualizing her personal vitality and spirit. Through Esperanza's epiphany, Cisneros confirms the potential (albeit at times hidden) for, as Esperanza's name suggests, "hope."

While charting Esperanza's experiences and insights, Cisneros does not ignore the "subaltern, adjunct" (Bhabha 1994, 168) reality, to draw from Homi Bhabha's theoretical readings about the location of culture, of life on Mango Street. Bhabha explains that this type of space "doesn't aggrandize the *presence* of the West but redraws its frontiers in the menacing agonistic boundary of cultural difference" (168). Through her short novel's distinct narrative strategy, Cisneros opposes forces of hegemony and seeks to break free from boundaries within which minority peoples are often confined. Esperanza's awareness and exploration of different perspectives, then, can be seen as "postcolonial" in, to adapt Bhabha's explanation, its refusal to "give a hegemony 'normality' to the uneven development and the differential, often disadvantaged histories of nations, races, communities, peoples" (171). Not restricting her perspective to a discourse about a victimized minority culture in America, however, Cisneros also addresses the dynamic interrelationship between spatiality and the formation of the individual and social subject. Specifically, she points to the transformative potential of socially responsible and individually creative thoughts and acts. With her protagonist exhibiting an enthusiasm and vigor for life, Cisneros shows how Esperanza learns to use this energy to build a will within herself. As she develops both a critical and creative awareness, she comes to accept her past and, at the same time, transform her present. By developing this strength of character, Esperanza finds herself able to move beyond assigned, contained, and disempowered mental and physical ghettoes, and live a meaningful and fulfilling life.

BIBLIOGRAPHY

Bakhtin, Mikhail Mikhailovich. 1981. "Discourse in the Novel." *The Dialogic Imagination: Four Essays*, trans. Caryl Emerson and Michael Holquist, ed. Holquist, 259–422. Austin: University of Texas Press.

Bhabha, Homi K. 1994. *The Location of Culture*. New York: Routledge.

Cisneros, Sandra. 1984. *The House on Mango Street*. New York: Vintage Contemporaries.

DeHay, Terry. 1994. "Narrating Memory." *Memory, Narrative, and Identity: New Essays in Ethnic American Literatures*, ed. Amritjit Singh, Joseph T. Skeriett Jr., and Robert E. Hogan, 26–44. Boston: Northeastern University Press.

Harlow, Barbara. 1991. "Sites of Struggle: Immigration, Deportation, Prison, and Exile." *Criticism in the Borderlands: Studies in Chicano Literature, Culture, and Ideology*, ed. Héctor Calderón and José David Saldívar, 149–163. Durham: Duke University Press, 1991.

McCracken, Ellen. 1989. "Sandra Cisneros's *The House on Mango Street*: Community-Oriented Introspection and the Demystification of Patriarchal Violence." In *Breaking Boundaries: Latina Writing and Critical Reading*, ed. Asunción Horno-Delgado, Eliana Ortega, Nina M. Scott, and Nancy Saporta Sternbach, 62–71. Amherst: University of Massachusetts Press.

Ortega, Eliana, and Nancy Saporta Sternbach. 1989. "At the Threshold of the Unnamed: Latina Literary Discourse in the Eighties." In *Breaking Boundaries*, 2–23.

Rosaldo, Renato. 1991. "Fables of the Fallen Guy." In *Criticism in the Borderlands*, 84–93.

Sandoval, Alberto. 1989. "Dolores Prida's *Coser y cantar*: Mapping the Dialectics of Ethnic Identity and Assimilation." In *Breaking Boundaries*, 201–220.

Soja, Edward W. 1989. *Postmodern Geographies: The Reassertion of Space in Critical Social Theory*. New York: Verso.

MICHELLE SCALISE SUGIYAMA

Of Woman Bondage:
The Eroticism of Feet in
The House on Mango Street

High heels must have been a man's idea—"Their asses will look good and they'll be crippled!"

—Rick Overton, *Comic Strip Live*, 1991

As a literary scholar, I am embarrassed to admit that I was well into my graduate career before I thought to ask, Why does Cinderella's fate hinge upon a *shoe*, of all things? Surely it is no accident that the foot (as opposed to some other body part) features so prominently in the tale. The question came to me when I was teaching Sandra Cisneros's *The House on Mango Street*, in which female feet and shoes are strangely and strikingly bound up with romance and sexuality. The answer began to take shape during a fortuitous study break spent on what turned out to be one of those rare, rich morsels of late-night television—namely, the observation by comedian Rick Overton cited above. What started as a little piece of mind-candy developed into an intellectual smorgasbord, with entrees from folklore, ethnography, Chicano studies, feminism, and human ethology. Although the following discussion addresses Cisneros's work in particular, its scope extends far beyond literature and even folklore: Cisneros's use of the foot/shoe motif sheds light on male manipulation of female sexuality and thus on the design and operations of the human mind.

From *The Midwest Quarterly* 41, no. 1 (Autumn 1999): 9–20. © 1999 by Pittsburgh State University.

In the chapter "The Family of Little Feet," Esperanza and her friends seem excessively excited by the experience of prancing around in the cast-off high heels which have been given to them: "Do you like these shoes? Rachel says yes and Lucy says yes and yes I say these are the best shoes. We will never go back to wearing the other kind again" (41).

Why all the excitement? The answer to this question lies in the girls' budding sexuality and its concomitant power. High heels accentuate the "female"—elongating the legs, elevating and making more prominent the buttocks, and causing the hips to sway pronouncedly. When the girls slip the shoes on, they suddenly discover, "We have legs"—legs that are "good to look at, and long" (40). Almost immediately after they put the shoes on, the girls begin acting in a sexually provocative manner: Rachel teaches Esperanza and Lucy how to "cross and uncross [their] legs" (40) and the three of them begin "strutting" (41) in their high heels. They are no doubt imitating the slightly older girls in the neighborhood who have already begun to attract sexual attention and of whom Esperanza speaks in admiring and envious tones. They have yet to realize, however, that like these older girls, they too possess sexual power—they seem surprised that their mocksexy posturing draws sexual attention: "On the avenue a boy on a home-made bicycle calls out: Ladies, lead me to heaven. But there is nobody around but us" (41).

Their resolution to "never go back to wearing the other kind" of shoe comes after they realize that the shoes make them sexually attractive to the men around them: Esperanza comments that they strut "[d]own to the corner where the men can't take their eyes off of us" (40). They also appear to sense that their strutting has an effect on women as well: "In front of the laundromat six girls with the same fat face pretend we are invisible. They are the cousins, Lucy says, and always jealous" (41).

This power to arouse men and to make women jealous initially exhilarates them—they "just keep strutting" (41), enjoying for the moment their position as the source rather than the object of power. This power begins to frighten them, however, when their bluff is called by a drunken bum who offers Rachel a dollar for a kiss.

A discussion of female power might seem out of place in a text which focuses primarily on the rigid control of women by men. However, even in a relentlessly partiarchal society, women have a power over men which only the aging process can take away: the power to sexually arouse. That the girls are at least subconsciously aware of the power the female physique has over the male libido is apparent in their deceptively innocent conversations: "You need them [hips] to dance" (49) says Lucy, to which Esperanza responds, "I don't care what kind I get. Just as long as I get hips" (51). And when Esperanza points out that you need hips to have children, Rachel cautions, "But don't have too many or your behind will spread" (50). The girls have observed this power in others and want it for themselves. In a reference to the precocious Sally, Esperanza's mother warns that "to wear black so young is dangerous" (82), but Esperanza wishes that she could wear shoes like Sally's "black ones made out of suede" (82) and wear "nylons the color of smoke" (81).

This power is ultimately a trap for the women of Mango Street, however, and this is illustrated through Cisneros's use of the shoe motif—most notably through the use of high heels. The effect that high heels have on the gait is not unlike the effect of footbinding, a practice notorious as an expression of male subjugation of women. Anyone who has ever worn high heels knows that they are uncomfortable at best and painful at worst; they slow the gait and make it virtually impossible to run. Overton inadvertently makes the connection between these distinct cultural practices quite clear in the observation that sparked this rumination: "High heels must have been a man's idea—'Their asses will look good and they'll be crippled!'" The responses of men to an attractive woman in high heels and to an attractive woman with bound feet are quite similar; indeed, the erotic appeal of bound feet is well documented. In her essay "The Bride-Show Custom and the Fairy-Story of Cinderella," Photeine Bourboulis cites the Chinese tale of "Miss A-pao," which features a beautiful young woman surrounded by a ring of admirers at a spring festival. The admirers' excitement intensifies as she stands up to leave, after which, Bourboulis emphasizes, the men "criticized her face and *discussed her feet*" (105). H.A. Giles, in his book *The Civilization of China*, observes that "any Chinaman will bear witness as to the seductive effect of a gaily dressed girl picking her way on tiny feet some three inches in length, her swaying movements and delightful appearance of instability, conveying a general sense of delicate grace quite beyond expression in words" (106).

Part of the appeal of bound feet is that, as Giles mentions, their growth is retarded, which dramatically decreases their length. High heels, too, cause the foot to appear smaller. Significantly, along with shoes, small feet are a recurring motif in *The House On Mango Street*. The first thing that is mentioned of Mamacita's physical appearance is her "tiny pink shoe" (76). An entire chapter is devoted to a "Family of Little Feet." And Esperanza's shame and embarrassment at having to wear *chanclas* with her new party dress is expressed as a feeling of "My feet growing bigger and bigger" and "My feet swell[ing] big and heavy like plungers" (47). On Mango Street, as in old China, female beauty is associated with foot size: because they make her feet feel large and clumsy, Esperanza feels "ugly" (47) in the *chanclas*.

An appearance of airy gracefulness is another of the appeals of bound feet mentioned by Giles: foot-binding causes a woman to sway from side to side as she walks. High heels cause a similar swaying—"tee-tottering" (40) is the word Esperanza uses, which suggests the "appearance of instability" Giles refers to. No doubt the "delightful" effect this "appearance of instability" has on the male psyche is due to the actual instability caused. A crippled woman is easier to control than a woman with healthy limbs. Esperanza unconsciously senses the link between high heels and footbinding: in "My Name" she observes that she was born in "the Chinese year of the horse which is supposed to be bad luck if you're born female—but I think this is a Chinese lie because the Chinese, like the Mexicans, don't like their women strong" (10).

Footbinding was practiced, of course, for precisely this reason: to make women weak. By making women physically unstable, men were able to curtail their movement and thereby prevent their sisters, wives, and daughters from engaging in any pre- and/or extra-marital sexual activity. As Laura Betzig suggests, "sexual modesty among women, including such strict institutions as veiling, footbinding, and claustration, might function to raise the paternal confidence of their consorts" (8; see also Dickemann). "Girls are like gold, like gems," says a Chinese interviewee to Giles at the turn of the century. "They ought to stay in their own house. If their feet are not bound they go here and they go there with unfitting associates; they have no good name. They are like defective gems that are rejected" (79). A woman whose feet were bound could not walk very far or for a sustained period of time, and had to be transported from place to place via palanquin. "Chinese ladies not walk abroad like Americans," says a Chinese woman interviewed by an American journalist in 1914. "In streets they go in sedan chairs, always with chaperone." This same woman was able to walk alone only with the aid of tables and chairs (Headland, 288). Thus a foot-bound woman was virtually a home-bound woman; for all practical purposes, she was cloistered.

Interestingly, the women of Mango Street are cloistered as well. The neighborhood is populated by women leaning out of windows, women who can't come outside, women who are literally or figuratively made prisoners in their homes. Marin can't come out of her house because she has to babysit all day—"but she stands in the doorway a lot" (23–24). Rafaela, who is "getting old from leaning out the window so much, gets locked indoors because her husband is afraid Rafaela will run away since she is too beautiful to look at" (79). Sally has to go straight home after school, to a "house [she] can't come out from" (82). Minerva "has many troubles, but the big one is her husband who left and keeps leaving" (85)—confining her to the home in effect by leaving her to raise two children all by herself. In short, the men in the story control women by controlling their feet—that is, by not letting them walk abroad. As Julián Olivares notes, for the women of Mango Street, the house represents "not the space of contentment but of sadness, and a dialectic of inside/outside. *The woman's place is one of domestic confinement*, not one of liberation and choice" (emphasis added, 163).

The subconscious logic behind such confinement is evident in one of the euphemisms for prostitute, *streetwalker*. A prostitute is an unchaste woman who roams the streets more or less freely. The confinement of a woman to the home can be seen as an attempt to keep her chaste. For it is not female movement per se but rather female sexuality that the men in the text are trying to control. In this way, shoes and feet ultimately come to symbolize female sexuality on Mango Street.

The association of shoes and/or feet with female sexuality is not without precedent. In an essay entitled "Psychoanalysis and Folklore," Ernest Jones discusses the obsolete custom of throwing an old shoe after departing newlyweds, which he claims is "a symbol for the (fruitful) female organ itself, an interpretation that may be supported by quoting the decidedly broad saying that used to accompany it—'May you fit her as well as my foot fits this ole shoe" (96). In an essay on "Cinderella in China," R.D. Jameson observes that the "use of the shoe in wedding ceremonies, the sanctification of the shoe in parts of China when it is brought to the temple in a ceremony to obtain children, the worship of a shoe as a characteristic symbol of a dead bride by a mourning groom, the gift of shoes by a bride to her husband in signification of her subordination to him and the gift of shoes among Manchus by a bride to her husband's brothers who share her with the husband all lead to the suggestion that we are here dealing with a very intimate and potent symbol" (88).

This "suggestion" is underscored by the vehemence with which the men of Mango Street guard their women. Ellen McCracken argues that "the men in these stories control or appropriate female sexuality by adopting one or another form of violence as if it were their innate right" (67). The text offers numerous examples attesting to this pattern. Consider, for example, Sally. The boys at school think she is pretty, to which her father responds by telling her that "to be this beautiful is trouble" (81). He makes her come straight home from school because, according to Sally, he thinks she is "going to run away like his sisters who made the family ashamed" (92). He beats her so severely when he catches her talking to a boy that she can't go to school for several days. Rafaela, too, is a domestic prisoner, only her jailer is her husband, who locks her in the house because he is afraid she will run off with someone else. As it turns out, Sally's father is not altogether wrong about beauty being trouble: in "The Monkey Garden," Tito and his friends steal Sally's keys and tell her "you can't get the keys back unless you kiss us" (96). Poor Sally is damned if she does and damned if she doesn't: if she kisses the boys, she risks her father finding out about it, for which she will probably be beaten;

if she doesn't kiss the boys, she will lose her keys, for which she may also be beaten. Regardless of which option she chooses (i.e., giving in to their blackmail or resisting it) one can easily imagine the situation escalating to rape. Indeed, Esperanza's great-grandmother's marriage was a virtual rape; she was abducted by Esperanza's great-grandfather, who "threw a sack over her head and carried her off. Just like that, as if she were a fancy chandelier" (11). And Esperanza herself is raped in "Red Clowns." The shoe motif and the use of violence by males to control female sexuality come together in the person of Mr. Benny, whose reaction to the high-heeled girls is, to say the least, extreme: "Them are dangerous, he says. You girls too young to be wearing shoes like that. Take them shoes off before I call the cops" (41). Mr. Benny's threat to summon the police confirms that control is indeed the issue: the police are agents of patriarchal power who use force (or threatened force) to control refractory members of society.

The shoe motif enables the reader to see that the power struggle taking place in the world of Mango Street is intrasexual as well as intersexual. The attempts of the men in the story to control female sexuality can be divided into two categories: (1) those that seek to blockade female sexuality, and (2) those that seek to bombard it. In other words, the male quest to control female sexuality is rooted either in fear (that the woman will lose her chastity and thereby shame the family) or desire (to possess the woman sexually), depending on the man's relationship to the woman in question. In either case, the plight of these women is much like that of Sally in the monkey garden, where "[o]ne of the boys invented the rules" (96). Women are pawns in a male struggle for status which is defined and determined, in part, by the control of female sexuality. The link between male socioeconomic status and female sexuality is made quite explicit by Giles, who claims that the motivation behind footbinding was "the social idea that small feet are both a mark of beauty and gentility" (430). This status derives in part from the fact that the feet of slave girls were not bound:

> The large-footed has to do rough work, does not sit in a sedan chair when she goes out, walks in the street barefooted, has no red clothes, does not eat the best food. She is wetted by the rain, tanned by the sun, blown upon by the wind. If unwilling to do all the rough work of the house she is called 'gourmandizing and lazy.' Perhaps she decides to go out as a servant. She has no fame and honour. To escape all this her parents bind her feet. (Giles, 79)

Thus, the foot-bound woman increased the socioeconomic status of those to whom she belonged—first her father and later her husband, which is revealed in the statement of one of Giles's interviewees that "One of a good family does not wish to marry a woman with long feet" (79).

The women of Mango Street are used in a similar way by their husbands. The men "bind" the feet of their wives and daughters by confining them to the home. This, in theory, renders the women chaste, which in turn makes the women "persons of respectability" (Giles, 79) and saves the family from being "ashamed" (Cisneros, 92). As Olivares notes, "A woman's place may be in the home but it is a patriarchic domain" (165).

It is not paradoxical that the home-bound girls of Mango Street yearn for houses. Prisoners in houses paled by their fathers, they seek escape in the only way they know how: by acquiring their own household to rule over—a house in which they might rule themselves. Unfortunately, the only means of acquiring a house which their rigorously patriarchal culture makes available to them is a husband. Hence, the women of Mango Street are forced into a kind of prostitution, using their sexuality to get husbands, houses, pillowcases, and plates (Cisneros, 101). They think they are escaping the bondage of their fathers but, as they realize too late, they are only exchanging "one repressive patriarchal prison for another" (McCracken, 68), leaving a "[domineering] father for a domineering husband" (Olivares, 164). A case in point is Sally, who gets married "young and not ready" in a state "where it's legal to get married before eighth grade" (101)—an obvious attempt to escape her brutally puritanical father. Sally says she is happy, but it is evident she is no better off than she was before:

> Sally says she likes being married because now she gets to buy her own things when her husband gives her money. She is happy except sometimes her husband gets angry and once he broke the door where his foot went through, though most days he is okay. Except he won't let her talk on the telephone. And he doesn't let her look out the window. And he doesn't like her friends, so nobody gets to visit her unless he is working.
>
> She sits at home because she is afraid to go outside without his permission. (101–02)

Olivares beautifully illustrates how Cisneros deromanticizes the idea of "sex and marriage as escape" through the image of the "tortilla star," Venus, which does not suggest love or romance but instead "means having to get up early, a rolling pin, and tortillas" (164).

The male definition of female beauty which results in marriages that are *de facto* prostitution and slavery is what Esperanza and her friends are becoming aware of in "The Family of Little Feet." They feel pretty when they put on the high heels, but this attractiveness results in their being propositioned by a bum, who offers Rachel a dollar for a kiss. As McCracken notes, this chapter narrates "the girls' discovery of the threatening nature of male sexual power that is frequently disguised as desirable male attention and positive validation of women, though what is, in fact, sexual reification" (67). This can be seen in "Chanclas," in which Esperanza's self-esteem is dependent upon arousing male sexual interest: "All night the boy who is a man watches me dance. He watched me dance" (48). The male definition of beauty, exemplified by high heels, is psychologically as well as physically crippling in that it requires, ultimately, submission and dependence. Compliance with this beauty standard is one of the ways in which, as María Herrera-Sobek puts it, "women are socialized into being participants in their own oppression" (173). This is perhaps best illustrated in the relationship between the tellingly named Sire and his girlfriend, "tiny and pretty" Lois, who is compared to a baby three times in the same paragraph (73). We are told not that she and Sire hold hands when they go on walks, but that she holds his hand, and that they stop periodically for him to tie her shoes. Whether or not Lois is faking this inability to tie her own shoes, the submission and dependence it results in are quite real: Esperanza tells us that "Sire *lets* Lois ride his bike around the block [emphasis added]" (implying that Lois has to ask Sire's permission) and that she "see[s] her sometimes running to the store for him" (73). The bum's solicitation of Rachel points out what is expected of women on Mango Street: that they should exchange their sexual services for economic support, and that they should not seek to earn a living in any other way. The girls ultimately reject the high heels because they don't want to be attractive on such terms. "But the truth is it is scarey to look down at your foot that is no longer yours and see attached a long long leg" (40) says Esperanza. "No longer yours" suggests the ugly truth of which they are becoming aware: their bodies are not their own, but belong to their fathers, brothers, boyfriends, and husbands in succession.

Thus female beauty, self-esteem, respectability, and subjugation are conflated in the image of the crippled foot. The similarities between high heels and footbinding enable us to see, however, that it is not tiny feet *per se* but the control of female sexuality they symbolize that is the root of male pleasure here. Footbinding and high heels function, in effect, as hobbles, making it easier for men to control the sexual activity of their sisters, wives, and daughters. As Martin Daly and Margo Wilson astutely observe, due to the age-old problem of paternity uncertainty, family (i.e., male) honor is to a large degree dependent upon the chastity of its women. What we see here, then, is the male psyche making, so to speak, a virtue of necessity: signs that a woman's chastity is well-guarded (e.g., footbinding) are perceived as sexually titillating stimuli. This phenomenon is visible in a comment made by one of Giles's interviewees: "Girls are like flowers, like the willow. It is important that their feet should be short, so that they can walk beautifully, with mincing steps, swaying gracefully, thus showing that they are persons of respectability" (79). Ultimately, then, female beauty is equated with bondage. This is sadly evidenced in the character of Marin, who wants to get a job downtown not because she wants to be financially independent but because "you always get to look beautiful and get to wear nice clothes and meet someone in the subway who might marry and take you to live in a big house far away" (26).

The parallel that Cisneros draws between Cinderella and the women of Mango Street is obvious. Like Cinderella, the women of Mango Street are confined to a life of domestic drudgery. Like Cinderella, their suitability as wives is symbolically determined by their shoes and feet. Like Cinderella, they use their sexuality to acquire a husband who they think will take them far, far away where they will live happily ever after. And like Cinderella, the women of Mango Street do not see that this escape is a trap. Hence the blind, unbounded joy of Esperanza and her friends when they first put on the high heels: "Hurray! Today we are Cinderella because our feet fit!" (40). Cisneros's work does not simply re-contextualize what some might consider to be a tired myth, however. Rather, by revealing the common motive underlying cultural practices seemingly far removed from each other in both space and time, Cisneros exposes the logic beneath an otherwise puzzlingly universal symbol. In the process, she presents us with an opportunity to deepen our understanding of human nature (particularly male sexual psychology), arguably one of the highest goals a literary work can hope to achieve. I can't speak for others, of course, but I know that I will never read the Cinderella story, in any of its multifold variations, quite the same way again.

BIBLIOGRAPHY

Betzig, Laura. "Mating and Parenting in Darwinian Perspective." *Human Reproductive Behaviour.* Eds. L. Betzig, M. Borgerhoff Mulder, and P. Turke. Cambridge: Cambridge University Press, 1988. 3–20.

Bourboulis, Photeine P. "The Bride-Show Custom and the Fairy-Story of Cinderella." *Cinderella: A Casebook.* Ed. A. Dundes. New York: Wildman Press, 1983. 98–109.

Cisneros, Sandra. *The House on Mango Street.* New York: Vintage-Random House, 1989.

Daly, Martin, and Margo Wilson. *Homicide.* New York: Aldine de Gruyter, 1988.

Dickemann, M. "Paternal Confidence and Dowry Competition: A Biocultural Analysis of Purdah." *Natural Selection and Social Behavior: Recent Research and New Theory.* Eds. R.D. Alexander and D.W. Tinkle. New York: Chiron Press, 1981. 417–38.

Dundes, Alan. *Cinderella: A Casebook.* New York: Wildman Press, 1983.

Giles, H.A. *Strange Stories from a Chinese Studio.* Vol. 1. London, 1880.

Headland, I.T. *Home Life in China.* London, 1914.

Herrera-Sobek, María. "The Politics of Rape: Sexual Transgression in Chicana Fiction." *Chicana Creativity and Criticism: Charting New Frontiers in American Literature.* Eds. M. Herrera-Sobek and H.M. Viramontes. Houston: Arte Publico, 1988. 171–81.

Jameson, R.D. "Cinderella in China." *Cinderella: A Casebook.* Ed. A. Dundes. New York: Wildman Press, 1983. 71–97.

Jones, Ernest. "Psychoanalysis and Folklore." *The Study of Folklore.* Ed. A. Dundes. Englewood Cliffs: Prentice-Hall, 1965. 88–102.

McCracken, Ellen. "Sandra Cisneros' *The House on Mango Street*: Community-Oriented Introspection and the Demystification of Patriarchal Violence." *Breaking Boundaries: Latina Writing and Critical Readings.* Eds. A. Horno-Delgado, E. Ortega, N.M. Scott, and N. Saporta Sternbach. Amherst: University of Massachusetts Press, 1989. 62–71.

Olivares, Julián. "Sandra Cisneros' *The House on Mango Street* and the Poetics of Space." *Chicana Creativity and Criticism: Charting New Frontiers in American Literature.* Eds. M. Herrera-Sobek and H.M. Viramontes. Houston: Arte Publico, 1988. 160–69.

MARIA SZADZIUK

Culture As Transition:
Becoming a Woman in Bi-ethnic Space

Issues created by post-national, multicultural societies involve not only questions about peaceful coexistence of different ethnic groups but also the variety of cultural influences to which members of these societies are exposed. What this means, in turn, is that culture can no longer be regarded as a static entity but must be viewed instead as something dynamic—"travelling cultures," as James Clifford titles one of his discussions of the topic. In the case of North American societies, this need to regard culture as an ongoing process may be seen especially in the emergence of studies concerned with the border between the United States and Mexico, such as those by Juan Flores and Nestor García-Canclini which focus on the cross-cultural indeterminacy of this meeting ground rather than on either of the two cultures in isolation.

This general perception of culture as a permeable space has its more intimate extension in the personal experience of those exposed to cross-cultural currents; if culture at the communal level involves the constant interaction of diverse elements, the same holds true of the microscopic mindscape. An individual in a multicultural society is also a site in which various cultures are rooted and transformed. Needless to say, a human psyche can also be a site of cultural conflict, as well as the place where individual mental "space" is invaded by incompatible cultural models and contradictory value systems. For

From *Mosaic* 32, no. 3 (September 1999): 109–29. © 1999 by *Mosaic*.

the individual, moreover, the notion of culture-as-transition often includes actual movement from one location to another, just as for the person writing about such experiences there is also frequently the problem of choosing amongst various discursive modes, plus of course the decision concerning the language in which to express oneself.

My overall concern in the following essay is to explore how the concept of culture-in-transition is played out in the autobiographical narratives of three women of Hispanic descent: *When I was Puerto Rican* by Esmeralda Santiago, *The House on Mango Street* by Sandra Cisneros, and *Loving in the War Years* by Cherríe Moraga. Although all three women have been integrated into U.S. urban culture, they respectively represent first, second, and third generation immigrants and thus three stages of removal from their ethnic origins—i.e., full immersion in a Spanish-speaking community. My specific concern, therefore, is with how progressive removal from the heritage of a minority culture affects the degree of conformity with dominant cultural standards, and how this relationship is reflected internally in terms of both content and narrative technique including the use of "ethnic" expressions and bilingual dialogue—and externally in terms of the re-publication of these texts in the language of the author's ethnic origins.

* * *

Although Santiago, Cisneros, and Moraga are all equally established writers, the reception of their autobiographical texts has been quite different. *When I was Puerto Rican*, Santiago's first book (her work had previously appeared in periodicals) was published in 1993 by Addison-Wesley and reprinted a year later in paperback by Vintage Books. A Spanish translation, by the author, also published by Vintage Books, appeared in October 1994. Cisneros's *The House on Mango Street* first appeared in 1984, thanks to a federal publication grant, and had six reprints by 1989. Its Spanish translation, by Elena Poniatowska, was published in 1994 by Vintage Books. Unlike Santiago and Cisneros, Moraga chose to remain on the margins as a radical feminist and a lesbian writer. Her *Loving in the War Years* was published in 1983, by South End Press, a small publisher targeting a niche market, and reached only selected audiences although the language of the original was English.

The varying degrees of commercial success of those texts seem to coincide with the degree to which the authors have complied with the majority culture's literary standards, as well as ideology and lifestyle. Santiago, who moved from Puerto Rico to New York as a teenager, consciously explores, and skillfully recreates, the exotic aspect of her childhood in Macún; Cisneros, born in Chicago, places her growing-up story against the background of a poor Hispanic neighborhood, where social issues are not overshadowed by guava trees. Whereas Santiago's autobiography takes the form of a sustained narrative of ambition, conquest and personal achievement, Cisneros's memoir consists of a series of vignettes and focuses on deprivation. Moraga, the daughter of a California-born Hispanic mother and Anglo father, turns the narrative of her life into a political manifesto, employing such modes as confessional self-exploration, a critique of the position of the Chicano woman in society, a poem and a short story. All of these modes are filled with explicit argumentation, making Moraga's ethnic protest a step beyond Cisneros's helpless longing for a different life and twice removed from Santiago's sincere eagerness to charm the reader. Rather than charm, Moraga's narrative aims at inflicting pain by pouring out and dissecting her own, as well as her people's, grievances.

As first/second/third generation immigrants, their writing respectively evidences an increasing movement toward non-conformity and protest. The tendency to take a radical stand against the mainstream culture becomes more pronounced with progressive abstraction from the individual's ethnic roots. Assimilation (Santiago), withdrawal (Cisneros), and active negation (Moraga) mark the general stance adopted by the three authors toward the dominant U.S. culture. Increasing distance from mainstream literature is also accompanied by increasing freedom of form, and is reflected in the degree of fragmentation in the various texts as well as in the greater variety of means of expression (e.g. the poems that Moraga includes).

* * *

In Santiago's *When I was Puerto Rican*, crossing culture involves travel in a literal, spatial sense, as well as travel in time. Featuring a protagonist/persona named Negi, the childhood narrative, which maintains the illusion of closely following the chronology of events, is bracketed by an opening fleeting glimpse of the narrator's adult life, where a detailed description of how guava fruit should be eaten both provokes a reflection on the tasteless predictability of the fruit staples in a New York supermarket and brings forward the entire childhood story, filled with long-forgotten smells and tastes. The other half of the narrative bracket, the final chapter, brings in another kind of flashback and a different cultural perspective: Negi, back from Harvard for a short visit, remembers old times with her former high school teacher, who reminds her how lucky she is to have escaped from her family's unglamorous existence and to have made her way into a higher social stratum. Here, the bright side of the American Dream comes to the fore and the reader gets a glimpse of the protagonist as a proud conqueror of the alien, privileged culture. "Do you ever think about how far you've come?" the teacher asks (269).

Santiago's view of the Puerto Rican element in Negi's life is thus ambivalent: on the one hand it represents a childhood paradise lost, but on the other a springboard for social advancement. This dual perspective reflects, obviously, a clash between "traditional" Puerto Rican values and those promoted by the American formula for success. Already incipient in her early life in Macún, the two cultural patterns between which young Negi is caught are personified by her parents, who struggle, reconcile, flee from and search for each other, causing suffering to those around them:

> Mami and Papi's arguments became unbearable. They screamed at each other, ruptured the night with insults and hate-filled words that echoed in my head for days. I lay in bed crying, *afraid to step into the room where I heard things breaking*, but the next morning there were no mismatched pieces, no chips or fragments, nothing to sweep away. We had breakfast in silence after Papi left for work, *Mami distant as another country*, shrouded by something dark and grievous *that we couldn't break through*. She served us, helped us dress, sent us off to school, and *left for her own job* in a fog of pain that obliterated all hope, all romance. *I tried to disappear within the hallways of Ramón Emeterio Betances School*, where children from happy homes crowded in cheery groups. *The school library became a refuge* from would-be friends, and I sat for hours reading fairy tales, *diving into them* as into a warm pool that washed away the fear, the sadness, the horror of living in a home where there was no love. (204, emphases mine)

The fact that even family struggles are conceived in terms of spatial demarcations suggests a curious continuity between material and metaphoric territories, boundaries, and distances. The fear of stepping into the room in which the parents are fighting is echoed by the fear of crossing the emotional boundary which the child perceives around her mother; the broken pieces which are not there and therefore cannot be removed suggest the same elusiveness and helpless feeling as "Mami distant as another country." The insult-filled night, with things happening on the other side of the forbidden threshold, gives way to a stony silence which closes each family member in a separate, unbreakable, emotional bubble.

The final outcome of this struggle is the mother's, and the daughter's, move from Puerto Rico to New York, while Negi's father decides to stay behind. The mother's resentment against her easy-going, careless partner (who refuses to marry her and is erratic in supporting the family) is related to her rebellion against the traditional role of women in Hispanic culture. Thus even before they emigrate to New York, the mother's search for dignity and independence results in increasingly frequent changes of scene for the family. These earlier ventures out of Macún were traumatic for the daughter, and her first return becomes a ritual regaining of the familiar ground: "The truck creaked to a stop, and I jumped out and ran into our yard, looking from one thing to the next, not knowing if what I was seeing was the same or different from what was there before because it didn't matter; I didn't care. I was home. And I never wanted to leave home again. [I walked] the land from post to post, trying to place myself within its borders" (46). Still, this symbolic repossessing of the land does not save Negi from uprooting.

Not surprisingly, life in New York does not conform to the family's expectations; living in Brooklyn, Negi learns about the danger of being mixed up in ethnic conflicts and has to face the reality of violent crime next door. Geographic closeness to the American culture does not preclude cultural deprivation which begins with the family's insufficient command of English. Living closer to the center, moreover, tends to restrict freedom of movement; North American cultural space proves even less permeable than that of Puerto Rico. Space restrictions, with each minority jealously defending its own territory and more affluent neighborhoods inaccessible, contribute to the feeling of claustrophobia. Walking alone is considered dangerous and playing with the neighborhood children is forbidden. Crossing the street may be treading on somebody else's turf. For Negi, staying at home most of the time is the only option, and for the family, the possibility of even moving out of the neighborhood is very remote. When Negi herself is finally able to transfer from Brooklyn to Manhattan, she achieves a feat comparable to her mother's crossing the ocean between Puerto Rico and New York. Her access to elite education frees her from the Brooklyn "ghetto" and accounts for a dramatic change in her life, a change that is not shared by other members of the family.

* * *

Such change does not happen in Cisneros's *Mango Street*, except in dreams, making this memoir in some ways more "realistic." Whereas Negi's cultural trajectory is far from typical for a first-generation immigrant, a second-generation immigrant could probably report an experience fairly similar to that of Esperanza, the narrator/protagonist of Cisneros's memoir. Born and educated in the United States, Esperanza is handicapped by her Hispanic background and the family's modest financial means. Having previously moved many times, when the family finally settles into the house on Mango Street, it seems their final dwelling as well as the limit of their mobility. The ghetto feeling in Cisneros's narrative is more pronounced than in Santiago's, since Esperanza's entire life is spent on Mango Street. The neighborhood-as-prison becomes a well-founded obsession and an echo of Negi's mobility can be found only in the initial fragment, where Esperanza remembers her past life as a series of different dwellings:

> We didn't always live on Mango Street. Before that we lived on Loomis on the third floor, and before that we lived on Keeler. Before Keeler it was Paulina, and before that I can't remember. But what I remember most is moving a lot. Each time it seemed there'd be more of us. By the time we got to Mango Street we were six—Mama, Papa, Carlos, Kiki, my sister Nenny and me.
>
> The house on Mango Street is ours and we don't have to pay rent to anybody or share the yard with the people downstairs or be careful not to make too much noise and there isn't a landlord banging on the ceiling with a broom.
>
> But even so, it's not the house we'd thought we'd get. (7)

Like Negi's disappointment with New York, the house on Mango Street is an ironic fulfillment of a dream, the family's long-expected permanent dwelling which by no means matches their expectations. As a child, Esperanza becomes painfully aware of the relationship between dwelling and social status, an awareness that initially stems from the shocked reaction of one of the nuns upon seeing the girl's house on Loomis Street. It is the outside world that sets a living standard and marginalizes those below it. Space available to a given ethnic group is restricted and determined by social status and income bracket. *Mango Street*'s poor neighborhood, however, is both a ghetto and an ethnic haven. "All brown all around, we are safe" states the narrator; "But watch us drive into a neighborhood of another color and our knees go shakity-shake and our car windows get rolled up tight and our eyes look straight" (29).

In *Mango Street*, the conception of space is clearly related to the house, which denotes both the disappointing place where one lives and the place to which one hopes to move some day, both confinement and the desire to fly away, both temporary roof over one's head and the mythical space associated with writing, dreaming, expanding, loving and any form of personal fulfilment that provides a way out. The house literally defines a person, as suggested by Esperanza's continual reference to people in terms of "she lives upstairs" (14) or "the lady who owns the big building next door, three apartments front and back" (64). Suggesting that each person is confined within a closed space, the house is a sign of oppression, often imposed on the Hispanic woman, but also symbolizes the American Dream of a better life which includes the notion of a better house. The house thus repeats the pattern set by the neighborhood, being both a safe haven and a prison.

The limits imposed by the actual space and by the oppressive dominant culture are reflected in the outcome of any attempts to transcend them. In one vignette we are told about the little boy who "learned to fly and dropped from the sky like a sugar donut, just like a falling star, and exploded down to earth" (31). Another vignette tells of the girl who loved fun and boys only to end up "happily" in her own house, looking at the manicured ceiling all day and only occasionally beaten by her husband. In the case of Esperanza herself, the delights of a new position are soured because she is too shy to join the others during lunch breaks; despite her efforts to join the "special" schoolmates who are allowed to eat in "the canteen," she is left eating her rice sandwich alone and crying. Lost chances and thwarted attempts to communicate are a recurrent motif in *Mango Street*. Esperanza is unable to make her blind aunt see the pictures in her book, or to share her favorite poem with the half-witted neighbor girl; she cannot keep her friend who prefers being with boys, and she is unable to be nice to an elderly co-worker without being sexually abused. On top of her rejection by the society at large or Mango Street itself, she is doomed to being alone with her dreams since they do not fit the local standards.

Whereas in Santiago's text, Negi's traveling through real spaces inhabited by varying blends of the Puerto Rican and North American cultures is echoed by her resolute upward mobility, in Cisneros's narrative any real movement is prohibited and escape is present only as a desire to escape. Thus while travel between two cultural poles—one related to childhood, home, mother, family, emotional ties, and the other to adult life, society, school, intellectual achievement—is the common element in both these narratives, the way it is realized varies considerably. Negi is determined to succeed whatever the culture in which she is immersed, and her curiosity and ambition seem to produce the right mixture of a willingness to conform and an "onward and upward" drive. Although her success has a price in terms of cultural identity, it is a success nevertheless. Esperanza, in contrast, tends to contemplate rather than argue and dream rather than move. Social mobility in *Mango Street* is more a desire than a fact, and in her essentially static world, it is only the protagonist's mind that travels.

* * *

Cherríe Moraga's *Loving in the War Years* documents a later stage both in the immigrant experience and in the narration of ethnicity: the admission into dominant, privileged culture is offered, partly achieved, and rejected. Although the protagonist, also named Cherríe like the author, is a white-skinned Anglo-Chicana, who is encouraged by her parents to "act white," she still feels alienated among her Anglo schoolmates and finally reaches out for her Hispanic roots as a result of her identification with the radical Latino movement. Unfortunately, for her the home-like cultural space is largely gone and needs, at best, redefining, rediscovering, or even recreating. On various levels, her attempts at cultural bonding seem to be systematically thwarted: she is too white-skinned to be tolerated by the Chicano radical groups, too independent to accept her woman's role in the sexist Chicano family pattern, too well-educated to feel at one with the working class. Her lesbianism is an additional dividing factor, which marginalizes her as a society member and, even more painfully, makes her an outcast from her mother's "brown" family, with which she tries desperately to identify.

Cherríe longs for her ethnic roots since they provide a way of self-definition, but in her case the roots are mostly gone. While for Santiago's Negi there is still a "real" Hispanic cultural space, a time and place that can be remembered, for Moraga's Cherríe there is no such thing. Santiago takes an explicit stand toward her origin in the introduction to the Spanish trans-lation of her memoir: "Here I am considered a Latina or a Hispanic ... I really don't know what it means.... But I do know what it means, for me, to be Puerto Rican. My being Puerto Rican includes my North-American life, my Spanglish.... Both cultures have enriched each other and they have enriched me" (xvii–xviii). For Santiago, being "Puerto Rican" is a matter of course and comes close to meaning simply "I," complete with the relevant cultural adjustments, while "Latina" is a label arbitrarily imposed and devoid of all personal meaning. This perfect balance of two different cultures is evi-dently not accessible to Moraga's Cherríe. For her it is the term "Latina" that is important; an all-embracing administrative label, it provides an instant I.D., saves a marginalized individual from alienation, and is equivalent to tak-ing a political stand.

"Latinas" who identify themselves as such are a group sharing radi-cal views on top of their loosely defined ethnicity. It is therefore significant that "La Güera"—Moraga's autobiographical sketch in *Loving in War*—first appeared in *This Bridge Called my Back*, a volume of texts by radical women of color which amounts to a collective autobiography of sorts, combining politi-cal statements with personal ones. While a testimonial aspect and an attempt to identify oneself through writing are present in Santiago's and Cisneros's narrations as well, those elements come to the fore in Moraga's text—i.e., with a progressive removal from the ethnic roots. Santiago presents her dou-ble identity—North American and Puerto Rican—as naturally integrated into her life; Cisneros's Esperanza both struggles against her ethnic and social background and is conscious of her mission to record it. For Moraga and other contributors to *This Bridge*, the mission and identity become one and come close to being the very reason for their writing. In the case of *Loving in War*, however, the return is to the roots which are not really there but have to be laboriously re-created as a race/gender/class myth.

Most of Moraga's narration involves painful self-examination, only to discover conflicting internal forces, which are also reflected in various stands that the narrator had taken during her lifetime:

> I think of how, even as a feminist lesbian, I have so wanted to ignore my own homophobia, my own hatred of myself for being queer. I have not wanted to admit that my deepest personal sense of myself has not quite "caught up" with my woman-identified politics. . . . I have sometimes taken society's fear and hatred of lesbians to bed with me. . . . For a lesbian trying to survive in a heterosexist society, there is no easy way around these emotions. Similarly, in a white-dominated world, there is little getting around racism and our own internalization of it. It's always there, embodied in someone we least expect to rub up against.
>
> When we do rub up against this person, *there* then is the challenge. *There* then is the opportunity to look at the nightmare within us. But we usually shrink from such a challenge. (57)

In this case, standards imposed by the white society are already part of a bicultural individual's mental makeup. Being a lesbian in Cherríe's case is only an additional complication; the pattern, according to her, is the same with her sexual orientation as with her race. Cultural barriers overcome by Santiago's Negi and felt painfully by Cisneros's Esperanza take the form of a divided mind in Moraga's text. The nature of oppression in the three texts moves from boundaries between cultural spaces (Santiago) through boundaries around the individual (Cisneros) to boundaries within the narrator's psyche (Moraga). The degree of oppression in Moraga's narrative is in some ways even greater than the others, since mobility seems to be confined to her own mind: "I know with my family that even as my writing functioned to separate me from them . . . it has freed me to love them from places in myself that had before been mired in unexpressed pain. Writing has ultimately brought me back to them" (v). Here, the concepts of movement and space acquire purely metaphorical meaning.

In Santiago's narrative, boundaries between cultures are still fluid. North American culture "reaches out" to transform Negi's life in Puerto Rico. Its presence is alternately incongruous (talks on proper nutrition without taking the local food staples into account); intrusive (the emblematic powdered milk which proves indigestible for the child); alluring (clothes sent by a grandmother from New York); and indispensable (effective treatment for Negi's little brother's foot). Various forms of "Americanism" are thus present in Negi's environment even before she is taken to live in New York. In Cisneros's *Mango Street*, cultures keep each other at bay, barricaded in their neighborhoods and wary of each other. In Moraga's *Loving in War*, the culture clash occurs inside the narrator's mind; having been pushed toward the Anglo culture by her family, she tries on her own accord to cling desperately to her mother's Hispanic roots. Increasing closeness to another culture seems to bring about first claustrophobia, then hostility and chaos.

* * *

In each of these three texts, family tends to be a privileged cultural space, a space which contributes decisively to the formation of a Hispanic child. Although in all three works families are presented as both closely knit and numerous, they are also divided by different cultural allegiances. Negi's black father is satisfied with the Puerto Rican way of life and refuses to move to New York, whereas her light-skinned mother is eager to embrace North American culture, which offers more independence and greater comfort. Whereas Negi, the only teenager in the family, has mixed feelings about their New York existence, her youngest brother and sister are instantly captivated by the new environment and their "American" grandmother who lets them spend entire days watching cartoons on TV and eating chocolate bars. The "middle" siblings, who arrive later, are wide-eyed and frightened by the new reality around them. Nevertheless, while differences in approaching culture run right through the family and divide it, the family tends to present a united front against the hardships of their Brooklyn life: "Mami was too proud to ask them for more than they volunteered, and we were all developing the same stubborn pride, behind which our frightened selves hid, pretending everything was all right" (254). The hostility which they encounter contributes to the family's forming a bond of solidarity against the outside world.

Cisneros's narrative similarly tends to stress family ties—Esperanza's instinctive communication with her sister (the house that "looks like Mexico" to both of them), the shared grief when her grandfather dies in Mexico. Still, the rift between Esperanza and her family is present and, even more obviously than in Santiago's text, is related to the traditional Hispanic family model in general and to the woman's role in it in particular. Esperanza is preoccupied with the way that her brothers ignore her in public even though at home they have a lot to say to both their sisters. The problem becomes even more acute in the case of other families that Cisneros describes, which add up to the collective "family portrait" of Mango Street. Women ill-treated by their fathers or partners are the norm rather than exception. Alicia, who studies at night, travels to college during the day and gets up with the "tortilla star" to prepare breakfast for her father, is considered deficient in her compliance with the culture's unwritten rules: a woman's sole duty is to prepare food, and staying up all night and going out during the day is suspicious. The social patterns here do not provide for a woman's education.

Negi's clear-eyed observation of her family members' attitudes and Esperanza's indirect comments on a Hispanic family situation are replaced in Moraga's text by a ruthless analysis of family patterns. In developing a theory of what is wrong with the family scene, Moraga attempts to show how woman's subjugation has to do with the *Malinche* stereotype—a woman considered a traitor to her own nation because of being a white man's lover—and the Chicano man's insecurity versus the white male. In Cherríe's own family, the mother's insistence on the women serving the men goes as far as requiring the daughter to serve drinks to her brother's teenage friends. The fact that next-door Anglo families do not enforce this sister-as-servant pattern is a factor in the girl's rebellion.

In all three narratives, the mother as a guardian and enforcer of cultural patterns figures prominently, but in each the mother is also the promoter of the daughter's ambitions. It is Cherríe's mother who encourages all her children to identify with the white culture and conform to its standards in order to achieve higher social status. Her own marrying an Anglo (she is the only one among her sisters who did) is also an attempt to break the "sacred circle" of her own culture even if she does enforce "decent" Chicano behavior in her family. Ironically, this act of miscegenation seems to turn against her, since the cherished white husband proves to be emotionally empty and sexually inadequate. As for her educated children, at least one of her daughters, Cherríe, declares herself unhappy with the education prescribed by her mother and with her own immersion in the dominant culture.

The mother's unfulfilled ambitions are also present in Cisneros's narrative. Esperanza's mother, who is a gifted singer and who left school only because she "didn't have nice clothes" even if she had brains, urges her daughter to study in order to become independent of men; she is unable to get over her own lost chance to be "somebody" (83–84). In Santiago's narrative, the mother's relationship with her children is more tumultuous; her unfulfilled aspirations make her turn against the children and vent her own frustrations on them. Negi's newly-won complicity with the dominant culture is a source of resentment, as when the mother shouts abuse at her for being late: "You think just because you speak a little English you can do anything you like!" (251). Nevertheless, the mother encourages the children to do well in school and her appreciation for the North American culture is a factor in shaping this attitude: "That's what you have to do in this country. . . . Anyone willing to work hard can get ahead" (246). Negi's command of English when she protests against being sent to a lower grade by the principal of her school in New York evokes the mother's surprise and admiration. Later, the prospect of Negi's winning admittance to the Performing Arts School seems to impress the mother more than the daughter: "'You'll be exposed to a different class of people,' she assured me, and I felt the force of her ambition" (263).

This ambiguous mother's role, encouraging as well as repressive, reflects a double standard: on the one hand, an attempt to become integrated in the dominant, North American culture, which provides access to economic and social privileges, and on the other, an effort to preserve one's own cultural identity by clinging to Hispanic traditions and stereotypes. Holding the family together, the traditional mother's role, also means resisting external cultural influences considered "bad," which are only too quickly assimilated by ambitious and strong-minded girls. At this point, it is obligatory to remember that the authors of the texts are themselves by no means typical. They have distanced themselves from their families' Hispanic culture by having mastered not only the "correct" American English but also the discourses of power within the society. In Moraga's narration, Cherríe's marginalized position is mostly a matter of her own choice; she is well capable of speaking the master's "white, masculine" language.

The dominant culture acquired by the daughters pushes the mothers into a subordinate position. In Santiago's text, the mother's last attempt to strike Negi is motivated by her rage at being dependent on her daughter's command of English, just as Negi's physical resistance on this occasion is another manifestation of her, already apparent, ability to dominate. Esperanza's mother in Cisneros's narration has spent her whole life in the city but "still doesn't know which subway train to take to get downtown" (83) and has to hold fast to her daughter's hand while they wait on the platform. Such dependence takes perhaps the most intimate form in Moraga's narrative, when the mother asks Cherríe for mediation in her failing sexual relationship with her husband, convinced of her daughter's ability to make herself heard.

Moraga's narrator and her specific mission of talking to her father almost in man-to-man fashion is the extreme manifestation of the trend apparent, in varying degrees, in all three texts: women's aspiring to "masculine" roles and positions, which goes against the grain of the Hispanic cultural stereotypes. As Cisneros's narrator fleetingly remarks, the Mexicans "don't like their women strong" (12). The woman's dependent position in Hispanic culture is also an issue that Moraga addresses when she speculates on the reasons for Hispanic men's fear of women's independence and explains it as due to a sub-liminal colonial horror of cultural and sexual aggression, which assumes that the woman's freedom to choose will make her opt for the privileged white man. Without commenting on the validity of this vision, I would like to stress the connection between women's seeking independence and power on the one hand and their insertion in the "aggressive" North American culture on the other. On top of being both dominant and expansive, the U.S. culture expects, and rewards, various forms of aggressive behavior. The adult Negi's playful remark about the school admitting her because of her "chutzpah" and not her talent may be a joke, but as a girl her being "rude" to the principal had won her a real concession on his part, to her mother's uncomprehending awe: "In Puerto Rico if I'd been so pushy, I would have been called *mal educada*," the daughter astutely observes (227). The fact that Negi happens to be right in her arguing on the basis of her intellectual ability is apparently of no con-sequence either in New York or in Puerto Rico.

By Hispanic standards, the women figures in these works step, in various ways, into their men's shoes, although in terms of self-identification they lean heavily toward feminine models. Cherríe's fervent embracing of her Chicana heritage is only one aspect of her passionate bonding with her mother who, ironically, reserves her unconditional love for the family's only son. While the link with the mother, which includes a fascination with the mother's body, is certainly to be expected in a memoir of childhood, Cisneros's Esperanza is particularly vivid when she evokes the smell of her mother's hair in describing sleeping with her parents as a child. In Santiago's narrative, not only are refer-ences to the mother's physical closeness innumerable, but Negi is also jealous of her mother and unhappy about having to share her with the other siblings. Cherríe's lesbian yearning to satisfy her mother sexually, that is to replace the father where he fails, can be regarded as an extension of this mother-centered attitude. Despite the fact that all of these young women are clearly superior to their mothers in terms of intellectual development and cultural assimilation, having acquired more of the state-regulated education, each daughter seems to long for the broken physical union with her mother.

Predictably, in each case the maturing young woman tends to relate her-self to other female figures. Curious and critical, young Negi "tries on" the *jamona* (old maid) pattern and declares that she would rather become *jamona* than be burdened with the grief of her partner's infidelity. Cisneros dedicates *Mango Street* "to the women" and presents a collection of feminine portraits which reveal directly the neighborhood subculture and, indirectly, various aspects of her identity. Like a typical adolescent girl, Esperanza searches for models among women and considers various personalities as she puts on her first, cast-off, high-heeled shoes. As for Moraga, her whole creative enterprise could be summed up as talking to, about, and against women and directed at women's bonding together, ideologically, affectively and sexually.

Being a descendant of a family line of women is also an integral part of each narration. The feminine heritage emerges as the sphere of unfulfilled dreams and ambitions but also as an anchor, cherished and remembered. Cherríe's recurrent remembering of her *abuela* (grandmother), who is both the past personified and the past gone, evokes joy and family reunions as well as sickness and death. Santiago's Negi takes crochet lessons from her paternal grandmother and is struck by a sense of unfulfilled expressiveness: "when Abuela came out from her prayers, we sat by the door, working our needles in, around, up, and out, silently making patterns with thread that might have told a story had either one of us known how to transform our feelings into shape" (99). The crochet work that "might have told a story" is given voice in *Mango Street* in the form of recollections by a female descendant who, according to Cisneros's metaphor, refuses to inherit her great-grandmother's "place by the window" even if she can't help carrying her name. This earlier Esperanza was "a wild horse of a woman, so wild she wouldn't marry until my great-grandfather threw a sack over her head and carried her off" (10). Esperanza, Hope, is an ironic name for a woman whose dreams of independence were never fulfilled.

Being a "woman" is, obviously, just a name, a word which means different things in different cultures. Unlike sex, which is considered by essentialist theories to be related to material, biological facts, gender is uniformly recognized as culture-based and discursively constructed, as Judith Butler amongst others has argued. This also means that the expectations attached to a female figure by various communities imply in fact much more than just patterns of dress and behavior and that the semantic fields of the term itself when employed by different cultures do overlap but do not necessarily coincide. Accordingly, a woman's transition from one culture to another may not only be expected to affect the way she conceives her gender role but may also interfere with gender identification. In the case of Moraga's narrative, Cherríe plainly states that her existence as a self-declared lesbian is possible only within the Anglo, as opposed to Chicano, culture. Determined to be both Chicana and a lesbian, she finds the two denominations incompatible since her original Hispanic culture does not accept lesbians as a group. The only viable way for Cherríe to exist in a society as a lesbian is, therefore, insertion in the Anglo culture, although she considers it alien and hostile for other reasons.

Although Cherríe's case is obviously the most clear-cut one in terms of multi-cultural identity crisis, the same latent incompatibility with cultural stereotypes seeps through the narratives by Santiago and Cisneros. The point at issue is self-definition through what Sylvia Molloy describes as "bonding illusions" (167) encoded in the discourse. Bonding through writing has to do with socially determined personality patterns evoked by the narrative voice, and as Molloy points out, this autobiographic bonding takes the form of reaching out toward the reader, either trying to lure the "real" audience into a vicarious sense of belonging or inscribing a "mirror figure" of the ideal reader into the text. In all three narratives, the bonding strategies are clearly directed toward women, and this feminine (as well as feminist) self-identification becomes more pronounced with progressive removal from ethnic roots. Although bonding with the mother has privileged status and is expressed in terms of affective and physical ties, this particular bond is also slightly condescending because of the daughter's complicity with the dominant culture and its discourses of power. The daughters' education sets them apart and marks them as different from the minority culture's feminine stereotypes.

Signs of this growing realization of being different are scattered throughout the memoirs of childhood in all three of these texts. Negi, for example, excels in school but her skills for domestic work are limited; her younger sister can do housework better and faster. In addition, her propensity for reading romances and daydreaming sets her apart. Cisneros's Esperanza is equally aware of her difference from other girls when she states: "I am an ugly daughter. I am the one nobody comes for" and concludes that she is not going to "grow up tame like the others who lay their necks on the threshold waiting for the ball and chain"; her "quiet war" consists of "leaving the table like a man, without putting back the chair or picking up the plate." The awareness that she does not fit the culture's feminine standards is related to her conscious appropriation of the "masculine" models of behavior. Also, she is fascinated with the model of a "beautiful and cruel" woman: "She is the one who drives the men crazy and laughs them all away. Her power is her own. She will not give it away" (82). Santiago's Negi acts according to similar principles when she engages in a tug-of-war against an abusive exhibitionist who, although excited by the prospect of victimizing her, quickly loses interest when Negi subverts his position of power by acting unfrightened and seductive. Cherríe's confessions in Moraga's narrative include the fact that she had behaved like a man (i.e. aggressively or possessively) in her lesbian relationships, subconsciously dissociating herself from a woman-victim role.

It seems that in a multicultural society which provides, on the one hand, an unacceptable woman-victim/man-aggressor gender pattern and on the other a woman-vamp stereotype, to meander between the aggressive "masculine" behavior and the "beautiful and cruel" self-image is a predictable choice for a girl who refuses to be victimized. The feminine/masculine roles and models and fluid gender identifications in the three narratives add up to one more example of what Debra A. Castillo describes as the "Subjunctive Mood" in multicultural writing, which allows for tuning into the cultural context and for adapting one's expression of self to multiple, and often conflicting, value systems. As she explains, the Subjunctive Mood "responds and corresponds to the need of the bicultural-bilingual writer to encode, in a more than trivial, more than superficial manner, her shifting set of mutually exclusive, equally valid alternate roles" and results in a life "attentive to nuance and capable of taking a cue from context without losing its autonomy" (292). In fact, Castillo's "Subjunctive Mood" is a flexible critical tool which may help describe very different phenomena relevant to multicultural autobiography, ranging from evaluation to motivation and self-positioning.

Particularly applicable here is the culture-as-space model which presupposes viewing culture as permeable and thus open to an infinite variety of possible positions and multicultural combinations. Castillo's emphasis on multiple, shifting roles and attention to the message conveyed by the cultural context can be related to the discursive element which functions in the (multi)cultural space, and which extends through discourse to the text in its literal, linguistic sense. Language is an element of culture and its use reflects an individual's position versus cultures, both in terms of deliberate self-expression (languages, dialects, vocabulary for which an author opts) and in terms of revealing the narrator's culturally-conditioned subconscious.

* * *

Linguistic adjustments are an integral part of bicultural reality and contribute to the "Subjunctive Mood" effect. In her introduction to the Spanish translation of *When I was Puerto Rican*, Santiago explains: "The life presented in this book was lived in Spanish but was initially written in English" (xv). In the memoir itself, Negi's family speak Spanish as a matter of course and their command of English is only rudimentary, while Negi herself learns English mostly from books and is less comfortable with its spoken variety. The girl uses a mixture of Spanish and English to communicate with her Hispanic school friends:

> "*Te preguntó* Mr. Barone, you know, *lo que querías hacer* when you grow up?" I asked.
> "*Si, pero*, I didn't know. *¿Y tu?*"
> "*Yo tampoco.* He said, *que* I like to help people" (258)

Cisneros's protagonist's immersion in the English-speaking community is much greater, although her family and most of her neighbors speak Spanish as well. The Mango Street neighborhood is in fact a linguistic shifting ground where the choice of language depends on the "context": the place, the occasion, the people involved. Speaking English in school is normal and expected, Spanish is reserved for familiar, oral use. In Moraga's narration, the fact that Cherríe was not taught Spanish and learned it only by listening to her family's conversations results in a grudge against her mother. What motivates the Chicana mother to favor English is obviously related to its importance as a tool for social advancement. English is the official language and a cultural weapon of sorts, both for the individual and for the state. When young Negi first hears about her island being a U.S. "colony," she immediately brings up the fact that English is an obligatory subject in Puerto Rican schools. Later, in New York, Negi's consistent effort to learn English is very much related to her ambition not to be pushed to a lower grade in school. Conversely, a protest against foreign culture can take the form of refusing to speak, and learn, its language. In Cisneros's narrative (in a vignette entitled "No Speak English"), a woman called Mamacita barricades herself against the English-speaking world only to be defeated within her own home: a TV commercial, learned and repeated by her baby son, is a reminder that even one's own home and family can't protect a person from intrusion. Ironically, the tune sung by the boy advertises Pepsi, one of North America's cultural symbols.

In these three narratives, while language is presented as an element of culture, and while its acquisition or refusal to acquire it is shown to mark a person's position within culture(s), the ways that varieties of English vs. Spanish are used by the three authors is also revealing. Like the mixture of Spanish and English that Negi uses to speak to her school friends, these three autobiographical works originally featured a bilingual hybrid form. Santiago's narrative is written in English but placed within an elaborate Spanish framework: an introductory poem, a proverb or a song fragment as a heading for each chapter, and frequent recourse to Spanish vocabulary when describing realities particular to the Puerto Rican culture. These untranslatable terms enhance both the impression of "authenticity" and a sense of the "exotic." A glossary of Spanish expressions at the end of this narrative is another reminder that cultures do resist attempts at their adaptation. In Cisneros's *The House on Mango Street*, the dedication "to the women" is immediately repeated in Spanish. Moraga's *Loving in the War Years* is subtitled "*lo que nunca pasó por sus labios*" (things that never passed though the lips), turning the composite title itself into a bilingual hybrid. In each of these texts, the protagonists' references to their parents and grandparents are almost invariably made in Spanish, suggesting that the family context is of this culture. Cisneros's use of Spanish words tends to be sparing; Moraga throws Spanish expressions into her English text seemingly at random, although again her use of Spanish tends to refer to her family and home. A guess about the reason can easily be attempted: Cherríe's public life, to paraphrase Santiago's text, is "lived in English." For Santiago, who is the author of the Spanish translation of her memoir, the memory of life in a Hispanic culture is still too vivid to be restricted to family life and thus Spanish expressions are pervasive even in the English text.

In the case of Santiago and Cisneros, a brief look at the respective translations is also instructive. Cisneros's Spanish text is preceded with standard acknowledgments, among them a word of recognition for the translator for helping to "*llegar a un eficaz compromiso entre las variedades de español habladas por los dos lados*" (arrive at an effective compromise between the varieties of Spanish spoken on either side [xii]). Santiago's introduction to her own translation is more explicit in addressing the problem of linguistic incompatibility; as she explains, Spanish spoken in the United States is not the same as Latin American Spanish, since day-to-day coexistence with English changes both the vocabulary and the syntax, and involves incorporating "adapted" English words to describe local realities (*mapo, panfletos*) and translating word-for-word English expressions (*llamar pa' atrás*). As her text suggests, this "pidginized" variety of Spanish is restricted to familiar, oral use. In view of this, the "effective compromise" for which Cisneros expresses her appreciation equals creating a non-existent variety of written Spanish.

Inventing a hybrid dialect which is in-between the Spanish spoken in Mexico or Puerto Rico (which are, of course, far from uniform in themselves) and "Spanglish," the anglicized U.S. form of Spanish, in order to translate autobiographic writings by the individuals who are themselves in various stages of hybridization is a perfect example of matching goals and means; both the reality recalled and its expressive medium are very much "neither here nor there." Bilingual autobiography seems to stress the unclaimed, uncharted spaces within the continuum of cultural transition, as opposed to well-defined landmarks along it. Santiago refers to frequently having the impression of being in a limbo as a part of her bilingual experience. This "*tiniebla idiomática frustrante*" (frustrating linguistic darkness [xv]) is also the mental space before the words are born. Yet putting things into words is also necessary and requires defining them as points or landmarks rather than assigning them to the fluid space in between. In order to express herself, the writer not only has to use language but also make a decision about what language she is to speak, and must in turn "*confiar*" (trust) both that her words have meaning and that the listener will understand them. For a bilingual, bicultural writer, between the idea and its spontaneous expression, there is a pause in the middle of nowhere.

Castillo's concept of Subjunctive Mood implies hovering between the choices, the ability to conform to whatever is required by the context, and hence the significance of the publication history of these works. Between the original and the translation, obviously, a cultural adjustment had been made. The appreciation of the original, English version, fed the translations, all the way from Cisneros's initial obscure, subsidized publication to a volume translated into Spanish by famous Elena Poniatowska and published by Vintage Books, a division of the market-oriented Random House. In Santiago's case, both the original and the translation resulted from a publisher's offer, being a clear case of the "context" asking for the book. The publication of both versions of Santiago's text, only a year apart, constitutes not only an instant fulfillment of the mainstream publisher's desire for a market success but also (or perhaps in fulfillment of this desire) a document of the author's coming to grips with her bicultural reality. Her memoir, first re-created and converted into an alien medium, English language, later translated into Spanish as the author speaks it today—and which she herself admits is different from the "real" Spanish of her childhood—required a reconstruction of linguistic, as well as factual, realities. Relating the story of a woman who wanted to be "*jíbara*" (a Puerto Rican country girl) as a child and who later wanted to be a North American teenager, only to end up being a "*jíbara norteamericana*" (xviii)—not only a hybrid but a "product" of all past transformations—Santiago's narrative mirrors her life in more ways than one.

The journey between the two cultural poles implies, in each case, an identity crisis and a series of translocations created by the conflicting forces of aspiration and rejection. In Santiago's story, although the narrative voice seems to have reached a certain kind of equilibrium, taking what she considers best for her from both cultures, there is still some bitterness and alienation. Cisneros's narrator ends up being an eyewitness to the reality which she feels tempted to discard and forget. The point of arrival of Moraga's Cherríe is a declared, if not factual, identification with the mother's ethnic heritage at the expense of her father's Anglo culture, which also amounts to rejecting her own efforts toward making a way for herself in the "white" world. The trajectories differ considerably but in the case of each of these three autobiographies the balance is precarious and the individual pays a high price for the adjustment—suggesting in turn that a multicultural environment, such as the one in which actually we all live, is a scene of internal, as well as external, conflict.

WORKS CITED

Butler, Judith. *Gender Trouble: Feminism and the Subversion of Identity*. New York: Routledge, 1990.

Castillo, Debra A. *Talking Back: Toward a Latin American Feminist Literary Criticism*. Ithaca: Cornell UP, 1992.

Cisneros, Sandra. *La casa en Mango Street*. Trans. Elena Poniatowska. New York: Vintage, 1994.

———. *The House on Mango Street*. 1984. Houston: Arte Publico, 1985.

Clifford, James. "Traveling Cultures." *Cultural Studies*. Ed. Lawrence Grossberg, Cary Nelson and Paula Treichner. New York: Routledge, 1992. 96–116.

Flores, Juan. "Cortijo's Revenge: New Mappings of Puerto Rican Culture." *On Edge: The Crisis of Contemporary Latin American Culture*. George Yudice, Jean Franco and Juan Flores. Minneapolis: U of Minnesota P, 1992. 187–206.

García Canclini, Nestor, and Patricia Safa. *Tijuana. La casa de toda la gente*. INAHENAH/ Programa Cultural de Las Fronteras/UAM-Iztapalapa/Conaculta, 1989.

Molloy, Sylvia. *At Face Value: Autobiographical Writing in Spanish America*. Cambridge: Cambridge UP, 1991.

Moraga, Cherríe. *Loving in the War Years. Lo que nunca pasó por sus labios*. Boston: South End, 1983.

———, and Gloria Anzaldúa, eds. *This Bridge Called my Back: Writings by Radical Women of Color*. New York: Kitchen Table, 1983.

Santiago, Esmeralda. *Cuando era puertorriqueña*. Trans. Esmeralda Santiago. New York: Vintage, 1994.

———. *When I was Puerto Rican*. 1993. New York: Vintage, 1994.

LESLIE PETTY

The "Dual"-ing Images of la Malinche and la Virgen de Guadalupe in Cisneros's The House on Mango Street

In "And Some More," a story from Sandra Cisneros's *The House on Mango Street*, two young girls discuss the nature of snow:

> There ain't thirty different kinds of snow, Lucy said. There are two kinds. The clean kind and the dirty kind, clean and dirty. Only two.
> There are a million zillion kinds, says Nenny. No two exactly alike. Only how do you remember which one is which? (35)

At first glance, the girls' conversation appears to be a bit of childish nonsense, and, on a surface level, it is. Read in a broader context, however, Nenny and Lucy's debate highlights a conflict that is at the heart of Cisneros's work: the insistence on culturally defining the world by a rigid set of black/white, good/bad, clean/dirty dualities, versus the reality of individuality, uniqueness, and infinite differentiation. Cisneros comments on the difficulties inherent in this clear-cut dichotomy, and she relates this binary specifically to the Mexican influences in her life and writing:

> Certainly that black–white issue, good–bad, it's very prevalent in my work and in other Latinas. We're raised with a Mexican culture that has two role models: La Malinche y la Virgen de Guadalupe.

From *MELUS* 25, no. 2 (Summer 2000): 119–32. © 2000 by *MELUS*.

And you know that's a hard route to go, one or the other, there's no in-betweens. (Rodríguez-Aranda 65)

According to Cisneros, then, females, like the snow, are not seen in Latino culture as unique individuals but are labeled as either "good" women or "bad" women, as "clean" or "dirty," as "virgins" or "*malinches*."

Cisneros is not the first writer to acknowledge the difficulties in dealing with this duality nor the cultural archetypes upon which it is based. As Luis Leal observes, "the characterization of women throughout Mexican literature has been profoundly influenced by two archetypes present in the Mexican psyche: that of the woman who has kept her virginity and that of the one who has lost it" (227).[1] These archetypes, embodied in the stories of la Malinche, the violated woman, and la Virgen de Guadalupe, the holy Mother, sharply define female roles in Mexican culture based on physical sexuality; however, as historical and mythical figures, these two archetypes take on both political and social significance that also influence perceptions of femininity in the Latin American world.

As the Mexican manifestation of the Virgin Mary, la Virgen de Guadalupe is the religious icon around which Mexican Catholicism centers. Consequently, versions of her historic origin are prevalent throughout the national literature. Although several variations of the story of the Virgin's initial apparitions exist, Stafford Poole identifies the version published in 1649 by the Vicar of Guadalupe, a priest named Luis Laso de la Vega, as the definitive source (26). According to Poole's translation of de la Vega,[2] la Virgen de Guadalupe originally appeared to a converted Indian, Juan Diego, in 1531, on the hill of Tepeyac, identifying herself as "mother of the great true deity God" (27). The Virgin tells Juan Diego that she "ardently wish[es] and greatly desire[s] that they build my temple for me here, where I will reveal . . . all my love, my compassion, my aid, and my protection" (27). Diego immediately proceeds to the bishop in Mexico City, but he is greeted with disbelief. On his second visit, the bishop asks Diego for proof of the apparition. The Virgin sends Diego to the top of the hill, where he gathers "every kind of precious Spanish flower," despite the fact that these flowers are out of season and do not grow on that hill, and the Virgin places them in his cloak (27). When Diego visits the bishop, the bishop's servants try to take some of the blossoms, but they turn into painted flowers. Finally, when Diego sees the bishop and opens his cloak, the flowers fall out, and an imprint of the Virgin is left on the lining of the cloak. The bishop becomes a believer, begs for forgiveness, and erects the shrine to la Virgen de Guadalupe on the hill of Tepeyac.

Several elements of this story are important in the development of the cult of la Virgen de Guadalupe that spread rapidly in Mexico after this apparition. As Octavio Paz observes, "The Virgin is the consolation of the poor, the shield of the weak, the help of the oppressed. In sum, she is the Mother of orphans" (76). In addition to her religious importance, Paz and others recognize the political significance of this nurturing aspect of the Virgin in the formation of a Mexican national identity. First, in *Quetzalcóatl and Guadalupe*, Jaques Lafaye makes the case that la Virgen de Guadalupe is a Christian transformation of Tonantzin, the pagan goddess who was originally worshipped on the hill of Tepeyac (216). This link with Aztec culture is important because it distinguishes the Mexican symbol from its Spanish counterpart, la Virgen de Guadalupe de Estremadura.[3] Therefore, as Leal notes, la Virgen de Guadalupe de Tepeyac is "an Indian symbol," and she is "identified with what is truly Mexican as opposed to what is foreign" (229). She is the "protector of the indigenous" (Leal 229). Appropriately, the image of the Virgin was used on banners promoting independence during the Mexican Revolution, and today she is revered as the "Queen of Hispandidad" (Lafaye 230), giving la Virgen de Guadalupe a political designation in Latin American tradition in addition to her religious significance.

The shrine of La Virgen de Guadalupe is a haven for the indigenous population of Mexico. As the incarnation of the Virgin Mary, Guadalupe represents the passive, pure female force. According to Paz, "Guadalupe is pure receptivity, and the benefits she bestows are of the same order: she consoles, quiets, dries tears, calms passion" (76). As such, she represents the holy, chaste woman, the embodiment of feminine purity as well as the virtues of nurturing and self-sacrifice. Thus, she is venerated in Mexican culture as the proper symbol for womanhood.

The antithesis of the pure maternal image of la Virgen de Guadalupe in the Mexican "dual representation of the mother" (Paz 75) is la Malinche, Cortés's interpreter and mistress during the conquest of Mexico. Like the Virgin, the popular perception of La Malinche is based more on legend than historical accuracy, and is therefore often romanticized and contradictory. Even her name is a source of contention. While Spanish accounts refer to her as "Doña Marina" or "Marina," indigenous Mexicans refer to her as "la Malinche," a name that implies the mythical persona as much as the historical woman. In "Marina/Malinche: Masks and Shadows," Rachel Phillips tries to deflate this myth as much as possible by using the small amount of historical documentation available to reconstruct a more factual account of Marina's life.[4] To begin with, while historians and contemporaries idealize Marina, identifying her as an "Indian Princess," Phillips shows that although she was from an indigenous Mexican tribe, she was far from royalty. Born in Painala, she grew up speaking Nahuatl and was either sold or given away as a child; therefore, she was enslaved by another tribe and moved to Tabasco where she learned to speak Mayan.

As a young woman, she was given to Cortés, along with nineteen other Indian slave women, as gifts from local Indian leaders. When Monteczuma's envoys came to Tabasco to find out information about Cortés, they spoke only Nahuatl while Cortés's Spanish translator spoke only Mayan. Marina was used to provide the missing link by translating the Nahuatl into Mayan. Marina soon learned Spanish and became Cortés's primary translator. Contemporary paintings and accounts show that Marina was near Cortés at all times and that her skill as a translator helped him defeat Monteczuma, furthering the cause of the Spanish conquest in Mexico. In addition to her role as translator, historical writings confirm that Cortés and Marina had a sexual relationship; she gave birth to his son, Martin. The last bit of information available about Marina is that some time after this birth, on an expedition to Honduras, Cortés gave her to one of his captains, Juan Jaramillo, to marry.

Although the historical facts about Marina are scant, the mythic implications of La Malinche in the Mexican psyche are just as complex and powerful as those of la Virgen de Guadalupe. Octavio Paz explains:

> If the Chingada[5] is a representation of the violated Mother, it is appropriate to associate her with the Conquest, which was also a violation, not only in the historical sense, but also in the very flesh of Indian women. The symbol of this violation is doña Malinche, the mistress of Cortés. It is true that she gave herself voluntarily to the conquistador, but he forgot her as soon as her usefulness was over.[6] Doña Marina becomes a figure representing the Indian women who were fascinated, violated, or seduced by the Spaniards. And, as a small boy will not forgive his mother if she abandons him to search for his father, the Mexican people have not forgiven La Malinche for her betrayal. (77)

Paz exposes the ambivalence that Mexicans feel for the la Malinche figure. While he equates her with the violated Mother at the beginning, he accuses her of betrayal at the end. The paradox is that Malinche embodies both the passivity and violation associated with the fallen woman while simultaneously representing the powerful act of treason as one who "betrays the homeland by aiding the enemy" (Leal 227). Both Malinche's betrayal and her violation threaten the Mexican concept of the Male; she either openly challenges his authority or is not saved by his protection. This dual threat makes her the symbol of the female sexuality that is both denigrated and controlled in Mexican society.

The work of a Chicana writer is threatened in a different way by the la Malinche archetype, a way that makes the role model of la Virgen de

Guadalupe just as dangerous. For Cisneros, the dilemma is creating a role model for herself and other Chicanas that is neither limited by this good/bad duality ingrained in Mexican culture, nor too "Anglicized" (Rodríguez-Aranda 65) to adequately represent their experience. When interviewing Cisneros, Pilar E. Rodríguez-Aranda observes, "the in-between is not ours. . . . So if you want to get out of these two roles, you feel you're betraying you're [sic] people" (65). In response to this dilemma, Cisneros claims that she and other Chicana women must learn the art of "revising" themselves by learning to "accept [their] culture, but not without adapting [themselves] as women" (66).

    The House on Mango Street is just such an adaptation. The author "revises" the significance of the Chicana archetypes of la Malinche and la Virgen de Guadalupe through her characterization of females in the book. By recasting these mythical stories from the female perspective, Cisneros shows how artificial and confining these cultural stereotypes are, and through her creation of Esperanza, imagines a protagonist who can embody both the violation associated with la Malinche and the nurturing associated with la Virgen de Guadalupe, all the while rejecting the feminine passivity that is promoted by both role models. Therefore, Esperanza transcends the good/bad dichotomy associated with these archetypes and becomes a new model for Chicana womanhood: an independent, autonomous artist whose house is of the heart, not of the worshiper, nor of the conqueror.

    Maria Elena de Valdés observes that in *The House on Mango Street*, Esperanza is "drawn to the women and girls [in the story] as would-be role models" (59). Not surprisingly, Esperanza does not find many lives that she would like to emulate. Her rejection of these role models stems from each character's close alliance with one of the two Mexican archetypes. Cisneros shows how being culturally defined by either of these two roles makes for an incomplete, frustrated life. While the Virgin Mother is a venerated role model, Cisneros complicates this veneration through her characterization of other maternal figures, most notably, Esperanza's mother and her aunt, Lupe.

    In "Hairs," Cisneros paints an intimate picture of Esperanza's relationship with her mother, whose hair holds "the smell when she makes room for you on her side of the bed still warm with her skin, and you sleep near her" (6). Like the Virgin, Esperanza's mother is a protector, a haven for her daughter during the rain. This idealized memory is marred somewhat in "A Smart Cookie," in which it is clear that Esperanza's mother is very talented, that she can "speak two languages" (90), and "can sing an opera" (90), but that she is not contented with her life. Mother says, "I could've been somebody, you know?" (91). Apparently, being the nurturing, self-sacrificing mother whose hair "smells like bread" is not sufficient to make Esperanza's mother's life complete. Instead of being a dependent female, Esperanza's mother tells her daughter that she has "[g]ot to take care all your own" (91), alluding to a culture that desires virgin-like women, but which does not reward the desired passivity with the care and adoration also reserved for the Virgin; instead, Mother mentions several friends who have fulfilled their roles as mothers but have consequently been left alone. Mother encourages her daughter to reject this self-sacrificing path that Mexican culture sees as noble, like the Virgin, and to choose instead to "study hard" (91) in school in order to prepare herself for independence.

A more forceful rejection of the Virgin archetype is evident in the characterization of Esperanza's aunt, Guadalupe. Like the mythic character for whom she is named, Aunt Lupe is a passive woman in a shrine, but in "Born Bad," this connection is corrupted with images of sickness, stagnation, and helplessness. Unlike Paz's assertion that "through suffering, our women become like our men: invulnerable, impassive and stoic" (30), there is nothing idyllic or positive about Cisneros's portrayal of a suffering woman. Instead of living in a resplendent holy place, Cisneros's Guadalupe lives in a cramped, filthy room with "dirty dishes in the sink" (60), and "ceilings dusty with flies" (60). The passivity of Lupe is the result of a debilitating illness that has caused her bones to go "limp as worms" (58). Guadalupe is chaste[7] like the Virgin, but her lack of sexual activity is not a sign of her moral superiority; it is again caused by her illness and associated with the frustration and longing of "the husband who wanted a wife again" (61).

Aunt Lupe, like Esperanza's mother, does provide a haven of sorts for the young protagonist, even though Esperanza "hate[s] to go there alone" (60). Esperanza says that she likes her aunt because "she listen[s] to every book, every poem I ever read her" (60). Aunt Lupe's home gives Esperanza a safe place to explore her passion for writing and her aspirations as a poet, and this protection is the most positive connection that Cisneros makes between Aunt Lupe and the Virgin. Aunt Lupe encourages Esperanza to "keep writing" because "[i]t will keep [her] free" (61). Ironically, the life that Aunt Lupe encourages Esperanza to follow is not one of passivity and self-sacrifice associated with the Holy Mother; instead Lupe gives Esperanza a push towards independence much like the one that the adolescent girl receives from her own mother. After Aunt Lupe dies, Esperanza begins to "dream the dreams" (61) of pursuing her education and her artistic aspirations.

While the primary female characters associated with the Virgin in *The House on Mango Street* are adult figures, and therefore distant and revered, the females aligned with la Malinche are adolescents, making them more accessible to Esperanza in her search for role models. The images of la Malinche are more widespread in Cisneros's book than those of the Virgin; in fact, images of the violated, abandoned, or enslaved woman are scattered from beginning to end, indicating that the unfortunate reality of Malinche/ Marina's life is a more likely scenario for women in the barrio than that of being worshipped as the ideal mother. Rosa Vargas, a woman with unruly children, "cries every day for the man who left without even leaving a dollar" (29); the abandonment seems to be the reason she is such a distracted, ineffective mother. The husband of another character, Rafaela, locks her "indoors because [he] is afraid [she] will run away since she is too beautiful to look at" (79). In this story, Rafaela, like Malinche, is enslaved because she and her sexuality are viewed as threats that must be contained. Another character, Minerva, who "is only a little bit older than [Esperanza]" (84), has already been abandoned by her husband, who leaves her to raise two children alone. Like Esperanza, Minerva is a poet, but her fate as a "*chingada*" makes her always sad, and her potential as an artist is consumed by her unlucky fate. As a young, frustrated writer, Minerva's story represents the probable path of Esperanza's life if she were to become inscribed in one of the typical roles for Mexican-American women.

While all of these women represent aspects of the Malinche archetype, perhaps the most sustained exploration of that archetype in *The House on Mango Street* can be found in the character of Marin, who, like Aunt Lupe, shares the name of the mythical figure she represents. By reading Marin's story through the lens of the la Malinche archetype, one gains insight into the pitfalls of this culturally proscribed role. In "Louie, His Cousin & His Other Cousin," the description of Marin immediately aligns her with the darker, more sexual side of Chicana femininity; she wears "dark nylons all the time and lots of makeup" (23) and is more worldly than Esperanza and the other girls. Like Malinche, Marin is living with people who are not her family, and in a sense, she is enslaved; she "can't come out—gotta baby-sit with Louie's sisters" (23).

It is Marin's aspirations, however, that most closely align her with Malinche. Marin says that,

> she's going to get a real job downtown, because that's where the best jobs are, since you always get to look beautiful and get to wear nice clothes and can meet someone in the subway who might marry you and take you to live in a big house far away. (26)

Like Malinche, Marin could be perceived as betraying her family and culture. By "getting a job downtown," she is leaving her neighborhood and her duty as babysitter to go where the "better jobs" are, in the more Anglo-oriented downtown area. However, Marin does not see her actions as an act of betrayal; she is hoping for self-improvement. Just as Malinche's position as translator for the powerful Cortés seems logically preferable to being a slave who "kneads bread"[8] for those in her own country, Marin's desire to escape her circumstances are justifiable. But, for Marin, and Malinche, this escape is inextricably tied to dependence on a man. The dream of marriage and a "big house far away" are Marin's sustaining thoughts, but the reality of her focus on sexuality leads to a denigration much like that of Malinche. While Marin believes that "what matters . . . is for the boys to see us and for us to see them" (27), this contact only provides a space for lewd sexual invitations from young men, who "say stupid things like I am in love with those two green apples you call eyes, give them to me why don't you" (27). Finally, Marin, like Malinche, is sent away because "she's too much trouble" (27).

Through these connections, Cisneros's text appropriates the Malinche myth, showing that this type of dependence on men for one's importance and security is what leads to violation and abandonment. The danger of Marin's "waiting for . . . someone to change her life" (27) lies in the possible result of this passivity. Paz comments on this potential for downfall: "This passivity, open to the outside world, causes her to lose her identity: she is the Chingada. She loses her name; she is no one; she disappears into nothingness; she is Nothingness. And yet she is the cruel incarnation of the feminine condition" (77). Cisneros seems to suggest that this "nothingness" is almost inevitable for women in the barrio.

Perhaps no one in *The House on Mango Street* more fully embodies the "cruel incarnation of the feminine condition" than Esperanza's friend, Sally. At different times in the book, Sally can be aligned with both la Malinche and la Virgen de Guadalupe, and her story reveals both the objectification and confinement associated with each archetype. In "Sally," her description, like Marin's, suggests a link with physical sexuality and desirability. She has "eyes like Egypt and nylons the color of smoke" (81), and her hair is "shiny black like raven feathers" (81). Unfortunately, Sally's attractiveness is the source of much unhappiness. Because her looks are perceived as a sign of promiscuity, she is stigmatized in her school; the boys tell stories about her in the coatroom, and she has very few female friends. More damaging, though, is the reaction of her father, who "says to be this beautiful is trouble" (81), and confines Sally to her room. Like la Malinche, Sally's sexuality is doubly threatening to her father's masculinity. Not only could she betray him by being promiscuous, but her beauty might also entice a man to violate her, which would threaten the father's role as protector. This perceived threat causes her father to erupt in horrific displays of violence, hitting his daughter until her "pretty face [is] beaten and black" (92) because "[h]e thinks [she's] going to run away like his sisters who made the family ashamed" (92). Sally's father uses force to deform her and to contain her threatening sexuality.

To get away from her father's abuse, Sally marries a marshmallow sales-man, "young and not ready but married just the same" (101). Sally "says she's in love, but . . . she did it to escape" (101). Sally perceives marriage as the path for leaving behind the "bad girl" image that links her to la Malinche as well as the violence she associates with this connection. As a wife she gains respectability and a propriety of which her culture approves; her sexuality has been contained within the proper confines of marriage, and now she has the potential to recreate the Virgin's role as nurturer and worshipped love.

In "Linoleum Roses," Cisneros again juxtaposes the reality of the female situation with its mythic counterpart. Significantly, the image of the "lino-leum roses on the floor" echoes the story of Juan Diego's flowers that heralded the need for a house of worship for the Virgin. Similarly, Sally's roses are proof of her status as a "good" female. Like the Virgin, Sally gets the home that she wants, but again the house functions more like a prison than a shrine. As Julian Olivares argues, the linoleum roses are a "trope for household con-finement and drudgery, and an ironic treatment of the garden motif, which is associated with freedom and the outdoors" (165). Sally "sits at home because she is afraid to go outside without [her husband's] permission" (102). Her only consolation is looking at the roses and the other "things they own" (102). Sally has not gained much from her crossing from one extreme to the other of the good/bad dichotomy that classifies Chicana women. The house of her husband is just as limiting as the house of her father.

Diane Klein has observed that in the stories that Esperanza tells of women in her barrio, the house functions as a place of confinement (23), and this sense of imprisonment exists whether the female is associated with la Vir-gen de Guadalupe, whose "house" is supposed to be a shrine, or la Malinche, who is enslaved in the metaphorical "house" of Cortés and the Spanish con-querors; Aunt Lupe is just as imprisoned in her home as Marin is in hers. Only Esperanza has a different vision for the house that she wants to inhabit, one that she says is "not a man's house. Not a daddy's" (108), but a "house all my own" (108). Esperanza's quest for a house is crucial in understand-ing how her character transcends the Malinche/Virgen de Guadalupe duality that defines and confines the other females in *The House on Mango Street*. As Valdés states, "the house she seeks is in reality her own person" (58), one that is labeled neither "good" nor "bad" by her society. This radical characterization unfolds in a series of vignettes in which Esperanza is alternately aligned with la Virgen de Guadalupe and la Malinche, finally fusing elements of the two archetypes at the end of the text. While Esperanza retains a connection to these myths, her art becomes the key to her transcendence of them.

The most obvious connection made between Esperanza and either of these archetypes is the protagonist's desire for a house, which resonates with la Virgen de Guadalupe's charge to Juan Diego that "they build my temple for me here" (Poole 27). In "Bums in the Attic," Esperanza, like the Virgin, wants "a house on a hill like the ones with the gardens" (86). Esperanza's hill is connected to the hill of Tepeyac, the location of la Virgen de Guadalupe's shrine, and the reference to the garden is easily associated with the flowers on the hill that the Virgin made grow as a sign of her divinity. Perhaps a more significant connection between the Virgin and Esperanza is Esperanza's plan for her house:

> One day I'll own my own house, but I won't forget who I am or where I came from. Passing bums will ask, Can I come in? I'll offer them the attic, ask them to stay, because I know how it is to be without a house. (87)

Esperanza's promise to take care of the bums is important for two reasons. First, it echoes the Virgin's promises to give "aid and . . . protection" to her followers, and to "hear their weeping . . . and heal all . . . their sufferings, and their sorrows" (Poole 27). Furthermore, Esperanza promises not to forget "where [she] came from," establishing a connection with her society that is reminiscent of the Virgin's position as the "truly Mexican" symbol. While some critics mistakenly interpret Esperanza's desire for a house as a betrayal of her heritage that is more in line with the negative aspects of the la Malinche myth,[9] her attitude toward the "bums" shows that she is not blind to the needs of those in her community, nor will she neglect her responsibility to that community. Although Esperanza's desire for a house is prompted by her desire for security and autonomy, it also encompasses a degree of compassion and nurturing that represents the noblest qualities of the Virgin archetype.

Esperanza's alignment with the Virgin, however, is complicated in the next story, "Beautiful and Cruel." Esperanza says she has "decided not to grow up tame like the others who lay their necks on the threshold waiting for the ball and chain" (88). Instead, she wants to be like the "beautiful and cruel" female in the movies, whose "power is her own" (89). Accordingly, Esperanza has "begun [her] own private war. . . . [she is] the one who leaves the table like a man" (89). In this story, Esperanza rejects the passivity associated with all women in her culture, whether they emulate the Virgin or Malinche. Instead, she imagines herself as Paz's "*mala mujer*," the woman who "comes and goes, . . . looks for men and then leaves them," whose "power is her own" (31). Paz sees this woman as the female equivalent to the Mexican "macho": "hard, impious and independent" (31). Still, this power is based on the mysterious, threatening existence of female sexuality that links Esperanza with la Malinche. While applauding Esperanza's refusal to be passive, the reader senses that if Esperanza relies on being "beautiful and cruel" to achieve her independence, she will follow a self-destructive path that will inscribe her on the "bad" side of Chicana femininity.

Not until "Red Clowns" is the heroine linked with the violation and forced passivity that are at the root of the la Malinche myth. While Esperanza waits for Sally at the carnival, she is raped by a male with a "sour mouth" who keeps repeating "I love you, Spanish girl, I love you" (100). Overcome with emotion while relating the story, Esperanza begs, "Please don't make me tell it all" (100), and then accuses Sally, saying "You're a liar. They all lied" (100). Like Malinche, Esperanza has been violated by someone outside her own culture, indicated by the rapist calling her "Spanish girl," which perhaps suggests that he himself is not Hispanic. The sad irony is that, also like Malinche, Esperanza is not Spanish, but Mexican, and this taunt falsely identifies her with a culture that is not her own.

This story also connects Malinche and Esperanza through a reference to language: Esperanza's saying, "Please don't make me tell it all" demonstrates just how painful recounting the story of one's own violation can be. As Cortés's translator, Malinche, too, was forced to "tell all" of the words that led to the violation of her country, and her son Martin was a nonverbal admission of the personal violation that Malinche herself suffered. Esperanza, like Malinche, understands the harsh reality of being a *chingada*. Maria Herrera-Sobek claims that Esperanza's accusations at the end of the story refer to this harsh reality and are directed at "the community of women who keep the truth [about female sexuality] from the younger generation of women in a conspiracy of silence" (178). This truth, according to the female characterizations in *The House on Mango Street*, is that, whether a woman follows the example of the Virgin, or of la Malinche, being reduced to either side of the good/bad dichotomy entails confinement, sacrifice, and violation.

It is Esperanza's dream for a house, a dream inextricably linked with her poetry, that keeps her from succumbing to her culture's demand that she be identified with one of these archetypes. Olivares interprets Esperanza's house as a "metaphor for the house of storytelling" (168). In such a metaphorical space, Esperanza can create for herself an identity that reconciles the violation and pain that she associates with Mango Street as well as the responsibility she feels to nurture and aid her community, the place in which she "belong[s] but do[es] not belong to" (110). Esperanza imagines:

One day I will pack my bags of books and paper. One day I will say goodbye to Mango. I am too strong for her to keep me here forever. One day I will go away.

> Friends and neighbors will say, What happened to that Espe-
> ranza? Where did she go with all those books and papers? Why
> did she march so far away?
>
> They will not know I have gone away to come back. For the
> ones I left behind. For the ones who cannot out. (110)

Elements of la Malinche and the Virgin are fused in Esperanza's plan. Like Malinche, Esperanza goes off into the world of the "conqueror," the more affluent, anglicized society outside the barrio, and also like Malinche, her motivations will be questioned. However, like the Virgin, Esperanza will return to support, protect, and aid those that need her within the barrio. Esperanza imagines herself as a bridge between these two worlds, and her writing is the tool that helps her create this connection: "I make a story for my life" (109). According to Wendy Kolmar, the "vision at the end of *The House on Mango Street* can only be achieved by the narrative's resistance of boundaries, separations, and dualisms" (246), and the most significant dualism that Esperanza rejects is the division of "good" versus "bad" females in her culture. Esperanza is neither "good" nor "bad"; she encompasses traits of both the Virgin and la Malinche, but she refuses passively to accept the label of either one. Instead, she sees her life, like her dream house, as a space "clean as paper before the poem" (108), with potential for creativity, autonomy, and most importantly, self-definition.

Not surprisingly, this self-definition is also a goal of Sandra Cisneros as a woman, as well as an author. In her essay, "Guadalupe the Sex Goddess: Unearthing the Racy Past of Mexico's Most Famous Virgin," Cisneros relates her own attempt to redefine what it means to be a Chicana artist by merging dichotomous images of the female: "To me, la Virgen de Guadalupe is also Coatlicue, the creative/destructive goddess.... Most days, I too feel like the creative/destructive goddess Coatlicue, especially the days I'm writing ... I am the Coatlicue-Lupe whose square column of body I see in so many Indian women.... I am obsessed with becoming a woman comfortable in her own skin" (46).

NOTES

1. Leal's article traces manifestations of the violated woman and the chaste woman in Mexican literature, dealing with some historical accounts from the 1660s, but focusing on works written between the 1860s and the 1960s. The author labels the various transformations of the stereotypes with terms such as "the available girl-friend" and the "pure sweetheart." Although Leal makes a convincing case for the existence of this duality, he does not develop a theory as to its significance, saying only that "Mexican literature, like all other literatures, reflects the prejudices of the

ages and creates types that are remolded within the limits of these prejudices, most of them derived from the past" (241).

2. My summary of this apparition is based almost exclusively on Poole's translation because it corresponds with and elaborates on the details of the apparition that are found in other sources, such as those given by Leal and Lafaye.

3. Interestingly, Cortés and his troops venerated this Spanish icon (Lafaye 217); perhaps this explains the Mexican insistence on distinction between the two.

4. I use "Marina" consistently in this summary because that is the name Phillips uses.

5. Paz gives a detailed definition of the usage of this term (67–71).

6. Because of her status as a slave, it would seem that Paz's assertion that Marina acted voluntarily is a matter of conjecture.

7. While "chaste" is often used to designate virginity, *The American Heritage College Dictionary* lists "celibacy" as a third definition. While Lupe is obviously not virginal, all signs indicate that she is currently, and permanently, celibate.

8. Phillips's article includes an eyewitness account that claims this was Marina's original job as a slave (103).

9. In her synthesis of the critical reception of *The House on Mango Street*, Valdés criticizes Rodríguez's interpretation that "Cisneros's novel expresses the traditional ideology of the American Dream, a large house in the suburbs and being away from the dirt and dirty of the *barrio* is happiness," and that accuses Esperanza of losing her ethnic identity (289).

Works Cited

Cisneros, Sandra. *The House on Mango Street*. New York: Vintage, 1991.

———. "Guadalupe the Sex Goddess: Unearthing the Racy Past of Mexico's Most Famous Virgin." *Ms.* July–August 1996: 43–46.

Herrera-Sobek, Maria. "The Politics of Rape: Sexual Transgression in Chicana Fiction." *The Americas Review* 15. 3–4 (1987): 171–88.

Klein, Diane. "Coming of Age in Novels by Rudolfo Anaya and Sandra Cisneros." *English Journal* 81.5 (1992): 21–26.

Kolmar, Wendy K. "'Dialectics of Connectedness': Supernatural Elements in Novels by Bambara, Cisneros, Grahn, and Erdrich." *Haunting the House of Fiction: Feminist Perspectives on Ghost Stories by Women*. Ed. Lynette Carpenter and Wendy K. Kolmar. Knoxville: U of Tennessee P, 1991. 236–49.

Lafaye, Jacques. *Quetzalcóatl and Guadalupe*. Chicago: U of Chicago P, 1976.

Leal, Luis. "Female Archetypes in Mexican Literature." *Women in Hispanic Literature: Icons and Fallen Idols*. Ed. Beth Miller. Berkeley: U of California P, 1983. 227–42.

Olivares, Julian. "Sandra Cisneros' *The House on Mango Street* and the Poetics of Space." *The Americas Review* 15. 3–4 (1987): 160–70.

Paz, Octavio. *The Labyrinth of Solitude*. Trans. Lysander Kemp. 1961. London: Penguin, 1967.

Phillips, Rachel. "Marina/Malinche: Masks and Shadows." *Women in Hispanic Literature: Icons and Fallen Idols*. Ed. Beth Miller. Berkeley: U of California P, 1983. 97–114.

Poole, Stafford. *Our Lady of Guadalupe*. Tucson: U of Arizona P, 1995.

Rodríguez, Juan. "*The House on Mango Street*, by Sandra Cisneros." *Austin Chronicle* (August 10, 1984). Cited in Maria Elena de Valdés. "The Critical Reception of Sandra

Cisneros's *The House on Mango Street.*" *Gender, Self and Society.* Ed. Renate von Barde-leben. Frankfurt: Peter Lang, 1993. 287–300.

Rodríguez-Aranda, Pilar E. "On the Solitary Fate of Being Mexican, Female, Wicked and Thirty-three: an Interview with the Writer Sandra Cisneros." *The Americas Review* 18.1 (1990): 64–80.

Valdés, Maria Elena de. "The Critical Reception of Sandra Cisneros' *The House on Mango Street.*" *Gender, Self, and Society.* Ed. Renate von Bardeleben. Frankfurt: Peter Lang, 1993. 287–300.

BETH L. BRUNK

En Otras Voces:
Multiple Voices in Sandra Cisneros'
The House on Mango Street

In *The House on Mango Street*, Sandra Cisneros creates a narrator, twelve-year-old Mexican-American Esperanza Cordero, who is fluent in a variety of voices. In this series of vignettes, Cisneros creates variations between an adolescent and a mature voice, between limited points of view and omniscience, and between a speaking voice and a writing voice. The fluidity of the narrative and the relationships created between the opposing voices make *The House on Mango Street* successful in detailing the people, places, and activities of Mango Street and Esperanza's life while also relaying the social and cultural messages that Cisneros deems significant.

Narrative Techniques: Point of View and Focalization
Linguist Roger Fowler identifies three facets of point of view: the psychological, ideological, and spaciotemporal perspectives. The psychological perspective examines the type and nature of the narrator. The ideological perspective reveals a set of values and beliefs communicated through the language of the text, in other words, the text's interpretation of the world. The spaciotemporal perspective includes the elements of space and time. To be more specific, the spatial perspective involves the distance from which the subject is viewed as well as its focus. Finally, the temporal perspective

From *Hispanófila* 133 (September 2001): 137–50. © 2001 by *Hispanófila*.

involves both the speed by which events progress and whether they proceed in a continuous chain or in isolated segments (*Linguistic Criticism* 127–30).

The psychological aspect of point of view leads Fowler to create four distinctions within narration. Types A and B narration are both internal narration where characters' states of mind, motives, and reactions, that which would be hidden from the common observer in reality, are revealed to the reader. In type A narration, the narrator is inside the events, is a character in the story. This point of view is limited to retrospective and present time. Any anterior narration, or the telling of what will happen, cannot be told with any certainty, but is pure speculation. Type B, however, involves an omniscient narrator, someone who is not a character in the story but has access to some or all characters' internal lives. Types C and D are both external narration where the narrator "constructs . . . the role of an unprivileged observer coming to a partial understanding of the fictional figures in a fragmentary way" (*Linguistics and the Novel* 89–90). In type C, the narrator accepts the privacy of other characters' experiences. Type D narration is an extreme of type C, stressing "the limitations of authorial knowledge, the inaccessibility of the characters' ideologies" (*Linguistic Criticism* 135).

Mieke Bal discriminates between narrator and focalizer, claiming that the terms "narrative situation" and "narrative viewpoint" do not create a clear distinction between "the vision through which the elements are being presented and . . . the identity of the voice that is verbalizing that vision" (100–101). In other words, these terms draw no lines between the point of view from which the story is told and the individual the readers assume to be the source and authority for the words used to tell the story. For various reasons, the focalizer may see, hear, or know some things that have not been witnessed by the narrator, thereby creating a distinction between the one who sees and the one who speaks. Many times, readers assume that the narrator is always the speaker, but Bal points out that this is not necessarily the case. She contends that it is quite important to determine which character focalizes which object or event, partly because focalization is the "most important, the most penetrating and most subtle means of manipulation" (116). The means by which the object or event is presented provides information about both it and the focalizer.

Gérard Genette proposes a three-pronged system for analyzing focalization: zero focalization, internal focalization, and external focalization. Zero focalization features an omniscient narrator who knows more than do the characters. Internal focalization can be further divided into fixed, where everything is relayed by the same person; varied, where there is predominantly one focalizer, but the focalization periodically shifts to other characters; and, multiple, where there are numerous focalizers who may relate the same event from different points of view, such as in epistolary novels. Finally, external focalization produces objective novels in which the reader can only observe actions, no thoughts or feelings are expressed. In this case, the characters know more than the focalizer tells (189–90).

An author will often utilize more than one focalizer or shift the angle of focalization by degrees. We will see that although *The House on Mango Street* is narrated by twelve-year-old Esperanza, or rather that it is her point of view from which the story is told, she is not always the focalizer. Neither are events and people always focalized in the same manner. *The House on Mango Street* is a mixture of Fowler's type A and type B narrative where the story is told through a narrator who reveals to us her own thoughts and feelings but is also occasionally able to express the thoughts and feelings of other characters. This utilizes both fixed internal focalization, where we get the thoughts and feelings of one character, and zero focalization, where we pay heed to an omniscient narrator. This creates an interesting case because zero focalization is not defined by Genette as being grounded in a character in the story; however, we could not argue that *The House on Mango Street* uses varied focalization because the others' internal thoughts are not revealed by the characters who hold them; they pass instead through Esperanza.

Esperanza's Narrative Technique

Adolescent/Mature Voices

In *The House on Mango Street*, the status of the focalizer is never fixed. Although the focalizer is always Esperanza, her angle of seeing is dynamic. Sometimes it is clearly a twelve year old's innocent, juvenile perspective. Other times it is an adolescent's thoughts embedded in a complex adult vocabulary. Still, other times the focalizer is not a twelve year old, but a more mature Esperanza with the experience of Mango Street within but behind her.

There are stories where Esperanza's telling of the situation suits that of a twelve year old. One fitting example is the story "And Some More," in which Esperanza, her sister Nenny, and her two friends, Lucy and Rachel, are discussing the thirty different names Eskimos have for snow and the various names for clouds. However, less than halfway through the story, they resort to name calling. "You know what you are, Esperanza? You are like the Cream of Wheat Cereal. You're like the lumps. Yeah, and you're foot fleas, that's you. Chicken lips.... Cockroach jelly.... Cold *frijoles*" (37). This name calling is indicative of their age. It is something that "children" do when they cannot think of anything else to argue but do not want to lose the linguistic war through silence. They believe that the name calling can hurt another as much as anything else they could say or do; and it does. However, at the end, one says that yelling "your ugly mama's toes" is "stupid." Esperanza writes "Who's stupid? Rachel, Lucy, Esperanza and Nenny" (38). This episode reveals her in-between age. She is not beyond the name calling game, but in the end shows that she is breaking away from this age, possibly maturing more quickly than the others.

Bal claims that perception "is a psychological process, strongly dependent on the position of the perceiving body; a small child sees things in a totally different way from an adult" (100). *The House on Mango Street* would, quite obviously, be different if narrated strictly from a child's or an adult's point of view. If it had been told in a strictly mature voice, as if it happened in the past, the childlike qualities of innocence and confusion would be forfeited. If it was told strictly through a child's point of view, the major insights and driving force of the book would be lost. A special effect is created between the child's innocent report of a situation and the readers' knowing interpretation. In this case, the child does not fully understand what is happening, but the reader does. There are two specific places where Esperanza's innocence is purposely played against the readers' knowledge. The most obvious example is found in "The Earl of Tennessee." Here, Esperanza claims that "the word is that Earl is married and has a wife somewhere." A number of people have seen her, but no one can agree on what this woman looks like. Mama thinks she is a "skinny thing, blond and pale like salamanders that have never seen the sun." The boys believe her to be a tall red-head who "wears tight pink pants and green glasses." Esperanza says that they "can never agree on what she looks like" but they all know that Earl and this woman "walk fast into the apartment, lock the door behind them and never stay long" (71). Esperanza does not understand that the reason why no one can agree on what this wife looks like is because "she" is never the same woman. Her childhood innocence prevents her from understanding that Earl's "wives" are more than likely prostitutes, something that an adult reader can easily infer.

Another instance is not as focused on Esperanza's lack of "adult" knowledge, but her lack of linguistic knowledge to identify tarot cards by name. Instead, she uses what Fowler calls "circumlocutions" to designate that for which she has no name: "blond men on horses and crazy baseball bats with thorns. Golden goblets, sad-looking women dressed in old-fashioned dresses, and roses that cry" (63). "The implication is that [she] has command of only part of [her] society's classification of objects" (*Linguistic Criticism* 134). Esperanza can describe what the images on the cards look like but is not capable of naming them appropriately.

Although there are times when Esperanza's voice is clearly that of a twelve year old and occasionally one that shows the beginnings of maturity, there are other times when the voice is much more mature, the voice of an adult looking back on past experiences. This mature voice appears primarily through the topic or content of the story and through prose of which only an experienced author is capable.

One example of an adult voice is found in "Darius and the Clouds" where Esperanza reflects on her surroundings:

> You can never have too much sky. You can fall asleep and wake up drunk on sky, and sky can keep you safe when you are sad. Here there is too much sadness and not enough sky. Butterflies are few and so are flowers and most things that are beautiful. Still, we take what we can get and make the most of it. (33)

Someone of Esperanza's young age would probably not notice that there is too little sky in the neighborhood and say that she just makes the best of what she has. This sounds like the voice of experience, someone who has been around awhile and knows how to cope pretty well. Another clue that this is a more mature voice is the use of the word "drunk" in "you can fall asleep and wake up drunk on sky." A twelve year old from Esperanza's family is not going to know the feeling of being drunk, especially since Esperanza assumes her mother feels sick because of too many tamales at the baptism reception until "Uncle Nacho says too many this and tilts his thumb to his lips" (47). Even then it is not clear that Esperanza knows what Uncle Nacho means by this gesture.

Another passage in which this mature voice appears through content includes "Mango Says Goodbye Sometimes." Esperanza says, "I put it down on paper and then the ghost does not ache so much. I write it down and Mango says goodbye sometimes. She does not hold me with both arms. She sets me free" (110). Again, this voice is much more mature than the twelve-year-old Esperanza who calls her friends "chicken lips." This is an author who realizes the value of writing down her life, who realizes what her writing will do for the others still living on Mango Street.

Cisneros says in her essay "Do You Know Me?" that she "wanted stories like poems, compact and lyrical and ending with a reverberation" (78). The techniques used to achieve this poetic effect, such as creative similes and metaphors, repetition, intertextuality identified by motifs, and conversations between the stories reveal a more mature voice, the polished style of an experienced author. It is still the viewpoint of twelve-year-old Esperanza but a different focalizer putting the words onto the paper. Esperanza describes Earl's dogs as not walking "like ordinary dogs" but they "leap and somersault like an apostrophe and a comma" (71). In "The Three Sisters" she describes

Lucy and Rachel's dead baby brother as a "little thumb of a human in a box like candy" (104). Her father tells her that her grandmother is dead and then "crumples like a coat and cries" (56). While Esperanza claims to have done some writing of her own, these similes are creative and fresh, a sign of an experienced writer. Additionally, Cisneros employs repetition at the end of stories for a poetic effect. "Those Who Don't" ends with "Yeah. That's how it goes and goes" (28). "Four Skinny Trees" ends with a series of repetitions for emphasis and a feeling of contemplation: "Four who grew despite concrete. Four who reach and do not forget to reach. Four whose only reason is to be and be" (75). With these techniques, Cisneros has created the poetic stories she desires and tells them through the eyes of Esperanza.

Cisneros also uses sentences too complex for a young writer. The best example is from "Sally" where Esperanza asks, "Sally, who taught you to paint your eyes like Cleopatra? And if I roll the little brush with my tongue and chew it to a point and dip it in the muddy cake, the one in the little red box, will you teach me?" Cisneros embeds her own author's voice into Esperanza's question. None of the words are beyond Esperanza, in fact, they are basic vocabulary. However, instead of Esperanza simply saying, "Will you show me how to put on eye liner?" the sentence is quite complex, not because Esperanza does not know how to ask a good question but because of Cisneros' stylistics seeping through Esperanza's voice.

Cisneros' use of intertextuality among the vignettes also signifies the work of an experienced author and not the "journal entries" of a twelve year old. In "Do You Know Me?" Cisneros claims that she intended for a reader to be able to pick up the collection and read any story without necessarily needing to know what came before or what comes after (78). While this kind of reading is entirely possible, the stories are tightly interwoven with motifs repeated throughout and a number of vignettes converse with each other, again, a sign of a skilled storyteller.

One recurring motif is that of a woman confined to the home but leaning out a window or standing in a doorway in a half-attempt to escape. Esperanza's great grandmother, for whom she was named, "looked out the window all her life, the way so many women sit their sadness on an elbow" (11). Rafaela is locked up by her husband on his domino nights and "leans out the window and leans on her elbow and dreams her hair is like Rapunzel's" (79). Marin cannot come out of the house because she is babysitting her cousins, but still "stands in the doorway a lot, all the time singing, clicking her fingers" (23–24). Mamacita "sits all day by the window and plays the Spanish radio show and sings all the homesick songs about her country in a voice that sounds like a seagull" (77). These women are confined to their space, but leaning through an opening allows them some degree of freedom; it allows them to see and to be seen. (Or, in Mamacita's case, to be heard.) Rafaela's dream that she is Rapunzel clearly suggests that she is waiting for someone to rescue her. Sally's new husband sees the potential danger in this "leaning" and "doesn't let her [even] look out the window" (102). This recurring window motif reflects the dismal situation of many women in Esperanza's neighborhood and larger social environment. The time these women spend at the window reflects their dissatisfaction with their confinement and the inability to break free of it on their own.

Another motif is that of shoes. Mamacita appears with tiny feet and "a dozen boxes of satin high heels" (77). Sire ties his girlfriend's shoes because she is unable to do so herself. The mother of "The Family of Little Feet" gives Esperanza and her friends a bag of high-heeled shoes. Through the wearing of these shoes, the girls discover that they "have legs . . . all our own, good to look at, and long" (40). Esperanza even eludes to the nursery rhyme "There Was an Old Woman Who Lived in a Shoe" in the story "There Was an Old Woman Who Had So Many Children She Didn't Know What to Do." However, this mother, Rosa Vargas, does not live in a shoe or "spank them all soundly and send them to bed." Instead she cannot control them, and every one in the neighborhood gives up caring about the kids and stops trying to help their mother. Perhaps Esperanza notices others' shoes and feet because she is preoccupied with her own. In a story dedicated to shoes, "Chanclas," Esperanza is mortified that she must go to her cousin's baptism in her new pink dress, new underclothes, new socks and the "old saddle shoes I wear to school. . . . My feet scuffed and round, the heels all crooked that look dumb with this dress" (47). In "The Monkey Garden" again she mentions looking at her "ugly round shoes" (98). The significance of all these shoes become evident in the last vignette. Here she says that she makes a story "for each step my brown shoe takes. I say, 'And so she trudged up the wooden stairs, her sad brown shoes taking her to the house she never liked'" (109). Even though shoes typically symbolize walking and transportation, most of the observed shoes really get the owners nowhere. Rosa Vargas is confined to her "shoe" full of children and missing a father/husband. Mamacita never ventures down the stairs despite her collection, and the shoes the girls teeter in for one afternoon are thrown away. Esperanza is the only one who ends up using her shoes to walk away from Mango Street—and she hated them for so long.

Another means by which Cisneros employs intertextuality is through the conversations continued between the stories. Esperanza's dying aunt tells her, "You remember to keep writing, Esperanza. You must keep writing. It will keep you free" (61). Later, the three sisters tell her that when she leaves Mango Street she "must remember always to come back . . . for the others. A circle, understand? You will always be Esperanza. You will always be Mango Street.

You can't erase what you know. You can't forget who you are.... You must remember to come back. For the ones who cannot leave as easily as you. You will remember?" (105). Finally, in "Mango Says Goodbye Sometimes" Esperanza has realized that her writing is the way to reveal who she is, where she has come from, what she knows and that this is the way to "come back for the ones [she] left behind. For the ones who cannot out" (110). She then continues with the opening lines of the book, "We didn't always live on Mango Street." The beginning and ending of the book echo each other. She declares at the end that she is going to tell us a story. She starts (or ends), "We didn't always live on Mango Street. Before that it was Loomis on the third floor, and before that we lived on Keeler. Before Keeler it was Paulina" (109). These words perfectly echo the beginning, but then the words then change with the year she has spent on Mango Street. In the opening, she states, "But what I remember most is moving a lot" (3). In the ending, she continues, "But what I remember most is Mango Street, sad red house, the house I belong but do not belong to" (110). She tells us she is going to now begin the story, but has, in effect, just ended it. The circle the three sisters said she must understand is now complete.

Limited/Omniscient Points of View

As one would expect in a description of a neighborhood, Esperanza spends a large amount of time describing the people who live there. Her descriptions indicate that it is the people, their hardships, and their relationships to one another that make this neighborhood a community. Out of the forty-four vignettes included in *The House on Mango Street*, fifteen (only four of which feature men) are descriptions of the people. Plus, a large number of the events Esperanza recounts reveal important and interesting information about others in the neighborhood. In these profiles, Esperanza starts with a brief description of how she knows the characters, where they live, what they look like, some general background and then, very subtly, enters their minds. Shlomith Rimmon-Kenan argues that "speaking/thinking and seeing need not come from the same agent. We need to allow for cases where the narrator undertakes to tell what another person sees or has seen" (72). Esperanza does this quite frequently with an assortment of her neighbors and friends on Mango Street. She easily sneaks in and out of Fowler's types A and B narrative, from a limited point of view where she can only report what she can see and hear to an omniscient point of view where the neighbors' own thoughts and feelings are expressed. This, incidentally, is done only with female characters; Esperanza appears less able to connect with the males in the neighborhood.

In "No Speak English," Esperanza describes the arrival of Mamacita, who "sits all day by the window and plays the Spanish radio shows and sings all the homesick songs about her country in a voice that sounds like a seagull" (77). This description of Mamacita, as well as that of other characters up to this point, is external, that which anyone passing through could observe by looking up to discover from where the strange seagull sounds come. However, the narrative continues:

> Home. Home. Home. Home is a house in a photograph, a pink house, pink as hollyhocks with lots of startled light. The man paints the walls of the apartment pink, but it's not the same you know. She still sighs for her pink house, and then I think she cries. I would. (77)

From the first "Home" to "it's not the same you know," Esperanza has entered into the feelings and thoughts of Mamacita; she has become privileged to know what she feels, what she misses, and what she is thinking. Esperanza also knows what goes on inside the apartment with no indication that she has actually been there. She knows that when Mamacita's baby boy starts to sing the Pepsi song from the commercial on TV—in English—that it "breaks [her] heart forever" (78).

This vignette clearly illustrates the division between Esperanza the character/narrator and Esperanza the focalizer. Esperanza the character has no means of obtaining this information. She says that after Mamacita arrived they "didn't see her" (77). The neighbors only catch a glance of her when she leans out the window and only hear her when she sings or fights with her husband. Esperanza the focalizer, however, is able to get into their apartment painted pink and into Mamacita's heart to know the deep longing she feels for her homeland.

Esperanza does the same in the next story, "Rafaela Who Drinks Coconut and Papaya Juice on Tuesdays." She explains that Rafaela is locked up on Tuesdays because that is the night her husband plays dominoes, and he is afraid that she "will run away since she is too beautiful to look at" (79). Esperanza explains that sometimes Rafaela throws down a dollar so the children will buy her a can of coconut or papaya juice, which is then sent upward via a paper bag and a clothesline. Yet, Esperanza tells us much more than what she can actually see. She says that Rafaela "dreams her hair is Rapunzel's," and she "wishes there were sweeter drinks, not bitter like an empty room, but sweet—sweet like the island, like the dance hall down the street where women much older than her throw green eyes so easily like dice and open homes with keys" (80). The goings-on in this dance hall would not be familiar to Esperanza, especially the minute detail of women throwing eyes like dice. She also reveals Rafaela's feelings with no indication that Rafaela has ever shared them with her. Once again, she taps into this woman's mind and heart to reveal her pain and sorrow.

This technique of jumping into certain neighbors' minds creates a more complete characterization of the neighbors—interestingly—more complete than twelve-year-old Esperanza understands them to be. It gives the reader an added flavor; it deepens the sorrow that so many, particularly women, experience on Mango Street. The only instances when men are shown to express sorrow is when Sally's father has realized he beats her too badly and when Esperanza's paternal grandmother dies. Esperanza never enters the hearts or minds of men. The men of Mango Street are strictly described from a limited point of view as if they do not have feelings or as if these feelings are simply not accessible to Esperanza.

"The Earl of Tennessee," which is filled with only those details that Esperanza can collect by looking and listening, perfectly illustrates the contrast. Any additional information is attributed to what she has been told by Earl. "Earl is a jukebox repairman. He learned his trade in the south he says. He speaks with a Southern accent, smokes cigars and wears a felt hat" (71). Even the rhythm of these choppy sentences, in comparison to the longer more poetic passages describing women, indicate her limited knowledge of the Mango Street men. In fact, she knows so little about him that she does not know that those women he escorts to his apartment are certainly not his wife.

Speaking/Writing Voices

In two vignettes, Esperanza directs her writing toward one specific person. It is here that the writing voice changes to a speaking voice, something that is intended to be said out loud. This makes readers feel as if we have overheard a very private conversation. These two vignettes are examples of uninterrupted free indirect discourse where all that is told is filtered through twelve-year-old Esperanza's interpretation. In both instances, this audience is her friend, Sally, who has "eyes like Egypt and nylons the color of smoke," who also comes to school "with her pretty face all beaten and black" (81, 92). Esperanza is fascinated with Sally. According to Jacqueline Doyle, Sally "represents danger and adventure," something that Esperanza knows little about (17). Esperanza tries to befriend Sally as best she knows how by inviting her to stay with her family when her father beats her too badly and by defending her against the boys who make her kiss them to get her house keys back.

In the first vignette to Sally, entitled "Sally," Esperanza begins with some introductions about Sally's beauty that is beyond her age and her father's worry that "to be this beautiful is trouble" (81). The rest is directed toward Sally—a conversation that Esperanza wishes to have, replete with questions that Sally is only able to answer through her actions. She starts with something superficial, "I like your black coat and those shoes you wear, where did you get them?" (82). Then she becomes more personal, "What do you think about when you close your eyes like that? And why do you always have to go straight home after school?" What comes next is really the most important question: "Sally do you sometimes wish you didn't have to go home?" (82). As the "conversation" progresses, Esperanza comes closer and closer to the heart of Sally's pain, believing that she has somehow understood the world that Sally lives in when she says, "when all you wanted, all you wanted, Sally, was to love and to love and to love and to love, and no one could call that crazy" (83).

After zeroing in on Sally's pain, Esperanza attempts to save her. She wants to take care of her, to try to eliminate the loneliness, sadness, and abuse she believes Sally experiences. However, the saving always fails, though not by Esperanza's lack of trying. In "The Monkey Garden," Esperanza does everything she can to save Sally from the abuse she is about to receive from the boys and is hurt to learn that Sally actually wants to go "behind the old blue pickup to kiss [them] and get her keys back." Even Sally tells her to "go home" (97). When Sally is invited to stay with Esperanza's family to keep her away from her abusive father, he soon comes to beg forgiveness and takes her home only to beat her again just for talking to a boy. There is nothing that Esperanza can do to keep her friend safe.

Although Esperanza has in some way taken responsibility for Sally, Sally does not feel nor do the same for her. The second direct address to Sally in "Red Clowns" shows not the pain that Esperanza believes Sally feels but the pain that Esperanza endures because Sally is not there for her when she is the one who needs saving.

> Sally you lied. It wasn't what you said at all . . . I like to be with you Sally. You're my friend. But that big boy, where did he take you? I waited such a long time . . . but you never came, you never came for me. Sally Sally a hundred times. Why didn't you hear me when I called? . . . Sally, make him stop. Why did you leave me all alone? You're a liar. . . . Sally, you lied, you lied. (99–100)

As Esperanza tells the experience of her sexual assault, possibly even rape (although that word is never used), she balances the injustice done to her by the boy with the injustice she feels Sally has done to her by not saving her and for lying about sex. "It wasn't what you said at all" (99). She is physically hurt by the boy who whispers "I love you Spanish girl" but even more emotionally damaged by Sally (99).

Esperanza is no longer concerned with Sally's feelings, yet she appears to feel some connection to her. Sally is probably the only person alive with whom she could share this experience even though she cannot "tell it all" (100). Others might blame her, but Sally might understand. Sally knows how it feels to be abused. Sadly, though, the reader gets the impression that, again, Esperanza's questions go unanswered. Sally does not care.

In the following story, "Linoleum Roses," we learn that Sally has married a marshmallow salesman "in another state where it's legal to get married before eighth grade" (101). Esperanza knows she likes being married because she gets to buy things, but sometimes her husband gets angry, will not let her talk on the phone, or go outside without permission. Esperanza no longer speaks to Sally directly, nor does she feel any need to save her. After Sally's cold dismissal in "Red Clowns," this story about Sally seems cold and lacking emotion on Esperanza's part.

Another place where a "you" is addressed is the last vignette, "Mango Says Goodbye Sometimes." In the last story, Esperanza focuses on her writing which she has mentioned previously throughout the book. She says, "I like to tell stories. I am going to tell *you* a story about a girl who didn't want to belong" (109, emphasis mine). She directly addresses her audience—whether it be the *mujeres*, the women, to whom the book is dedicated, those who symbolically live on Mango Street, or anyone who has cared to read this account of Esperanza and her experience on Mango Street—who realizes that the story Esperanza believes she is about to tell is the one she has already told. This "you" gives the story direction, a recipient. Just as we realize the vignettes employing free indirect discourse have an intended audience, Esperanza realizes that she has an audience for the entire story she now has to tell/has already told. While it seems that many of the previous stories were told simply for the sake of telling, this direct address to the audience at the end blankets the entire book, gives the entire story meaning. It has been (or will be) told with the intention of someone hearing it.

Conclusions

What do these variations in ways of telling accomplish for Esperanza and her story? They both reflect and enhance the tensions that Cisneros hopes to express of being female, of being a child, of living in the *barrio*, of being something other than white. These tensions work with the plot and the social messages that Cisneros intends to send her audience. In an interview,

Cisneros expresses her frustration with those writers who "make our *barrios* look like Sesame Street." She continues that "poor neighborhoods lose their charm after dark. . . . I was writing about it in the most real sense that I know, as a person walking those neighborhoods with a vagina" (Aranda 69). So, Cisneros' goal is to tell the real story, to show the reality of an Esperanza's life. The shifts in the focalizer, the different ways of telling, help her do just that.

By telling the story through twelve-year-old Esperanza's point of view, Cisneros is empowering someone who is normally not seen as possessing authority in the world—a young, Hispanic female. Esperanza is given a voice. Her entire community is discriminated against both for being a minority (albeit a large one) and for being poor. In addition, we see through the stories Esperanza tells that she is at risk of being discriminated against *within* that community because she is soon to be a woman.

We learn in "My Name" that "in English [her] name means hope" (10). By giving Esperanza this voice, Cisneros is expressing optimism, optimism that the situation can change, that Esperanza and others like her will not have to spend their lives leaning out windows, that she will not have to be "sorry because she couldn't be all the things she wanted to be" like her great grandmother, that she will not succumb to the shame that kept her mother, "a smart cookie then," from continuing with school (11, 91). At the age of twelve, Esperanza dares to rebel against her oppressive world. She "has begun [her] own quiet war." She is the "one who leaves the table like a man, without putting back the chair or picking up the plate" (89). We are certain by the end of the text that through Esperanza's writing she will not inherit her mothers' sadness and shame, and she will help those who cannot physically move beyond their station to break free in their own private way; she will help them to move beyond the windows and doorways. Esperanza will give them all the key that Rafaela wishes she could possess.

The shifts in point of view, from Esperanza's adolescent voice to a mature one, from a limited point of view to omniscience, from writing to speaking help to reveal the social realities of Esperanza's world, where women are locked up by their husbands and confined by their sadness, where little girls are beaten by their fathers because they are too beautiful, where those who do not "belong" to this country are allowed to die without a last name, where twelve year olds are raped and fear that they will be the ones to be blamed. These shifts allow the reader to gaze into more lives than just one and thereby receive a more complete picture of the community of Mango Street. These allow us to see the impact of the realities twelve-year-old Esperanza may not fully realize at this time, but the more mature Esperanza who has been transported beyond Mango Street through her writing has. They show us that Esperanza has a voice she can use to speak out, and although she is taking small steps now, she will likely come to find her strong voice soon.

Interestingly, one voice Esperanza does not speak in, or perhaps is not capable of using, is Spanish, the language which ties the community together. For the most part, the only Spanish she uses is that from others' dialogue. Her father says, "Your *abuelito* is dead. . . . *Está muerto*" (56). Elinita, the witch woman, declares that "*los espíritus*" have joined them (63). Esperanza's mother tells her to "look at my *comadres*" (91). While Esperanza appears to understand what is meant by the Spanish words, she fails to speak the language with a couple exceptions. One is when she and her friends are creating jump rope rhymes. "I want to be Tahiti. Or *merengue*. Or electricity. Or *tembleque!*" (51). Here the words mean little but are simply a part of the rhyming game. Another instance is in regard to Geraldo, no last name, when she says that he was just another "*brazer* who didn't speak English. Just another wetback" (66). This seems to be not her own word, but one she heard others use to describe this man.

Wanting to know when they will return home, Mamacita cries to her husband, "*¿Cuándo, Cuándo, Cuándo?*" He replies, "*¡Ay, Caray!* . . . Speak English. Speak English. Christ" (78). He cries out to her both in anger and frustration to speak English, to assimilate. In effect, that is what Esperanza and her friends have done; they have assimilated as best they can. Although her parents' and others' English is seasoned with Spanish, there is very little of that language in the children's speech. Perhaps this is indicative of passive bilingualism, where the children know and understand the language but do not speak it. However, this limited Spanish could also be a statement from Cisneros. She refuses to let Esperanza speak it. Esperanza's silence in this language is symbolic of her ability to break out of this neighborhood and the larger culture that have the power to oppress her. If she fails to speak the language, she cannot be confined by it.

Works Cited

Aranda, Pilar E. Rodriguez. "On the Solitary Fate of Being Mexican, Female, Wicked and Thirty-Three: An Interview with Writer Sandra Cisneros." *The Americas Review* 18 (1990): 66–80.

Bal, Mieke. *Narratology: Introduction to the Theory of Narrative*. Trans. Christine van Boheemen. Toronto: U of Toronto P, 1985.

Cisneros, Sandra. "Do You Know Me?: I Wrote *The House on Mango Street*." *The Americas Review* 15 (1987): 77–79.

———. *The House on Mango Street*. 1984. New York: Vintage, 1989.

Doyle, Jacqueline. "More Room of Her Own: Sandra Cisneros' *The House on Mango Street*." *MELUS* 19.4 (1994): 5–35.

Fowler, Robert. *Linguistics and the Novel*. London: Methuen & Co. Ltd., 1977.

————. *Linguistic Criticism*. Oxford: Oxford UP, 1986.

Genette, Gérard. *Narrative Discourse: An Essay in Method*. Trans. Jane E. Lewin. Ithaca: Cornell UP, 1980.

Rimmon-Kenan, Shlomith. *Narrative Fiction: Contemporary Poetics*. London: Methuen, 1983.

KELLY WISSMAN

"Writing Will Keep You Free": Allusions to and Recreations of the Fairy Tale Heroine in The House on Mango Street

In describing the forty-four vignettes that comprise *The House on Mango Street*, Sandra Cisneros (1987a) has explained, "I wanted stories like poems, compact and lyrical and ending with a reverberation" (p. 78).[1] Indeed, Cisneros's vignettes contain powerfully poetic and often poignantly haunting images of women: of a young woman entrapped in her home because her husband claims she is "too beautiful to look at"; of women who "sit their sadness on a window" and long for different lives; of a young woman pursuing dreams of higher education amidst fears of "four-legged fur. And fathers." Suggestive of a social reality in which women's lives are often constrained by social mores and male violence, these images are juxtaposed against the narrator's own coming-of-age story. Told through the voice of young Esperanza Cordero who lives in a working-class Latino neighborhood in Chicago, *The House on Mango Street* reverberates not only with images of women acquiescing to or suffering in their social worlds, but also of vibrant women imagining and inventing alternative psychic and physical spaces.

Cisneros has contended that in her work she is writing against the stereotypes of Latinas[2] and is instead working to illuminate what she calls "fierce" women who are strong despite adversity:

From *Children's Literature in Education* 38 (2007): 17–34. © 2006 by Springer Science+Business Media.

I have to say that the traditional role is kind of a myth. I think that
the traditional Mexican woman is a fierce woman. There's a lot of
victimization but we are also fierce. We are very fierce. Our mothers
had been fierce. Our women may be victimized but they are still
very, very fierce and very strong. I really do believe that. (Jussawalla
& Dasenbrock, 1992, p. 300)

With her acute sensitivity to the limitations placed on the women around
her and her relentless struggle to construct new possibilities for herself, Esperanza, as her name suggests, is indeed a figure of hope, a "fierce woman" on a
complex pursuit for personal and community transformation.

As a testimony to the resonant quality of this coming-of-age story,
The House on Mango Street is widely incorporated in settings ranging from
elementary school classrooms (Hammemberg, 2001) to middle school book
clubs (Schaafsma, Tendero, & Tendero, 1999) to graduate level seminars
(Addington, 2001) 20 years after its initial publication. Although not written specifically for audiences of children or adolescents, the widespread use
of this novel is suggestive of its broad appeal and its continuing impact on
generations of readers (Klein, 1992; O'Malley, 1997). Given that the text
rewards close readings of both its aesthetic qualities as well as its embedded
social commentary, the novel also has great potential for continuing to enrich
emerging frameworks for feminist literary criticism and for providing feminist teachers of literature with a novel that can promote reflection on gender
issues and social injustice. A compelling feature of this text, for example, is
that in tracing Esperanza's confrontations with and challenges to the roles
of women in her community, Cisneros employs allusions to classic Euro-
pean fairy tales. Cisneros utilizes and recasts these tales in a way that reveals
their troubled legacy in the lives of many women on Mango Street, drawing
attention to how they transmit the mythologies of heterosexual romance that
obscure women's economic, physical, and psychic vulnerability in patriarchal
contexts. Spencer (1997), for instance, has referred to some of the stories
in *The House on Mango Street* as "revisionist fairy tales," writing, "Cisneros's
version of these fables reveal the true-to-life consequences for women who
are socialized to live their lives waiting for the happy ending" (p. 278). Close
readings of allusions to fairy tales in the novel, coupled with an analysis of
the social construction of gender, can provide opportunities for students and
teachers to consider how these tales function as powerful and seductive cur-
rency in the lives of the women in the novel.

In this article, I explore in further depth the images of fairy tale heroines and fairy tale narratives in *The House on Mango Street*. I do this with the
intent, however, to consider not only how Cisneros renders the "true-to-life

consequences" of these mythologies in women's everyday lives, but also how Cisneros renders possibilities for a re-writing of the scripts of passivity, victimization, and powerlessness embedded in the popularized versions of these tales that circulate heavily in popular culture and in the public imagination. I suggest that through Esperanza the outlines appear of feminist heroine who does not simply rebel against tradition, but who also creates new possibilities for herself and her community. The significance of this analysis rests in the recognition that the literature and lives of women of color are often marginalized within discussions of feminist literary criticism in children's and young adult literature. While a number of recent articles attest to the development and refinement of feminist literary theory and feature re-readings of fairy tales in order to do so (Joosen, 2005; Marshall, 2004; Parsons, 2004), fewer articles have incorporated discussions of literature featuring heroines from diverse cultural backgrounds or theoretical frameworks attuned to racial and ethnic diversity. I suggest that incorporating culturally attuned theoretical models, like Latina feminism, and discussion of a diversity of ways that gender is enacted and shaped by race, culture, and ethnicity, can enrich the field of feminist literary criticism and may also help facilitate the continuing creation and diversification of feminist heroines within children's and young adult literature.

Before considering specific images of fairy tale heroines in *The House on Mango Street*, I first outline feminist critiques of traditional fairy tales. My intent in laying this foundation is not to cover this growing body of knowledge in an exhaustive manner, but to introduce a set of concepts, images, and critiques that will inform the discussion of allusions to fairy tale heroines in Cisneros's work. This discussion is animated by a desire to show how Cisneros's novel resonates with, and even enacts, the critiques lodged at fairy tales by revealing the problematic ways in which these tales often elide social realities and put forward limiting constructions of women. Importantly, this discussion is also meant to provide a framework through which to consider how Cisneros re-imagines a feminist heroine through Esperanza. Because Cisneros refers to fairy tales and to feminism when describing her own life, I also draw upon her autobiographical writing and interviews to forward my analysis. By incorporating multiple theorizations of Latina feminism at the end of the article, I conclude with a final articulation of how Esperanza can be read as a feminist heroine by harnessing the power of writing as an act of personal freedom and social transformation.

Feminist Critiques of Fairy Tales and *The House on Mango Street*

For many of the women in *The House on Mango Street*, fairy tale promises of romance and happiness hover, swirl, and linger over their lives. Cisneros, however, juxtaposes these airy dreams against concrete social realities in which they become severely complicated. In considering these allusions, Cisneros's novel can be read as embodying many of the feminist critiques of fairy tales as put forward by a proliferation of literary critics beginning in the early 1970s. Feminist critiques of fairy tales expose how the tales promote damaging images of women and expose how the tales obscure the social reality of women's lives after courtship and marriage. Lieberman's (1972) analysis of Andrew Lang's popular collection of fairy tales, *The Blue Fairy Book*, provided one of the earliest and most extensive critiques of the representation of women in these tales. Lieberman stresses that these tales serve to "acculturate" children to proscribed gender roles by making a "major contribution in forming the sexual role concept of children, and in suggesting to them the limitations that are imposed by sex upon a person's chances of success in various endeavors" (p. 384).[3] Lieberman argues that for women in these fairy tales, "success" is won through allegiance to following a code of behavior that is highly rigid, highly intolerant of imperfection, and highly dependent on physical beauty and passivity. She states quite plainly that, "The system of rewards in fairy tales, then, equates these three factors: being beautiful, being chosen, getting rich" (p. 387).

The salience of beauty is noted often in feminist critiques of fairy tales due to the pervasive use of this descriptor for heroines as their primary attribute around which the plot proceeds. Lieberman contends that the "beauty contest is a constant and primary device in many of the stories" (p. 385), while Moore (1975) asserts to be proclaimed beautiful in a fairy tale lends women their "highest value" (quoted in Zipes, 1986, p. 6). Lieberman (1972) and Moore (1975) both further contend that women's beauty is equated with such character traits as goodness, morality, and sensitivity. While Stone (1975), Rowe (1986), Yolen (1977), and Spencer (1997) also note these connections between beauty and virtue, they also point out how the tales promote another link: that of beauty with passivity. In Stone's (1975) and Yolen's (1977) analyses of the fairy tale heroines popularized by Charles Perrault, the Grimm Brothers, and Walt Disney, both critics trace how the heroines in these tales progressively lose the initiative, spirit, and active natures that characterized these same heroines in versions drawn from earlier centuries and non-European countries. Stone (1975) contends that in Disney's hands these once vital and resilient heroines become "not only passive and pretty, but also unusually patient, obedient, industrious, and quiet" (p. 44).

The pervasiveness of passive heroines in popular versions of fairy tales relates directly to Lieberman's second factor of success in fairy tales, that of "being chosen" for heterosexual romance and marriage. Lieberman writes:

So many of the heroines of fairy stories, including the well-known Rapunzel, are locked up in towers, locked into a magic sleep, imprisoned by giants, or otherwise enslaved, and waiting to be rescued by a passing prince, that the helpless, imprisoned maiden is the quintessential heroine of the fairy tale. (p. 389)

As suggested here, feminist critics have further noted that heroines are actually rewarded for their endurance of suffering, ill-treatment, and loneliness by "being chosen" for marriage (Moore, 1975; Stone, 1975). As Lieberman states, "The girl in tears is invariably the heroine" (p. 390). Adolescence, as Rowe (1986) and Stone (1975) contend, serves as the defining period of life for most heroines who wait and suffer until their luck changes. Rowe (1986) has further argued that it is often female characters in the form of stepmothers, witches, and fairies who serve as primary impediments to any form of self-determination among heroines. "Evil" stepmothers and witches often imprison, physically abuse, or demand labor from heroines. Female characters such as fairy godmothers who are not "evil" serve to guide their young charges and to create conditions where they can be in the best position to be "chosen." As Lieberman contends, however, even these fairies underscore that passivity is a rewarded virtue and that power is an undesirable trait for women. She writes:

[Fairy godmothers] are not human beings, they are asexual, and many of them are old. They are not examples of powerful women with whom children can identify as role models; they do not provide meaningful alternatives to the stereotype of the younger, passive heroine. (p. 391)

If to be beautiful leads to being chosen, then it is most often the case that to be chosen, particularly for marriage, leads to Lieberman's final tier of success for the fairy tale heroine, "getting rich." Zipes (1986) argues that traditional fairy tales "implicitly yoke sexual awakening and surrender to the prince with social elevation and materialistic gain" (p. 217). Rowe (1986) also suggests a causal link between the heroine's embrace of "conventional female virtues" and "getting rich." She writes:

Because the heroine adopts conventional female virtues, that is, patience, sacrifice, and dependency, and *because* she submits to patriarchal needs, she consequently receives both the prince and a guarantee of social and financial security through marriage. (emphasis in original, p. 217)

Lieberman (1972) makes a key point in noting that eighteen of the thirty stories in *The Blue Fairy Book* come to abrupt conclusions after the heroine has married. Very few images of married life therefore populate fairy tales, enabling the "happily-ever-after" conclusion to locate courtship and weddings as the defining moments in a woman's life.

To a great degree, the three-tiered "system of rewards" that Lieberman identifies in fairy tales is ever-present in the dream lives of many women in *The House on Mango Street*; however, as I explore below, this system becomes severely challenged, and often not realized, in their actual lives.

Being Beautiful

In *The House on Mango Street*, physical beauty does not position women as inevitable protagonists who will be rewarded with marriage and economic security. Rather, to be beautiful often engenders danger, confinement, and sexual assault. In Cisneros's powerful re-writing of the Cinderella story in "The Family of Little Feet," for example, physical beauty is linked to young girls' awakening (hetero)sexuality, but this awakening is, in effect, a very rude awakening. In the beginning of the story, Esperanza and her friends Lucy and Rachel are given multiple pairs of second-hand shoes by their neighbors. They playfully exclaim, "Hurray! Today we are Cinderella because our feet fit exactly" (p. 40). Only on the verge of adolescence, they still wear girls' "grey socks" and sport "satin scars where scabs were picked"; yet, in the high heels, they discover their legs are "all our own, good to look at, and long" (p. 40). The girls spend a delightful time learning how to walk in these "magic high heels," with Rachel providing instruction on how to "strut," cross and uncross their legs, and walk so "that the shoes talk back to you with every step" (p. 40).

The real "magic" of these shoes, however, results from the effects they have on the men around them, on how the girls' increased vulnerability due to shoes that make them "tee-totter" plays into the societal constructs of women's sexuality: "Lucy, Rachel, me tee-tottering like so. Down to the corner where the men can't take their eyes off us" (p. 40). Suddenly, their legs are no longer "all their own." Instead, under these gazes, their legs and the girls themselves become offerings or gifts to others. In the midst of this attention, for example, the girls think, "We must be Christmas" (p. 40). Their delight quickly becomes shaded by fear and confusion as they encounter individuals who convey a variety of messages to them about women's beauty. The grocer scolds them, warning, "Them are dangerous. You girls too young to be wearing shoes like that. Take them shoes off before I call the cops" (p. 41). The grocer underscores how women's sexuality is often regulated, not just by ordinary men in the community, but also by law enforcement (Saldívar, 1990). Next, a boy rides by the girls on a bicycle, surprises them by calling them "ladies," and pleads, "lead me to heaven" (p. 41). This boy underscores again how women's bodies and their sexuality are often constructed as tools for men's gratification. Finally, the girls are approached by a "bum man" who makes Rachel "dizzy" with his compliments and offers her a dollar if she will kiss him. Here, women's beauty is a blatant commodity. With mounting fear, the girls then run, "fast and far away, our high heels shoes taking us all the way" back to Mango Street. "We are tired of being beautiful," (p. 42) they admit, and they hide the shoes under Lucy's porch.

In this Cinderella story, the "magic high heels" have lost their magic. They are not the magical glass slippers of the popularized Cinderella story, promising the heroines a pathway to a handsome prince and marriage. Rather than transporting the heroines to a festive ball filled with prospective mates, these shoes instead transport them to streets filled with desirous and lecherous men. Unlike the Cinderella popularized by Disney, who waits in expectation of the prince who will return the glass slipper and thus recapture the magic and promise of the royal ball, Esperanza, Lucy, and Rachel hide their shoes and thus the memory of their frightening exposure to male control and desire. The girls' joy in their emerging sexuality and its intoxicating effects on themselves and the men around them becomes quickly and quite dramatically undercut by the day's events. The myth of beauty as a steppingstone to happiness is troubled, if not shattered, in this vignette.

For Sally, a girl with "eyes like Egypt and nylons the color of smoke" (p. 81), beauty at first appears to be an attribute that will indeed enable her to escape her troubled home life and promise her a happy future, much like many fairy tale heroines. Sally is described as beautiful, yet this beauty is again linked to sexuality and endangerment. To the boys at school, Sally's beauty, her hair "shiny black like raven feathers" (p. 81), and her playful laughter, inspire attention of a sexual nature. Beyond the watchful eyes of adults, under the cover of night, and behind abandoned cars in the vignette, "Monkey Garden," a group of boys convince Sally to kiss each one of them in exchange for giving her back her car keys which they have confiscated. Beauty here is linked to sexual coercion in a setting far from the pastoral countryside of many fairy tales; there are no promises of marriage here, only promises of giving back to Sally what is already hers.

Sally's beauty is also linked to her confinement in her father's home. Her father contends that, "to be this beautiful is trouble" (p. 81) and orders her to come home directly from school everyday, often not to emerge until the following morning. Beauty here is dangerous and provocative; it requires regulation by fathers. When Sally disobeys her father and he sees her talking with a boy, "the next day she doesn't come to school. And the next" because her father "just went crazy, he just forgot he was her father between the buckle and the belt" (p. 93). Beauty is linked to male control of female bodies and breeds forms of violence to maintain that control. Although Sally's beauty is a factor that enables her to marry young, just like many fairy tale heroines, this marriage is less about the fulfillment of her own happiness, but rather an escape from her father's physical abuse. Here, too, however, Sally's beauty imprisons her; in her new home, she is not allowed to talk on the phone or even look out the window. Her "happily-ever-after" has not arrived. In a striking internalization of the lessons she's learned about the dangerous nature of beauty and the control of men in both her father's and husband's houses, Sally is afraid to go outside without her husband's permission.[4]

Being Chosen

As noted above, Lieberman has argued that the "helpless, imprisoned maiden is the quintessential heroine of the fairy tale" (p. 389). While most heroines of fairy tales are eventually rewarded for their confinement and isolation, for the women of *The House on Mango Street*, these rewards are rarely realized. Nonetheless, the mythology of waiting for a better life to supersede the limitations of present situations of poverty, violence, and constriction to home is ever-present. Cisneros carefully draws the character of Marin in a way that suggests the seductive dream of waiting for a man to serve as her escape route. In "Louie, His Cousin, & His Other Cousin," Cisneros deftly links both Marin's isolation and her resultant faith in love to overcome it:

> She can't come out—gotta baby-sit with Louie's sisters—but she stands in the doorway a lot, singing, clicking her fingers, the same song:
>
> *Apples, peaches, pumpkin pah-ay,*
> *You're in love and so am ah-ay.* (pp. 23–24)

Marin's duties as a baby-sitter for her cousins, her status as a young woman from Puerto Rico under the care of relatives, and her emergent sexuality keep her bound to the home and to the ideal of rescue through love, which she recounts again and again through her singing of the "same song."

In the next vignette entitled "Marin," Cisneros again describes the dreams of romance that are bred through confinement. Esperanza tells us, "We never see Marin until her aunt comes home from work, and even then she can only stay out in front" (p. 27). Every night Marin stands outside, despite the cold and despite the boredom, in order to be seen. Cisneros accentuates Marin's desire to project herself as a sexual being by describing her wearing of "dark nylons" and "lots of make-up" (p. 23). As Esperanza recounts:

> What matters, Marin says, is for the boys to see us and for us to see them. And since Marin's skirts are shorter and since her eyes are pretty, and since Marin is already older than us in many ways, the boys who do pass by say stupid things like I am in love with those two green apples you call eyes, give them to me why don't you. And Marin just looks at them without even blinking and is not afraid. (p. 27)

Despite Marin's explicit use of her sexuality and her brave responses to male attention, there is a remarkable innocence and poignancy in Marin's waiting and wanting to be noticed. Her waiting, standing, and posing are embedded in her dreams for a different, as yet unrealized, life. Cisneros's writing seems to be at its most lyrical and moving when she writes, "Marin, under the streetlight, dancing by herself, is singing the same song somewhere. I know. Is waiting for a car to stop, a star to fall, someone to change her life" (p. 27). Here, Cisneros projects Marin's loneliness unto a future date, still dancing by herself, still singing her same song. These words ring of tragedy, of unrealized dreams still longing to be fulfilled. Whether it is through a car stopping, a magical star falling, or a possible prince passing by, Marin holds steadfast to her belief that she might meet someone—on the street, in the subway, in a "real job downtown—who might marry you and take you to live in a big house far away" (p. 26). Marin's yearning for romance, tied as it is to the concrete conditions of her life and her wishes for a future of economic security, retains a dream-like fragility and the rarity of a falling star. She does not appear in the text again, leaving us to wonder if she is indeed still longing for the elusive opportunity to be chosen.

Cisneros further complicates the archetype of fairy tale heroine waiting to be chosen through her description of Esperanza's great-grandmother. In the space of only a few sentences, we learn that Esperanza's great-grandmother was once a "wild horse of a woman" who refused to marry until Esperanza's great-grandfather "threw a sack over her head and carried her off" (p. 11). In a striking passage that upsets the romanticism inherent in the "being chosen" mythology, her great-grandmother is not simply chosen, but literally *captured*. Cisneros underscores Esperanza's great-grandfather's sense of entitlement to claiming this woman "as if she were a fancy chandelier," (p. 11), as if she were a piece of property to be used for his own enjoyment and utility. Esperanza's great-grandmother then lost her wildness and her verve, and never forgiving him, "she looked out the window her whole life" (p. 11). Esperanza's own mother is wracked with feelings of missed opportunities resulting from marriage as well. She can sing operas with "velvety lungs powerful as morning glories," (p. 90), speak in two languages, and fix televisions, but she sighs while cooking and wishes for a life where she could maneuver with independence. She wistfully recalls that she was once a "smart cookie" (p. 91). For both Esperanza's great-grandmother and mother, then, being chosen for marriage shuts down possibilities, talents, and vitality instead of opening up new worlds. In effect, marriage returns them to the suffering, isolation, and wistful hopes of the adolescent heroines in classic fairy tales.

Getting Rich

In *The House on Mango Street*, Lieberman's third tier of success for fairy tale heroines, "getting rich," and therefore living "happily ever after" through marriage is problematized to an even larger degree than the mythos surrounding being beautiful and being chosen. Images abound throughout the text of married women who are beleaguered by children, poverty, isolation, or husbands who are abusive or absent. Often, the women are suffering in situations where they must contend with more than one of these debilitating life issues. Rosa Vargas's "happily ever after," for instance, consists of the interrelated and crushing realities of having too many children, not enough money, and a husband who has deserted her. In the vignette entitled "There Was an Old Woman She Had So Many Children She Didn't Know What to Do," Cisneros imbues the Mother Goose rhyme with a distinct poignancy in Rosa's context:

> Rosa Vargas' kids are too many and too much. It's not her fault, you know, except she is their mother and only one against so many.
>
> They are bad those Vargases, and how can they help it with only one mother who is tired all the time from buttoning and bottling and babying and cries every day for the man who left without even leaving a dollar for bologna or a note explaining how come. (p. 29)

Although Minerva's husband also disappears after the wedding and after children, he intermittently returns, often violently. A victim of recurring domestic abuse, Minerva struggles for a sense of control in her life, a control that she can never quite keep due to her husband's violence, his promises to change, and her love for him. Cisneros writes:

> One day she is through and lets him know enough is enough. Out the door he goes. Clothes, records, shoes. Out the window and the door locked. But that night he comes back and sends a big rock

through the window. Then he is sorry and she opens the door again. Same story. (p. 85)

Cisneros's use of the phrase, "same story," is striking here because it poetically and sparingly captures the plight of many survivors of domestic violence whose lives become crippled by on-going cycles of abuse, broken promises, and pleas for forgiveness. It is also resonant with Sally's post-nuptial life in which the abuse she endured from her father becomes the "same story" of abuse in her marriage.

Like heroines of traditional fairy tales, the women in *The House on Mango Street* often invest the prospect of marriage with hopes for a happy and fulfilling life; however, the women of Mango Street continue to long for different lives even after they are married. As explored above, Esperanza's great-grandmother and mother contend with lingering disappointments resulting from marriage. Ruthie, too, lost opportunities due to her decision to marry and to move away to a "pretty house outside the city" (p. 69). Her fairy tale becomes even further eroded when her husband leaves her and she is forced to return to Mango Street and live with her mother. Ruthie waits and retains hope despite her circumstances. As Cisneros writes, " . . . but she says she's just visiting and next weekend her husband's going to take her home. But the weekends come and go and Ruthie stays" (p. 68).

After her marriage, Rafaela, who "dreams her hair is like Rapunzel's" (p. 79), remains confined to her home because of her beauty and continues to dream of rescue and a sweeter life. Because this vignette contains some of the novel's most striking and troubling imagery of the fairy tale mythology, it is illuminating to quote at length:

And then Rafaela, who is still young but getting old from leaning out the window so much, gets locked indoors because her husband is afraid Rafaela will run away since she is too beautiful to look at.

Rafaela leans out the window and leans on her elbow and dreams her hair is like Rapunzel's. On the corner there is music from the bar, and Rafaela wishes she could go there and dance before she gets old . . .

Rafaela who drinks and drinks coconut and papaya juice on Tuesdays and wishes there were sweeter drinks, not bitter like an empty room, but sweet—sweet like the island, like the dance hall down the street where women much older than her throw green eyes easily like dice and open homes with keys. And always there is someone offering sweeter drinks, someone promising to keep them on a silver string. (pp. 79–80)

Within this vignette, Rafaela's longing is palpable, perhaps made even more so by our knowledge that although she has already been rescued once by a "prince," she is now re-confined in the bitterness of an empty room that is infused with music from the dance hall and Rafaela's own dreams for the freedom to dance, to open her home with her own key, to drink sweeter drinks. There is an almost unbearable sadness here, a sadness made even more profound by the final lines which suggest there will always be a longing and a desire for the fulfillment of elusive promises.

As evidenced throughout this analysis, Cisneros artfully employs allusions to fairy tales in these vignettes. This imagery serves both to reveal women's faith in fairy tale promises and to reveal how these promises are often shattered in the lives of the women on Mango Street. Because of Cisneros's often exquisite use of poetic language, her fierce indictments of the victimization of women in patriarchal structures and her powerful portrayals of the women's resounding, yet muffled, longing for different lives may not be obvious on a first or even second read of the text. In "The Red Clowns," however, Cisneros provides perhaps the most graphic reference to women's victimization and the most chilling indictment of the romantic dream. In this excerpt from the vignette, Esperanza's severe pain and disillusionment are revealed in her railing against the lies of romance promulgated by her girlfriend Sally, books, magazines, and the wider culture:

> Why did you leave me all alone? I waited my whole life. You're a liar. They all lied. All the books and the magazines, everything that told it wrong. Only his dirty fingernails against my skin, only his sour smell again. The moon that watched. The tilt-a-whirl. The red clowns laughing their thick-tongue laugh.
>
> Then the colors began to whirl. Sky tipped. Their high black gym shoes ran. Sally, you lied, you lied. He wouldn't let me go. He said I love you, I love you, Spanish girl. (p. 100)

As horrific as this experience is for Esperanza—filled as it is with a sexual assault, a racial slur, and abandonment by a girlfriend she trusted—her story does not end here. As our guide through Mango Street, Esperanza has witnessed and experienced gender-based oppressions and the severe complication of popular fairy tale mythologies within a patriarchal context; however, she has also encountered women whose lives do not follow these fractured and painful scripts and who find ways to live their lives with independence and strength. Importantly, "The Red Clowns" is also framed by stories that suggest Esperanza's own emergence as a young woman "whose power is her own" (p. 89) and who, as I explore next, we may read as an emergent feminist heroine who develops her own alternative script for success.

Imagining Social Transformation:
Feminist Fairy Tales and *The House on Mango Street*

While feminist literary scholars have taken as their project the examination and critique of portrayals of women in fairy tales, a proliferation of new fairy tales written by feminist-oriented writers have emerged in tandem. Although it is beyond the scope of this article to survey this young, though rich and substantial genre, it is illuminating to call attention to some of the characteristics of it that resonate in some ways, but not in others, with the work of Cisneros in *The House on Mango Street*. Feminist writers of fairy tales are most often animated by a desire to invert, and often subvert, fairy tale narratives in a manner intended to criticize and perhaps transform social conditions. As Zipes (1986) contends, feminist fairy tales are characterized by "symbolical representations of the authors' critique of the patriarchal status quo and of their desire to change the current socialisation process" (p. xii). There is great variation, however, in how these critiques find expression.

Altmann (1994) has contended that many feminist fairy tales can be considered parodies of traditional tales in that they often simply replace male characters with female ones and do not promote images of more egalitarian social relationships. She contends that a feminist fairy tale as parody "looks back" by relying on traditional forms, inverts rather than subverts gender hierarchies, and relies upon a pre-existing knowledge of literary conventions for its effect. As she writes:

> In feminist fairy tales that are straightforward parodies, the point, usually the main joke, is oversetting the readers' previously formed expectations, and in the process challenging the inevitably of those expectations. That is, parody looks back, plays with a particular genre or narrative form to comment on that form and on the meaning that has already been made with it. (p. 23)

This "main joke," as Altmann sees it, may provide amusement to readers and may even invoke indictment of patriarchal structures, but it does not move us forward in imagining how to transform those structures.

Altmann (1994) makes an insightful distinction between "parody" and "poesis" in feminist fairy tales. While she argues that feminist fairy tales of parody leave us "still trapped in a hierarchical structure of power relations" (p. 22), a feminist fairy tale of poesis, on the other hand, "offers a new and wider world of meaning through reconfigured events and characters directly" (p. 23). Altmann contends that feminist fairy tales as poesis create new visions of social relations and gender roles rather than merely "contesting the old" (p. 28). It is within this context of maintaining of what she calls the "the power of the wonder tale" (p. 28) where feminist reconstructions of fairy tales hold the most socially transformative potential.

Cisneros's treatment of Esperanza at times suggests parody of patriarchal norms. I say "at times" because Esperanza's is indeed a coming-of-age story and as such we witness her thoughts and assertions as they arise and as other thoughts and assertions follow that complicate, if not contradict, them. At certain points in Esperanza's quest, for example, she decisively and with touches of parody rejects the three-tiered model of success for fairy tale heroines put forward by Lieberman. In "Beautiful and Cruel," for instance, Esperanza asserts that she will not rely on her beauty as a device to attract a mate, but will instead utilize her beauty like a movie star heroine who is "cruel." As Cisneros writes, "She is the one who drives men crazy and laughs them all away" (p. 89). In this way, Esperanza rejects the archetype of a beautiful, passive princess; however, by doing so, she uses as her model a woman who manipulates men and who does not therefore refigure more egalitarian relationships with them.

Esperanza also explicitly rejects the imperative to wait passively to be chosen. In the same vignette she contends that she will refuse to "grow up tame" and wait for a husband. Instead, she begins her "own quiet war" against the societal structures that inhibit her independence. She endeavors to "leave the table like a man, without putting back the chair or picking up the plate" (pp. 88–89). In the vignette, she positions herself in opposition to the traditional role of a woman in her refusal to keep her hair combed and her blouse clean in order to attract and keep a mate; yet, she then embraces a stereotypical male role of claiming absolute power in the household and irresponsibility for its upkeep. She does not reconfigure these gender roles or work to redress the imbalances of power; instead, she inverts these roles and thus leaves power unproblematized.

Esperanza also firmly rejects and supplants the final tier of success for the fairy tale heroine: to use one's beauty to acquire marital status in order to attain economic security. Instead, Esperanza desires a house of her own where she is free to write and free from taking care of others. She describes this place, "Not a flat. Not an apartment in back. Not a man's house. Not a daddy's. A house all my own" (p. 108). Esperanza imagines a life and future for herself in direct opposition to the constricting life she has experienced and witnessed in the women around her. It is in this place where Esperanza's radical re-thinking of gender roles and possibilities are seeded. It is in this place of imagination—filled as it is with Esperanza's own books and poems and where she is free to pursue her creative desires—where visions of Esperanza as feminist heroine in a tale of poesis emerge most strongly, as I explore next.

Sandra Cisneros and Esperanza Cordero: Making a Story for Their Lives

To a great degree, Esperanza's journey through Mango Street is not only emblematic of her rejection or inversion of the three-tiered system of rewards that allures and holds hostage many women of Mango Street. Rather, Esperanza creates a new set of guiding life principles for "success." Her discovery of these alternative ways of being and experiencing the world as a woman serves to position her as a heroine of her own life. I suggest that we can take from Esperanza a distinctly feminist model of a heroine who locates the vocation of writing as the fulcrum through which she realizes self-definition, freedom, and independence. Esperanza's emergence as a young woman writer is connected to her clear-sighted observations of the lives of the women and girls around her; to her interactions with women who offer advice and the possibilities of more fulfilling life choices; and to her desire to take responsibility for imagining a transformative social reality for herself and her community.

In Esperanza's system, then, success becomes contingent on these three factors: *bearing witness* to oppression of others and self; *seeking guidance* and alternative models from other women; and *imagining social transformation* that promotes self and community empowerment. In this discussion of the facets of Esperanza's emergence as a feminist heroine whose textured "happily ever after" comes through bearing witness, seeking guidance, and recreating possibilities, compelling parallels can be made to Cisneros's own life and Latina feminist theory.

Bearing Witness

As the narrator of *The House on Mango Street*, Esperanza allows the reader to see the world through her eyes as she describes and imbues with significance the details of her lived experience and the lives of the women she meets along the way. Esperanza bears witness to her life and the lives of other women, revealing how social constrictions of poverty, gender, culture, and ethnicity touch upon her life and those around her. In the final vignette of *The House on Mango Street*, "Mango Says Goodbye Sometimes," Esperanza draws upon the particulars of her experiences to claim an identity as a storyteller of her life; therefore, the very life that she sees and experiences every day becomes the subject of her writing. She asserts, "I make a story for my life, for each step my brown shoe takes. I say, 'And so she trudged up the wooden stairs, her sad brown shoes taking her to the house she never liked'" (p. 109).

Cisneros herself has described the presence of a narrator's voice recounting the everyday experiences she lived and witnessed in her own childhood mind as being the precursor to her writing. This voice described her days lived in a succession of apartments in Chicago neighborhoods. The only daughter in a family of six sons, Cisneros sought refuge in books, a past time that soon suggested her vocation as a writer in a parallel way to Esperanza. This literature, as well as her lived experiences, found expression in her internal narrator, as she recounts here:

> About this time I began hearing a voice in my head, a narrator—
> just like the ones in the books, chronicling the ordinary events
> that made up my life: "I want you to go the store and get me a
> loaf of bread and a gallon of milk. Bring back all the change and
> don't let them gyp you like they did last time." In my head my
> narrator would add: *she said in a voice that was neither reproachful
> nor tender. Thus clutching the coins in her pocket, our hero was off
> under a sky so blue and a wind so sweet she wondered it didn't make
> her dizzy.* This is how I glamorized my days living in the third-
> floor flats and shabby neighborhoods where the best friend I
> was always waiting for never materialized. (emphasis in original,
> 1987b, p. 70)

Unlike Esperanza, who comes to the realization in adolescence that the lives she has borne witness to, including her own, could serve as the fertile ground of her creative energies, Cisneros's epiphany did not come until much later. Although Cisneros nurtured this narrator's voice in her head as a child, it was not until she left Chicago and enrolled in the Iowa Writers' Workshop at age 23 that she realized this voice and the experiences it recounted "were worthy of writing about." Cisneros (1987b) writes:

> It seems crazy, but until Iowa I had never felt my home, family,
> and neighborhood unique or worthy of writing about. I took for
> granted the homes around me, the women sitting at their windows,
> the strange speech of my neighbors, the extraordinary lives of my
> family and relatives which was nothing like the family in "Father
> Knows Best." ... That's precisely what I chose to write: about
> third–floor flats, and fear of rats, and drunk husbands sending rocks
> through windows, anything as far from the poetic as possible. And
> this is when I discovered the voice I'd been suppressing all along
> without realizing it. (pp. 72–73)

Third-floor flats, rats, and drunken husbands certainly populate the pages of *The House on Mango Street*, suggesting that these lived experiences and observations found expression through the voice Cisneros initially had suppressed.

As I explored above, a recurring image in the book is also that of "the women sitting at their windows," an image highly resonant with the plight of fairy tale heroine, Rapunzel, locked in a tower, waiting for rescue. Cisneros may have witnessed many women like this during her childhood; however, throughout her essays and poetry, Cisneros has commented on her own decisive distancing from a life shaped exclusively by the seeking and attaining of marriage. She credits her mother for nurturing this break with tradition, asserting, "I'm here because my mother let me stay in my room reading and studying, perhaps because she didn't want me to inherit her sadness and her rolling pin" (1987d, p. 75). It is noteworthy that Esperanza also disavows the "inheritance" of her maternal grandmother's namesake and place by the window. Early in the novel in "My Name," Esperanza asserts, "She looked out the window all her life, the way so many women sit their sadness on an elbow . . . Esperanza. I have inherited her name, but I don't want to inherit her place at the window" (p. 11). In some ways, then, both Cisneros and Esperanza are almost "anti-Rapunzels" who refuse their place by the window (and the associated waiting, passivity, self-effacement that this could render) for the vocation of writing. Here, bearing witness serves as a way to identify and name the limitations one sees in women's lives and serves to facilitate a process of self-definition in opposition to these limitations.

It is worthwhile to note, too, that Cisneros explicitly names two other fairy tales when describing her childhood journey toward becoming a writer in her reflective piece, "Ghosts and Voices: Writing from Obsession." In this segment, she invokes both the "Six Swans" and "The Ugly Duckling" and describes how she "dreamed" herself into these tales, inserting herself and her experiences directly into the stories:

> I dreamed myself the sister in the "Six Swans" fairy tale. She too was an only daughter in a family of six sons. The brothers had been changed into swans by an evil spell only the sister could break. Was it no coincidence my family name translated "keeper of the swans?" I dreamed myself Andersen's "Ugly Duckling." Ridiculous, ugly, perennially the new kid. But one day the spell would wear off. I kept telling myself, "Temporary." (1987b, p. 71)

Here, the young Cisneros imagines herself the powerful sister who can break the spells of her brothers' curse. As a child, she recognizes her marginal status as the only girl among six brothers and as the "ridiculous, ugly, perennially the new kid" due to her family's frequent moves in Chicago neighborhoods and between Chicago and Mexico City; yet, in her reading of both tales she also imagines a reworking of those conditions. When she dreams herself into the tales, she imagines possibilities of her own agency, of an improved life where she breaks certain spells and where other spells would wear off. Could this young Cisneros's reading of the "Six Swans" and "The Ugly Duckling" be the inspiration for Esperanza's own forthright naming of her loneliness and ugliness in "Beautiful and Cruel": "I am the ugly daughter. I am the one nobody comes for" (p. 88)? And who, in only a few lines later, asserts her rejection of an adolescence spent waiting for a prince, by proclaiming, "I have decided not to grow up tame like the others who lay their necks on the threshold waiting for the ball and chain" (p. 88)?

Esperanza's experiences of witnessing women's oppression, poverty, and loneliness and these beginning stirrings of desires not to fall victim to the ravages of the social world are suggestive of her journey to critique and also recreate her life. Alternative models, however, not just oppositional ones, have yet to be created. The next stage of Esperanza's quest is to seek out concrete models of women who are not "tame" and who provide guidance in fashioning a life capable of providing outlets for her restless desires for freedom and creativity.

Seeking Guidance

Although Esperanza encounters women imprisoned in their homes, young girls who are emotionally and physically abused, and women trying to raise children in homes abandoned by fathers, she also encounters Minerva, a woman who writes poems in spite of her abusive husband; Alicia, a young woman who attends university despite her father's lack of support; and her Aunt Guadalupe who encourages her to write. These women provide concrete advice and concrete models of women who work against limiting conditions in order to retain their independence, pursue their ambitions, and cultivate their sources of creativity. Esperanza's friend, Alicia, for example, studies late into the night despite having to rise with the "tortilla star" and despite her father's admonitions that "a woman's place is sleeping" (p. 31). Alicia, who "inherited her mama's rolling pin," does not acquiesce to these limitations. Despite the challenges of her life and despite her fears of her father, she takes on a lengthy commute to college and endures her father's chiding for studying too much.

While Alicia provides Esperanza with a model of a young woman pursuing her ambitions despite obstacles, Guadalupe (who Esperanza proudly describes as "my aunt who listened to my poems") provides support and encouragement for Esperanza's emerging talents as a writer. After Esperanza reads a poem that she has written, Guadalupe responds:

That's nice. That's very good ... You must remember to keep writing, Esperanza. You must keep writing. It will keep you free, and I said yes, but at that time I didn't know what she meant. (p. 61)

Here, Guadalupe tells Esperanza directly that she must keep writing and links this act to her freedom. Though not quite certain of what her aunt's words mean at this point in the novel and in her quest, these words resonate in Esperanza's mind and are recalled when Esperanza invokes her writing as an avenue to freedom on the last page of the novel. She says, "I write it down and Mango Street says goodbye sometimes. She does not hold me with both arms. She sets me free" (p. 110). These "fierce women," as Cisneros might call them, are essential to Esperanza's journey toward becoming a writer. Unlike the evil stepmothers and conniving witches of fairy tales who heroines must struggle against, these women illuminate possibility and nurture Esperanza's desires for a creative life.

Perhaps the most influential women, however, are the ethereal and mysterious three sisters who visit Esperanza when she attends the funeral of a young child. It is these women, wise and powerful like fairy godmothers in a feminist fairy tale, who stir Esperanza's conscience. They serve an integral role in helping Esperanza move on to her final stage of her journey, that of embracing her talent as a writer who does not refute her heritage, but works towards its transformation. The three sisters suggest the faith, hope, and a touch of magic needed for the young Esperanza to realize her role as a heroine and as a writer. They therefore imbue *The House on Mango Street* with some of its most perceptible traits as a wonder tale in a distinctly feminist vein.

Imagining Social Transformation

While Esperanza has borne witness to and critiqued the lives of the women around her, and while she has caught glimpses of alternative realities through the guidance and support of mentors, the true significance of her defiance and creativity rests in her ability to connect her writing to self and community empowerment. For Esperanza to imagine social transformation requires a complex movement in which she embraces her cultural heritage, while also working to transform its most limiting attributes. Cisneros's own life suggests a similar drive. Esperanza's defiant claim in the "Beautiful & Cruel" vignette that she will not "grow up tame" is a compelling precursor to Cisneros's 1987 book of poetry entitled, *My Wicked, Wicked Ways*, in which she foregrounds her own vocational and sexual independence. As Cisneros has noted and as the ending of *The House on Mango Street* suggests, however, a refusal to grow up tame or an embrace of "wicked, wicked ways" are not symbolic of wholesale rejection of her cultural background.

Instead, they suggest a woman's complex process of both acceptance and revision of Latino culture in a way highly attuned to gender oppression. As Cisneros contends, "I felt, as a teenager, that I could not inherit my culture intact without revising some parts of it" (Aranda, 1990, p. 66). She also draws specific attention to gender as the part of her culture she needs to revise, stating, "We accept our culture, but not without adapting ourselves as women" (Aranda, 1990, p. 67).

Both Cisneros and Esperanza embody a complex inheritance and transformation of Latino culture and female identity that are reflective of multiple strands of Latina feminism. Yarbro-Bejarano (1996) defines Latina feminism as a recognition that a Latina's "experience as a woman is inextricable from her experience as a member of an oppressed working-class racial minority and a culture which is not the dominant culture" (p. 214). Yarbro-Bejarano further contends that the writing and theorizing of Latinas function to affirm a sense of solidarity with other oppressed groups and link women and men in joint struggles for economic and political justice, while also embedding a critique of oppressive gender relations within the Latino community itself. Anzaldúa (1990) also calls attention to these multiple identities and sources of oppression for Latinas and argues that a "mestiza consciousness" emerges when women move between and among these forces. As Anzaldúa writes:

> From this racial, ideological, cultural and biological cross-pollinization, an "alien" consciousness is presently in the making—a new *mestiza consciousness, una conciencia de mujer.* It is a consciousness of the Borderlands. (emphasis in original, p. 377).

Anzaldúa herself writes from these Borderlands, encouraging other women to draw upon and enact a mestiza consciousness as she describes here: "She communicates that rupture, documents the struggle. She reinterprets history and, using new symbols, she shapes new myths" (p. 381). For Cisneros, a similar sense of urgency and purpose animates her writing of the struggles and complexities of her life and that of other Latinas. She asserts:

> There's no luxury or leisure in our lives for us to write of landscapes and sunsets and tulips in a vase. Instead of writing by inspiration, it seems we write by obsession, of that which is most violently tugging at our psyche. (1987b, p. 73)

Also driven by what is "violently tugging at [her] psyche," and drawing from the guidance of numerous women in the community, Esperanza begins to understand her vocation as a writer in a manner that keeps her connected to her heritage, but does not foreclose her opportunities for independence and self-fulfillment. McCracken (1999), Saldívar (1990), and Olivares (1996) have written persuasively of Esperanza's evolving recognition of the dialectic between self and community, emphasizing Esperanza's growing "awareness of the connections between the privately created self and its public responsibilities" (Saldívar, 1990, p. 184).

I would argue, though, that characterizing the complex realizations Esperanza comes to at the end of the novel as a dialectic between self and community does not perhaps capture the full range of the socially transformative work Cisneros is imagining here. I would contend that Esperanza's multifaceted identity work is better reflected in Anzaldúa's notion of "mestiza consciousness" in that Esperanza is navigating multiple identities, while creating new and revolutionary roles for herself in a social environment shaped by racial, gender, and economic inequity. It seems this is nowhere better expressed than in her assertion that she will go "away to come back. For the ones I left behind" (p. 110). Perhaps even more significant to a complication of this dialectic is that it is the women in Esperanza's life who guide her to this realization. In "The Three Sisters," the mysterious woman with "marble hands" peers into Esperanza's face and tells her, "You will always be Esperanza. You will always be Mango Street. You can't erase what you know. You can't forget who you are" (p. 105). Alicia later says to her in markedly similar language, "Like it or not you are Mango Street, and one day you will come back too" (p. 107). In addition, a fortuneteller informs Esperanza that she sees "a home in the heart" (p. 64). These women suggest to Esperanza that she is Mango Street, she does not simply have a relation to it. Esperanza therefore holds within her both the restrictive and potentially transformative power of Mango Street and it is this power that she must claim as a writer. She claims this role on the final page of the novel when she asserts the link between her writing and her freedom, "I put it down on paper and then the ghost does not ache so much. I write it down and Mango says goodbye sometimes. She does not hold me with both arms. She sets me free" (p. 110).

The lyricism and transparent beauty of Cisneros's prose, coupled with her unflinching portrayals of the harsh realities of women's social worlds, saturate Esperanza's journey toward adulthood with a unique fairy tale wonder all its own. When Esperanza whispers her own poem to her Aunt Guadalupe,

One day I'll jump
out of my skin.
I'll shake the sky
like a hundred violins (pp. 60–61)

She transmits to her aunt and to the reader an image of a young woman whose power is emergent from the uniqueness of her worldview, is made tangible through her writing, and is realized through a life connected to, yet sometimes defiant of, her Latino heritage. Esperanza's coming-of-age story is one of concrete struggles and joys, but is clearly also one of everyday magic, hope in new possibilities, and visions of transformative opportunities for women. Through the voice of the young heroine, Cisneros boldly suggests a transformative social project that can continue to inform feminist analyses of children's and young adult literature and inspire the development of heroines from a wide range of cultural backgrounds. From these new analyzes and these new creations, it may be possible for Esperanza to continue to emerge as a figure of hope to many generations of young readers.

Notes

1. In reference to critics who have praised the "childlike" character of the narrator's voice, Cisneros has argued that the voice is instead reflective of language use in Spanish. She says, "The syntax, the sensibility, the diminutives, the way of looking at inanimate objects—that's not a child's voice as is sometimes said. That's Spanish!" (Jussawalla & Dasenbrock, 1992, p. 288).

2. Although Cisneros interchangeably names herself as "Mexicana," "Chicana," and "Latina," for the sake of clarity I use the term "Latina" to refer to women in this article.

3. Zipes (1986) takes issue with some feminist notions of the role of fairy tales in the acculturation of children into stereotyped gender roles and argues instead for a more subtle analysis that emphasizes how fairy tales are more *reflective* of social realities, rather than as responsible for creating them.

4. It is noteworthy, too, that in both the Cinderella and Rapunzel stories, it is women in the stories who imprison and abuse the heroines; Cisneros suggests a striking reversal of this thematic by casting men in these roles in the series of vignettes related to Sally and the Cinderella story.

References

Addington, A. (2001). Talking about literature in university book club and seminar settings. *Research in the Teaching of English*, 36(2), 212–248.

Altmann, A. (1994). Parody and poesis in feminist fairy tales. *Canadian Children's Literature*, 73(20), 22–31.

Anzaldúa, G. (1990). La conciencia de la mestiza: Towards a new consciousness. In G. Anzaldúa, (Ed.), *Making face, making soul: Creative and critical perspectives by women of color* (pp. 377–389). San Francisco: Aunt Lute Foundation Books.

Aranda, P. E. R. (1990). On the solitary fate of being Mexican, female, wicked, and thirty-three: An interview with writer Sandra Cisneros. *The Americas Review*, 18(1), 64–80.

Cisneros, S. (1984). *The house on mango street*. New York: Vintage Books.

Cisneros, S. (1986). The softly insistent voice of a poet. *Austin American Statesman*, March 11, pp. 14–15.

Cisneros, S. (1987a). Do you know me?: I wrote *The House on Mango Street*. *The Americas Review*, 15(1), 77–79.

Cisneros, Sandra. (1987b). Ghosts and voices: Writing from obsession. *The Americas Review*, 15(1), 69–73.

Cisneros, S. (1987c). *My wicked, wicked ways*. Berkeley, CA: Third Woman Press.

Cisneros, S. (1987d). Notes to a young(er) writer. *The Americas Review*, 15(1), 74–76.

Hammerberg, D. (2001). Reading and writing 'hypertextually': Children's literature, technology, and early writing instruction. *Language Arts*, 78(3), 207–216.

Joosen, V. (2005). Fairy-tale retellings between art and pedagogy. *Children's Literature in Education*, 36(2), 129–139.

Jussawalla, F., & Dasenbrock, R. W. (1992). Sandra Cisneros. In F. Jussawalla & R. W. Dasenbrock (Eds.), *Interviews with writers of the post-colonial world*, (pp. 286–306). Jackson: University Press of Mississippi.

Klein, D. (1992). Coming of age in novels by Rudolfo Anaya and Sandra Cisneros. *English Journal*, 81(5), 2126.

Lieberman, M. (1972). 'Some day my prince will come': Female acculturation through the fairy tale. *College English*, 34, 383–395.

Marshall, E. (2004). Stripping for the wolf: Rethinking representations of gender in children's literature. *Reading Research Quarterly*, 39(3), 256–270.

McCracken, E. (1999). *New Latina narrative. The feminine space of postmodern ethnicity*. Tucson: The University of Arizona Press.

Moore, R. (1975). From rags to witches: Stereotypes, distortions and antihumanism in fairy tales. *Interracial Books for Children*, 6, 1–3

Olivares, J. (1996). Entering *The House on Mango Street*. In J. R. Maitino & D. R. Peck (Eds.), *Teaching American ethnic literatures*, (pp. 209–235). Albuquerque, NM: University of New Mexico Press.

O'Malley, T. (1997). A ride down mango street. *English Journal*, 86(8), 35–37.

Parsons, L. (2004). Ella evolving: Cinderella stories and the construction of gender-appropriate behavior. *Children's Literature in Education*, 35(2), 135–154.

Rowe, K. (1986). Feminism and fairy tales. In J. Zipes (Ed.), *Don't bet on the prince. Contemporary feminist fairy tales in North America and England*, (pp. 209–226). New York: Methuen.

Saldívar, R. (1990). *Chicano narrative: The dialectics of difference*. Madison, WI: The University of Wisconsin Press.

Schaafsma, D., Tendero, A., & Tendero, J. (1999). Making it real: Girls' stories, social change, and moral struggle. *English Journal*, 88(5), 28–36.

Spencer, L. G. (1997). Fairy tales and opera: The fate of the heroine in the work of Sandra Cisneros. In J. C. Reesman (Ed.), *Speaking the other self: American women writers*, (pp. 278–287). Athens: The University of Georgia Press.

Stone, K. (1975). Things Walt Disney never told us. In C. R. Farrer (Ed.), *Women and folklore: Images and genres*, (pp. 42–50). Prospect Heights, IL: Waveland Press, Inc.

Yarbro-Bejarano, Y. (1996). Chicana literature from a Chicana feminist perspective. In M. Herrera-Sobek & H. M. Viramontes (Eds.), *Chicana creativity and criticism: New frontiers in American literature*, (pp. 213–219). Albuquerque: University of New Mexico Press.

Yolen, J. (1977). America's Cinderella. *Children's Literature in Education*, 8(1), 21–29.

Zipes, J. (1986). Introduction, in *Don't bet on the prince: Contemporary feminist fairy tales in North America and England*, (pp. 138). New York: Methuen.

Chronology

1954	Sandra Cisneros was born on December 20 in Chicago, the only daughter and third child in a family of seven children. Her father was born in Mexico and came to the United States in pursuit of higher education. Her mother was a Mexican American living in Chicago. The family moved many times before residing on Chicago's north side.
1976	Graduates from Loyola University with a bachelor of arts degree.
1978	Graduates with a master's degree from the University of Iowa Writers' Workshop.
1978–80	Teacher at Latino Youth Alternative High School in Chicago. In 1980, publishes *Bad Boys*, a book of poems.
1981–82	College recruiter and counselor for minority students at Loyola University. In 1982, a National Endowment for the Arts fellow.
1983	Artist-in-residence at Foundation Michael Karolyi, Vence, France.
1984	Publishes *The House on Mango Street*, a novel.
1984–85	Literature director at the Guadalupe Cultural Arts Center, San Antonio. In 1985, publishes *The Rodrigo Poems*; receives American Book Award for *The House on Mango Street*.

1987–88	Guest professor, California State University, Chico; in 1987 publishes *My Wicked, Wicked Ways*, a book of poems. In 1988, guest professor at the University of California, Berkeley, and National Endowment for the Arts fellow.
1990	Guest professor at the University of California, Irvine, and the University of Michigan, Ann Arbor.
1991	Guest professor at the University of New Mexico, Albuquerque. Publishes *Woman Hollering Creek and Other Stories*. It wins the PEN Center West Award for Best Fiction and other awards and is selected as a noteworthy book of the year by *The New York Times*.
1994	Publishes *Hairs/Pelitos*, a bilingual children's book, and *Loose Woman*, a book of poems.
1995	Macarthur fellow.
2002	Publishes *Caramelo*, a novel. Title is selected a notable book of the year by *The New York Times* and several other newspapers.
2004	Publishes *Vintage Cisneros*, featuring excerpts from her previously published works.

Contributors

HAROLD BLOOM is Sterling Professor of the Humanities at Yale University. He is the author of 30 books, including *Shelley's Mythmaking*, *The Visionary Company*, *Blake's Apocalypse*, *Yeats*, *A Map of Misreading*, *Kabbalah and Criticism*, *Agon: Toward a Theory of Revisionism*, *The American Religion*, *The Western Canon*, and *Omens of Millennium: The Gnosis of Angels, Dreams, and Resurrection*. *The Anxiety of Influence* sets forth Professor Bloom's provocative theory of the literary relationships between the great writers and their predecessors. His most recent books include *Shakespeare: The Invention of the Human*, a 1998 National Book Award finalist, *How to Read and Why*, *Genius: A Mosaic of One Hundred Exemplary Creative Minds*, *Hamlet: Poem Unlimited*, *Where Shall Wisdom Be Found?*, and *Jesus and Yahweh: The Names Divine*. In 1999, Professor Bloom received the prestigious American Academy of Arts and Letters Gold Medal for Criticism. He has also received the International Prize of Catalonia, the Alfonso Reyes Prize of Mexico, and the Hans Christian Andersen Bicentennial Prize of Denmark.

MARIA ELENA DE VALDÉS, now Maria Elena Valdés-Corbeil, has taught at the University of Texas at Brownsville/Texas Southmost College. She co-authored *Approaches to Teaching Garcia Marquez's* One Hundred Years of Solitude.

JACQUELINE DOYLE is a professor at California State University, East Bay, where she is also coordinator of graduate studies. She has published essays and reviews in various journals and specializes in nineteenth-century American literature and women's studies.

183

THOMAS MATCHIE is an emeritus professor at North Dakota State University. His interests include nineteenth- and twentieth-century American, Native American, and regional literature; Victorian literature; and contemporary drama.

ANNIE O. EYSTUROY has taught American literature in the United States, Spain, and the Faroe Islands. She co-edited *This Is About Vision: Interviews with Southwestern Writers.*

NICHOLAS SLOBODA is a professor at the University of Wisconsin–Superior. He has published essays on Barthelme, Zukofsky, Erdrich, Melnyczuk, and Charlotte Sherman. He also has been the English language book review editor for the *New Novel Review.*

MICHELLE SCALISE SUGIYAMA is affiliated with the Institute for Cognitive and Decision Sciences and the English Department at the University of Oregon, Eugene, where she teaches classes on the prehistory of narrative and art behavior. She has published many articles in journals, including *Philosophy and Literature* and *Mosaic.*

MARIA SZADZIUK is a translator of Polish, English, Spanish, and Russian. In addition to multicultural issues, her interests include Spanish Golden Age prose and drama. She has written on irony in *Don Quixote.*

LESLIE PETTY is an assistant professor at Rhodes College. She is the author of *Romancing the Vote: Feminist Activism in American Fiction, 1870–1920.*

BETH L. BRUNK, now Beth Brunk-Chavez, teaches at the University of Texas at El Paso, where she also is the director of first-year composition. She is co-author of the forthcoming *Explorations: Guided Inquiry into Writing.* She also has been published in journals and edited collections.

KELLY WISSMAN is an assistant professor in the School of Education at the University at Albany, State University of New York. Her research interests include literacy and literature in the lives of urban youth and feminist approaches to the study and teaching of children's literature. She has been published in several journals, including the *English Journal.*

Bibliography

Aceituno, Yolanda. "Double Revolutions: Chicana Fiction and the Revitalisation of the Social Function of Literary Discourse: Sandra Cisneros' Example." *Caballero; Grove: Working Papers on English Studies* 11 (2004): 25–36.

Bolaki, Stella. "'The Bridge We Call Home': Crossing and Bridging Spaces in Sandra Cisneros's *The House on Mango Street*." *eSharp: Electronic Social Sciences, Humanities, and Arts Review for Postgraduates* 5 (Summer 2005): 1–14.

———. "Weaving Stories of Self and Community through Vignettes in Sandra Cisneros's *The House on Mango Street*." In *Narratives of Community: Women's Short Story Sequences*, edited by Roxanne Harde, pp. 14–36. Newcastle upon Tyne, England: Cambridge Scholars, 2007.

Busch, Juan Daniel. "Self-Baptizing the Wicked Esperanza: Chicana Feminism and Cultural Contact in *The House on Mango Street*." *Mester* 22–23 (Fall 1993–Spring 1994): 123–34.

Carter, Nancy Corson. "Claiming the Bittersweet Matrix: Alice Walker, Sandra Cisneros, and Adrienne Rich." *Critique: Studies in Contemporary Fiction* 35, no. 4 (Summer 1994): 195–204.

Chakravartee, Moutushi. "Shock Therapy: Sandra Cisneros' *The House on Mango Street*." *Indian Journal of American Studies* 24, no. 2 (Summer 1994): 21–25.

Cutting, Rose Marie. "Power and Powerlessness: Names in the Fiction of Sandra Cisneros." *Xavier Review* 18, no. 2 (1998): 33–42.

Dalleo, Raphael. "How Cristina Garcia Lost Her Accent, and Other Latina Conversations." *Latino Studies* 3, no. 1 (April 2005): 3–18.

Dwyer, June. "Ethnic Home Improvement: Gentrifying the Ghetto, Spicing Up the Suburbs." *Isle: Interdisciplinary Studies in Literature and Environment* 14, no. 2 (Summer 2007): 165–82.

Frydman, Jason. "Upward Mobility as a Neurotic Condition in Sandra Cisneros' *The House on Mango Street*." *Exit 9: The Rutgers Journal of Comparative Literature* 8 (2007): 15–23.

Ganz, Robin. "Sandra Cisneros: Border Crossings and Beyond." *MELUS* 19, no. 1 (Spring 1994): 19–29.

Gibson, Michelle. "The 'Unrealistic' Narrator in *The House on Mango Street*." *San Jose Studies* 19, no. 2 (1993): 40–44.

Giles, James R. *Violence in the Contemporary American Novel: An End to Innocence*. Columbia: University of South Carolina Press, 2000.

Gonzalez, Maria. "Love and Conflict: Mexican American Women Writers as Daughters." In *Women of Color: Mother-Daughter Relationships in 20th-Century Literature*, edited by Elizabeth Brown-Guillory, 153–71. Austin: University of Texas Press, 1996.

Gutiérrez-Jones, Leslie S. "Different Voices: The Re-Bildung of the Barrio in Sandra Cisneros' *The House on Mango Street*." In *Anxious Power: Reading, Writing, and Ambivalence in Narrative by Women*, edited by Carol J. Singley and Susan Elizabeth Sweeney, pp. 295–312. Albany: State University of New York Press, 1993.

Herrera, Andrea O'Reilly. "'Chambers of Consciousness': Sandra Cisneros and the Development of the Self in the BIG House on Mango Street." *Bucknell Review: A Scholarly Journal of Letters, Arts and Sciences* 39, no. 1 (1995): 191–204.

Herrera-Sobek, María. "The Politics of Rape: Sexual Transgression in Chicana Fiction." *Chicana Creativity and Criticism: New Frontiers in American Literature*, edited by María Herrera-Sobek and Helena María Viramontes, pp. 245–56. Albuquerque: University of New Mexico Press, 1996.

Kanoza, Theresa. "Esperanza's Mango Street: Home for Keeps." *Notes on Contemporary Literature* 25, no. 3 (May 1995): 9.

Karafilis, Maria. "Crossing the Borders of Genre: Revisions of the Bildungsroman in Sandra Cisneros's *The House on Mango Street* and Jamaica Kincaid's *Annie John*." *Journal of the Midwest Modern Language Association* 31, no. 2 (Winter 1998): 63–78.

Kelley, Margot. "A Minor Revolution: Chicano/a Composite Novels and the Limits of Genre." In *Ethnicity and the American Short Story*, edited by Julia Brown, pp. 63–84. New York: Garland, 1997.

Kessler, Elizabeth A. "A Sociolinguistic Study of Male-Female Interaction in Cisneros' *The House on Mango Street*." *Conference of College Teachers of English Proceedings*, 55 (1995): 10–17.

Kuribayashi, Tomoko. "The Chicana Girl Writes Her Way In and Out: Space and Bilingualism in Sandra Cisneros' *The House on Mango Street*." In *Creating Safe Space: Violence and Women's Writing*, edited by Tomoko Kuribayashi and Julie Tharp, pp. 165–77. Albany: State University of New York Press, 1997.

Madsen, D. L. "(Dis)continuous Narrative: The Articulation of a Chicana Feminist Voice in Sandra Cisneros's *The House on Mango Street*." *Journal of the Short Story in English/Les Cahiers de la Nouvelle* 27 (1996): 13–28.

Marek, Jayne E. "Difference, Identity, and Sandra Cisneros's *The House on Mango Street*." *Hungarian Journal of English and American Studies* 1 (1996): 173–87.

Marino, Simona. "Sandra Cisneros's Bilingual House of Fiction: Open Doors and Closed Borders." In *America Today: Highways and Labyrinths*, edited by Gigliola Nocera, pp. 230–37. Siracusa, Italy: Grafià, 2003.

McCay, Mary A. "Sandra Cisneros: Crossing Borders." In *Uneasy Alliance: Twentieth-Century American Literature, Culture and Biography*, edited by Hans Bak, pp. 302–21. Amsterdam, Netherlands: Rodopi, 2004.

McCracken, Ellen. "Sandra Cisneros' *The House on Mango Street*: Community-Oriented Introspection and the Demystification of Patriarchal Violence." In *Breaking Boundaries: Latina Writing and Critical Readings*, edited by Asunción Horno-Delgado, Eliana Ortega, Nina M. Scott, and Nancy Saporta Sternbach, pp. 62–71. Amherst: University of Massachusetts Press, 1989.

Norton, Jody. "History, Rememory, Transformation: Actualizing Literary Value." *The Centennial Review* 38, no. 3 (Fall 1994): 589–602.

Ochoa Fernández, Ma Luisa. "Family as the Patriarchal Confinement of Women in Sandra Cisneros' *The House on Mango Street* and Loida M. Pérez's *Geographies of Home*." In *Evolving Origins, Transplanting Cultures: Literary Legacies of the New Americans*, edited by Laura P. Alonso Gallo, pp. 119–28. Huelva, Spain: Universidad de Huelva, 2002.

Olivares, Julián. "Sandra Cisneros' *The House on Mango Street*, and the Poetics of Space." *The Americas Review: A Review of Hispanic Literature and Art of the USA* 15, nos. 3–4 (Fall–Winter 1987): 160–70.

———. "Sandra Cisneros' *The House on Mango Street*, and the Poetics of Space." In *Chicana Creativity and Criticism: New Frontiers in American Literature*, edited by Maria Herrera-Sobek and Helena Viramontes, pp. 233–44. Albuquerque: University of New Mexico Press, 1996.

Pagán, Darlene. "Girls and Women in Sandra Cisneros' *The House on Mango Street* (1984)." In *Women in Literature: Reading through the Lens of Gender*, edited by Jerilyn Fisher and Ellen S. Silber, pp. 141–43. Westport, Conn.: Greenwood, 2003.

Pollack, Harriet, ed. *Having Our Way: Women Rewriting Tradition in Twentieth-Century America*. Lewisburg, Pa.: Bucknell University Press; London: Associated University Presses, 1995.

Pollock, Mary S. "'A Woman with One Foot in the World and One Foot in That': The Bilingual Perspective of Sandra Cisneros." *Journal of the Short Story in English* 21 (Autumn 1993): 53–61.

———. "The Raw Edges of the Mind: Sandra Cisneros Reads Mercè Rodoreda." *Catalan Review: International Journal of Catalan Culture* 12, no. 1 (1998): 87–100.

Rosaldo, Renato. "Sandra Cisneros: The Fading of the Warrior Hero." In *The Latino/a Condition: A Critical Reader*, edited by Richard Delgado and Jean Stefancic, pp. 644–48. New York: New York University Press, 1998.

Salazar, Inés. "Can You Go Home Again? Trangression and Transformation in African-American Women's and Chicana Literary Practice." In *Postcolonial Theory and the United States: Race, Ethnicity, and Literature*, edited by Amritjit Singh and Peter Schmidt, pp. 388–411. Jackson: University Press of Mississippi, 2000.

Sanborn, Geoffrey. "Keeping Her Distance: Cisneros, Dickinson, and the Politics of Private Enjoyment." *PMLA: Publications of the Modern Language Association of America* 116, no. 5 (October 2001): 1334–48.

Spencer, Laura Gutierrez. "Fairy Tales and Opera: The Fate of the Heroine in the Work of Sandra Cisneros." In *Speaking the Other Self: American Women Writers*, edited by Jeanne Campbell Reesman, pp. 278–87. Athens: University of Georgia Press, 1997.

de Valdés, María Elena. "The Critical Reception of Sandra Cisneros's *The House on Mango Street*." In *Gender, Self, and Society*, edited by Renate von Bardeleben, pp. 287–300. Frankfurt: Peter Lang, 1993.

———. "In Search of Identity in Cisneros's *The House on Mango Street*." *Canadian Review of American Studies* 23, no. 1 (Fall 1992): 55–72.

Weddle-Mulholland, Katona D. "Sandra Cisneros: A Cicana's Search for Identity." *Publications of the Missouri Philological Association* 24 (1999): 68–75.

Weldt-Basson, Helene C. "Silence as Narrative Strategy in Sandra Cisneros's *The House on Mango Street*." *Cuadernos de Aldeeu* 16, no. 1 (2000): 201–9.

———. "Women and the City: Sexual Initiation of Female Protagonists in Marta Brunet, María Luisa Bombal, Sandra Cisneros and Rosario Castellanos." *Torre: Revista de la Universidad de Puerto Rico* 11, no. 39 (January–March 2006): 65–78.

Acknowledgments

Maria Elena de Valdés, "In Search of Identity in Cisneros's *The House on Mango Street*" From *Canadian Review of American Studies* 23, no. 1 (Fall 1992): 55–72. © 1992 by University of Toronto Press, www.utpjournals.com. Reprinted by permission of Canadian Association for American Studies.

Jacqueline Doyle, "More Room of Her Own: Sandra Cisneros's *The House on Mango Street*" was first published in *MELUS: The Journal of the Society for the Study of Multi-Ethnic Literature of the United States* 19.4 (Winter 1994) and is reprinted here with the permission of *MELUS*.

Thomas Matchie, "Literary Continuity in Sandra Cisneros's *The House on Mango Street*. From *The Midwest Quarterly* 37, no. 1 (Autumn 1995): 67–79. © 1995 by Pittsburgh State University.

Annie O. Eysturoy, "*The House on Mango Street*: A Space of Her Own." From *Daughters of Self-Creation: The Contemporary Chicana Novel*. Copyright © 1996 University of New Mexico Press.

Nicholas Sloboda, "A Home in the Heart: Sandra Cisneros's *The House on Mango Street*." From *Aztlán: A Journal of Chicano Studies* 22, no. 2 (Fall 1997): 89–106. © 1997 by the UCLA Chicano Studies Research Center. Reprinted with permission of the Regents of the University of California. Not for further reproduction.

Michelle Scalise Sugiyama, "Of Woman Bondage: The Eroticism of Feet in *The House on Mango Street.*" From *The Midwest Quarterly* 41, no. 1 (Autumn 1999): 9–20. © 1999 by Pittsburgh State University.

Maria Szadziuk, "Culture As Transition: Becoming a Woman in Bi-ethnic Space." This essay originally appeared in *Mosaic*, a journal for the interdisciplinary study of literature, vol. 32, issue 3 (September 1999): 109–29.

Leslie Petty, "The 'Dual'-ing Images of la Malinche and la Virgen de Guadalupe in Cisneros's *The House on Mango Street*" was first published in *MELUS: The Journal of the Society for the Study of Multi-Ethnic Literature of the United States* 25.2 (Summer 2000) and is reprinted here with the permission of *MELUS*.

Beth L. Brunk, "*En Otras Voces*: Multiple Voices in Sandra Cisneros' *The House on Mango Street.*" From *Hispanófila* 133 (September 2001): 137–50. © 2001 by *Hispanófila*.

Kelly Wissman, "'Writing Will Keep You Free': Allusions to and Recreations of the Fairy Tale Heroine in *The House on Mango Street.*" From *Children's Literature in Education* 38 (2007): 17–34. © 2006 and reprinted with kind permission of Springer Science and Business Media.

Index